G000310714

HAILSHAM AND ITS ENVIRONS

HAILSHAM
and its
ENVIRONS

Charles A. Robertson

Phillimore

1982

Published by
PHILLIMORE & CO. LTD.
London and Chichester

Head Office: Shopwyke Hall,
Chichester, Sussex, England

© C. A. Robertson, 1982

ISBN 0 85033 434 9

Typeset in the United Kingdom by
Fidelity Processes - Selsey - Sussex
Printed and bound in Great Britain at
The Camelot Press Ltd, Southampton

To
Kathleen,
Jennifer
and Susan

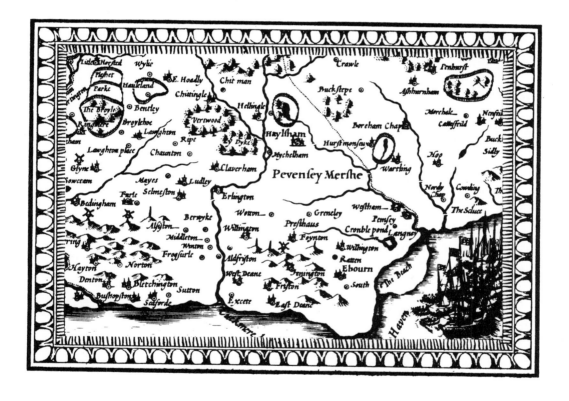

CONTENTS

LIST OF PLATES

(between pages 112 and 113)

ACKNOWLEDGEMENTS FOR PLATES

I would like to thank the following for their permission to use their photographs:
Roger Blackwell, 1, 8, 19, 20, 21, 43; Robert Girling, 2, 10, 14, 22, 28, 32, 36,
37; David Calvert, A.I.I.P., A.M.P.A., 3, 5; Cambridge University Collection, 4;
Gordon Head, 7, 30, 34, 39 (photographed by kind permission of Mr. and Mrs.
Edward Burchett of Halland Park Farm); Robin Falk, 17; Patricia Stevens, 18;
Sussex Archaeological Society, 24; Thomas Buckeridge, 35; Jennifer Berkett, 42.
  All other photographs are by the author.

LIST OF TEXT FIGURES

FROM:

THE RT. HON. LORD HAILSHAM OF ST. MARYLEBONE, C.H., F.R.S., D.C.L.

HOUSE OF LORDS,
SW1A 0PW

29 June 86

Though I may no longer live at Carter's Corner, at the junction of the parishes of Hellingly, Hailsham, Warbleton and Herstmonceux, these parishes are, as they have been, since 1917, and always will be, my home.

I wish this book, which recounts the varying fortunes and worthies of Hailsham and its neighbourhood, every success.

Hailsham of St Marylebone

INTRODUCTION

This book first appeared in 1981 as a private edition of forty numbered copies, each illustrated with documents and maps, together with some engravings of a merit that happily encouraged the pleasure of hand-tinting.

From its beginning as a series of somewhat casual yet exciting explorations into parish church histories, the research imperceptibly widened ultimately to embrace those events and phases of English history that affected the people of Hailsham and the surrounding villages. Much time was taken up and so absorbing had become the research and writing that it was with some reluctance, even after four years, that the work was ended and binding put in hand.

With the edition finished, books were allocated to libraries, to descendents of people in the history and to friends where an interest had prompted the seeking of a copy. But this small and rather personal edition proved not to be the end, for kind Press notices provoked a curiosity and awareness that seemed to confirm a genuine need for this second edition.

Thus, there followed some re-writing in greater detail, where the need to be concise had caused a previous entry to be all too brief, and more important, writing of those occasions in history on which research demanded much more time than even a delayed private edition could allow. Indeed in the part of East Sussex with which we are concerned, many books remain to be written on its immensely varied history and the people who lived with it.

The county of Sussex with neighbouring Kent have together suffered from being that part of England closest to a Continent often unfriendly and seldom long without a dire threat of war. And in spite of protection given by the narrow waters of the English Channel, Sussex has endured the cruelty and destruction of countless raids apart from the Norman invasion that devastated much of East Sussex, struck down England's King and eventually changed the course of English history.

From the truly momentous date of 1066, a date perhaps without parallel in changing the course of English history, this book lists through its pages in chronological order, other dates recording events in history and the vast changes in the lives and fortunes of the people who lived in a particular part of East Sussex.

As the times in history changed, so the lives of the people suffered unrest, poverty, cruelty, the impact of war, the bitter persecution of religious differences and the later beginnings of human charity. Through the centuries both farming and industry brought many fine houses and the unique parish churches of great age, some of whose first crude stones were shaped and laid nearly a thousand years ago. Sixteen such remarkable churches are within a mere five miles of Hailsham and they all have countless links with the past, having seen every phase of history and the joys, sorrows and turbulence of countless generations.

The hundreds of date entries that attempt a time span of a thousand years mean this book can only in truth be a presumption, albeit well meant, for both people and events are recorded in all too few words. But wherever a gap may be, then surely there is an enticement for those who may care to follow.

Hailsham   C. A. R.
September 1982

ACKNOWLEDGEMENTS

Many people have been both patient and kind with my seeking answers to countless questions and I am grateful to them all. Those mentioned below have been particularly helpful and generous with their time:

John S. Berkett, A.B. (U.S.A.); Gilbert Catt; Susan Robertson; Clare Clutterbuck, B.A.; Joyce Crow, B.A., A.L.A.; Judith DePue, Ed.D. (U.S.A.); Alan Hibbs, A.L.A.; Jean Linford-Jones; Martyn Owen, B.Sc.; Ernest Pitcher; Elizabeth Talbot Rice, T.D., M.A.; Pauline Tear.

Some years ago when this work was first discussed, Dr. Louis Salzman of the Sussex Archaeological Society was also of help and this gesture from such a man was very much appreciated. Sadly, he is no longer with us.

The following establishments have been of considerable assistance: British Library; Dr. William's Library (London); East Sussex Record Office; Geological Museum; House of Lords Record Office; National Army Museum; New York Historical Society; Ordnance Survey, Archaeology Branch; Public Record Office, Kew; Royal Archives, Windsor Castle; Southern Water Authority; Victoria and Albert Museum; Wesleyan University (Conn. U.S.A.); and public libraries at Brighton, Eastbourne, Hailsham and Westminster. In particular, the library of the Sussex Archaeological Society at Barbican House in Lewes was always a source of kind help whenever the need arose.

HAILSHAM AND ITS ENVIRONS

c. 340

THE ROMAN CASTLE (or Fort) called Anderida was built at Pevensey to defend the coast against the fierce and persistent raids by the Saxons. The Roman road out of Pevensey was inevitably westward, for the other three sides of the fort could only be approached by sea of varying depths according to the tide.

The main Gateway of the Castle was between the enormous circular Bastions at the west end and close to the site of the future church, in an area to become Westham. Outside the main gate was a heavy wooden bridge spanning an eighteen foot wide ditch and from here the Romans built a road to travel west on its important route towards Lewes. (For the route of the Roman Road *see* appendix 'A').

c. 410

The Roman garrison finally withdrew from Pevensey Castle and its anchorage, known to have been a Roman naval port, enabling the local Britons to take possession of the area.

491

Anderida, to become known as Pevensey, was attacked by the Saxon chief Ella whose onslaught was determined and hard, but when finally the persistent Saxon hordes broke through there was a fury that led to the massacre of every man, woman and child. In the Saxon's own Anglo-Saxon Chronicle it records:

> . . . and slew all that dwelt therein so that not a single Briton was there left . . .

It is considered that this merciless battle, after many other deadly Saxon raids on the settlements of Britons, served to mark the ending of the Roman Briton era in Sussex.

1066

William, Duke of Normandy, claimed he was promised the throne of England and about this there must be some doubt, but clearly it was his determination to be King that set in motion the long and detailed planning that made possible William's invasion of England.

For such an operation, there was the immense task of transporting across the English Channel an army with a strength of up to eleven thousand men; the number cannot be agreed, but with them was the extremely hazardous problem of taking some three thousand horses for the Norman mounted troops.

To carry out this complicated venture nearly seven hundred boats were assembled on the French coast, numbers of which were required to be specially built. Many were needed to transport timbers, weapons, food, pre-fabricated assemblies

1

for forts and the tools and equipment for essential tradesmen, some of whom were carpenters, shipwrights, sailmakers, farriers, shoemakers, leather workers, butchers, cooks and others dealing with the daily life of thousands of men.

With William's Norman troops were many who had travelled far to join the expedition, for much was promised and such men would fight only for the plunder that victory would bring. There was also support from the Pope, who gave his blessing to the plans of William with the knowledge that to conquer England would spread the religion of Rome.

After several early set-backs, the army and its huge invasion fleet were ready at St Valery on the north coast of France. But again there was delay, for William now awaited a reasonable wind from the south to ensure a safe crossing to Pevensey; here, with its shallow lagoon, his boats could shelter and his men disembark. However, not until nearly six weeks had passed did a southerly wind finally enable William to set sail at the head of hundreds of heavily laden boats. It was a strict order for the invading boats to stay close together that allowed, after some twenty-four hours on the water, almost the entire fleet to reach Pevensey on 28th September.

Amid turmoil and noise the long and complicated task of disembarking men, animals, equipment and stores went ahead and it was to the immense advantage of William, Duke of Normandy, to learn that Harold, the man he planned to defeat, was some two hundred and sixty miles away at Stamford Bridge near York. It was here only three days previously, he had fought a hard battle against an army of invading Vikings from Norway. Fighting a numerically superior force, Harold had in the end routed the enemy, but upon hearing of William landing at Pevensey it was a depleted and tired army that then sped south to a battle which was to change the course of English history.

And so, merely days after his savage encounter involving thousands of warriors, Harold was soon to confront an even more powerful enemy, an enemy who had long coveted his land and plotted his downfall. At this moment, Harold was faced with a crisis that physically and mentally would prove to be the ultimate test, and upon his response rested the fate of England.

But what manner of man was King Harold? Now aged forty-four, just six years older than William, his home had been at Bosham in west Sussex where he worshipped in a church that still stands. He was of common stock with Danish ancestry, a powerful man and a hard, experienced warrior.

Harold had been crowned King in great haste barely ten months previously in Westminster Abbey just a few hours after the burial in the same place of King Edward, known as the Confessor. He was not a descendant of the dead King but merely his brother-in-law. However, the choice had been made and it had been decided that here was the man most suitable to be crowned. But it was a choice that was disputed and none more so than by William, Duke of Normandy, who was the dead King's cousin.

Soon after landing on English soil, William rode with a party on an early reconnaissance around the waters that then extended inland from Pevensey. It was a ride that can only have produced a stark fear in the people of the villages near the edge of the water. Of this moment, William of Poitiers, a chronicler and former chaplain to William, Duke of Normandy, wrote:

> . . . having been carried to Pevensey by a prosperous wind he disembarked without opposition . . . William quickly explored the places, and the inhabitants, himself, accompanied by a band of not more than 25 soldiers . . . returning from this on foot on account of the roughness of the bye-paths . . .

But the needs and characteristics of such an army as William led were perhaps more aptly expressed by the historian Brigadier C. N. Barclay:

> . . . the Norman horseman rode far and wide from their coastal base, mainly one supposes in quest of supplies for men and animals, and as a protective measure to make certain that there was no large English force in the vicinity. In doing this they seemed to have behaved with the customary barbarity of the times — killing the inhabitants and burning their farms and cottages . . .

Such was the ferocity shown by the invading Normans to the people of the villages within reach of Pevensey, with their intention to quell the population and to take animals and food wherever they found it, that Edwin Tellow in his 'The Enigma of Hastings' records:

> . . . among the villages which the Normans are known to have ravished were: Ashburnham, Bexhill, Crowhurst, Herstmonceux, Ninfield, Sedlescombe and Whatlingham, and while the then market town of Pevensey also received such treatment so, . . . others named in the Domesday Survey cannot be identified, for the pitiful reason that they were so thoroughly despoiled that they were never rebuilt . . .

Hailsham on higher ground was then almost at the water's edge, and it would certainly have been ridden into by the invaders, whose vital needs would have been fiercely sought and ruthlessly taken.

Somewhat to William's surprise, Harold and his men arrived in Sussex on 13 October and both sides made last minute preparations, each on the high ground of their choice, just under two miles apart.

It was thought to be between nine and ten o'clock the next day, the fateful 14th October, with both armies having moved forward to their final positions, that the Normans opened their attack. Hour after hour the battle raged with William's men repeatedly attacking the solid English defensive position on Senlac Hill, using to their advantage hundreds of archers and even greater numbers of cavalry, neither of which were in Harold's army.

> . . . never it was said, had the Normans met foot-soldiers of this stubbornness . . .

As the day wore on with the dead and wounded mounting, so the fighting became more confused with each side in turn having periods of domination, until late in the afternoon, outnumbering the Saxons and showing a greater degree of discipline, the Normans finally broke through the last lines in front of Harold.

In a Norman account of the battle, it was said that a group of knights reached the English King and hacked him to pieces and this manner of death is accepted, but of the fate of Harold's remains, and their removal from the battlefield, there is much doubt. Differing versions exist both in French and in English telling of burials, but conclusive evidence is lacking.

That he could invade and fight with the support of the most powerful knights, William, Duke of Normandy, had promised them lavish rewards of land and booty. And so with victory, and William becoming known as the Conqueror, property and huge areas of land were granted to those who had stood with him against the unyielding English.

Arrogant and ruthless, and now with great power, the Normans settled on their new lands and exerted utter domination over every form of life, regardless of the horror and cruelty they practised on the helpless poor. The renowned G. M. Trevelyan has described the Normans as:

> ... quite as inhumane as the Anglo-Saxons or Danes of contemporary England, and being more active and industrious they committed many more deeds of revolting cruelty. The lopping-off of hands and feet, and the gouging out of eyes of prisoners ...

Life for the defeated was indeed one of oppression with the conquerors taking everything, often with devastating results.

> ... Before the Conquest the lord of the manor was an Englishman, mixing freely with his tenants, but now he was a Norman living remotely in a wooden fort on top of a mound; a foreigner speaking unintelligible French, and the cows, pigs and sheep that the English villein bred and killed for him became the beef, pork and mutton of his table. It was a harsh and rigid system, for the villein was desperately poor ...

But these hated conquerors from Normandy still needed to fight and suppress, for while by victory in Sussex they had quelled the south-east, there still remained the England of the west, the Midlands and the north. In the long years before all resistance was gone, there were still places where the invaders were made to fight hard and on such occasions, both the humans and animals of a district could be wiped out. And yet the Saxon hate was towards a people who were ultimately to unite and strengthen the country against the once deadly Viking raids.

Such a presence was also to see the beginning of a succession of ten Kings of England, all with Norman blood. While the Norman knights, with their vast land and power, were often in the centuries ahead to emerge with a place in history, having introduced the first generations of some of the future great families of England.

Slowly, as the Normans began to take their place in the daily life of the country, their language from France mixing with the English of conquered Saxons, it was perhaps in religion that their influence first began to be apparent. The control of the church was soon firmly in the hands of Norman clergy who replaced not only English priests but most other positions of power in the church hierarchy.

There was also an eventual progress in the fields of administration and law, while later, in more settled times, there emerged the need and desire to enrich their church buildings with fine craftsmanship wherever it could be used. Today, nearly a thousand years on, there can still be seen the clearest evidence of such progress in the remains of castles, as at Lewes, of priories and more fortunately, those parts of cathedrals as at Chichester, that still stand secure with great strength and dignity.

But near to everyone, is the evidence to be found today in many of the parish churches close to Hailsham and indeed throughout Sussex. Of these countless, simple stone churches there can be few where part of the structure, however small, does not bear witness to having been built under the influence of the Normans. And where such a church was built under the care of a powerful and meticulous knight, then there could be simple but outstanding carving in the fine, clean stone from Caen in Normandy.

1066

On Christmas Day, mere months after his victory, William the Conqueror was crowned King William the First of England in Westminster Abbey.

Immediately following the coronation, with the urgent need to ensure the defence of London, fortifications were hastily erected on a site by the Thames. This structure was followed in 1078 by the building of a tall and formidable Keep, parts of which were of white Caen stone from France. The Keep, of great importance to the King, was the beginning of a castle to be known centuries into the future as the Tower of London.

1067

William the Conqueror set sail from Pevensey to return to Normandy where he was awaited by his jubilant people. With him on the journey were taken English hostages of some importance.

c. 1070

Following his victory at Senlac Hill, William the Conqueror rewarded his Knights with land and property and Robert, Count of Mortain, a half brother of William, was granted immense areas of land in several counties. This gift of land included an acreage amounting to almost a sixth of Sussex including fifty-four manors and what remained of the extensive Roman castle at Pevensey. So lavish were the rewards of land by the Conqueror to his followers that calculations have indicated barely 10 per cent of English land remained in the hands of Englishmen.

It was at this time that extensive repairs were undertaken to strengthen the ancient Roman walls. Most of the repair work was in the eastern half of the castle and to make this end secure against attack, a wide ditch was dug, and an earth bank thrown up on which a palisade was erected of heavy spiked stakes set close together.

From this hasty and urgent beginning mostly at the hands of Saxon men, there came in time replacement by the formidable stone defences of the Norman Castle set within the old, but now repaired outer Roman walls. And so the rape of Sussex land given by a grateful and victorious William to Robert of Mortain, was now secure with a castle that dominated the port of Pevensey.

With the same protection of land in mind, the remaining four Norman barons similarly rewarded with a Sussex rape, each built their castles at Hastings, Lewes, Bramber and Arundel.

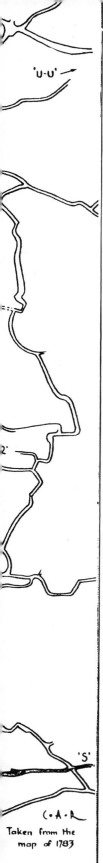

Taken from the
map of 1783

KEY to MAP indicating route of Roman Road westward from Pevensey Castle

A	CARTERS CORNER PLACE	OO	DOWNASH
B	THE BROAD	P	ARLINGTON
C	HELLINGLY CHURCH	Q	BOSHIP
D	HIDE FARM	R	HORSE EYE
E	HORSELUNGES	S	KETCHEM CORNER
F	KNOCKHATCH	T	LOWER HORSEBRIDGE
FF	YEARSHAM (ERSHAM)	TT	HEMPSTEAD LANE
G	MICHELHAM PRIORY	U	MAGHAM DOWN
H	OTHAM ABBEY (Site of)	UU	HERSTMONCEUX
J	POLEGATE STATION (Site of)	V	MARSHFOOT LANE
K	PRIESTHAWES	VV	HAREBEATING
KK	MONTAGUE	W	MILTON HIDE
L	SESSINGHAM	X	NASH STREET
M	THORNWELL COTTAGE	Y	STONE CROSS
N	WILMINGTON PRIORY	YY	PEELINGS
NN	FOLKINGTON	Z	UPPER DICKER
O	COLDTHORN LANE		

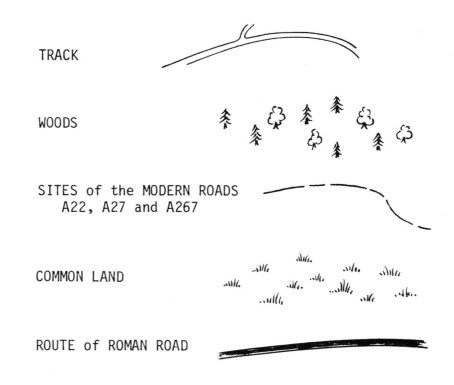

TRACK

WOODS

SITES of the MODERN ROADS
A22, A27 and A267

COMMON LAND

ROUTE of ROMAN ROAD

HAILSHAM COMMON POND

1086

With the need to know more about England and in particular the value of its villages and towns, that they may be fairly assessed for tax, the Saxon Chronicle recorded at the time that in 1085 . . .

> . . . at Gloucester at midwinter . . . the King had deep speech with his counsellors . . . and sent men all over England to each shire . . . to find out . . . what or how much each land holder held . . . in land and livestock and what it was worth . . .

The survey that followed in 1086 was remarkable and at that time, unmatched. The need was that the counsellor's returns should be true and on occasions in pursuit of this, other counsellors were later sent to check their figures. When false results were revealed, punishment followed.

The King's Counsellors visited Hailsham and part of their survey was:

> . . . William holds one hide and a half of the Earl of Hamelesham . . . There is land for 4 ploughs. There are 4 bordars (smallholders) with one ox, and 2 salterns (houses) of 7 shillings. In the time of King Edward (1065) they were worth 100 and ten shillings. Now 20 shillings . . .

There is little doubt that with the need to support the animals and men of an invading army many villages near to Pevensey would have been robbed of cattle, corn and whatever else could be found. The desolation wrought by the invaders is revealed by the low village values recorded in the Domesday Book compared with the values of pre-conquest times. In Herstmonceux the decline was from 120s. 0d. to a mere 20s. 0d., the same as Hailsham.

A year after the survey, entries in the Domesday Book revealed that Hailsham at the time was smaller than most of its surrounding hamlets or villages. The larger populations being in Pevensey on the coast, with Hooe, Wartling and Hertsmonceux, each on small headlands jutting out into the waters that with the passing of many centuries was to become Pevensey Marsh.

But at this early time of the Norman invaders, the waterway behind Pevensey allowed at high tide, boats to be sailed in to villages around the edge of the inland water. Over the years a number of such waterside villages or small ports, were able to develop a modest trade with boats that could navigate the rivers to villages further inland.

It is accepted that the origin of the name Hailsham is: Hoegeles Ham (Hoegeles = a name, Ham = a settlement).

1088

Following the death of the Conqueror in 1087, Pevensey Castle was besieged by William the Conqueror's son William II, known more as William Rufus. The castle, held by Odo, Bishop of Bayeux, withstood all assaults but the inhabitants were finally, after a siege of six months, starved into submission.

1100
1101

An unsuccessful rebellion against Henry I, the Conqueror's youngest son, resulted in William, Count of Mortain, being forced to give up Pevensey Castle. The Castle was later to pass into the possession of the Aquila family whose earlier members had fought at Senlac Hill.

c. 1130

Arising from the dominating influence of Norman noblemen in England, descendants of the Conqueror's army, a Benedictine Priory was founded at Hooe. Its site was on land now known as the Parish Field adjacent to the parish church which was itself largely rebuilt by the Normans.

Hooe at this time was a village that still lived off the waters of Pevensey as indeed it had done for hundreds of years for the salt water tides as they came inland allowed exceptional activity in salt-making, a vital substance for people who relied on fish for a large part of their diet.

In later years, the Benedictine Priory named St Martins in the Wood, was given to the Abbey of Bec in Normandy causing it as an alien priory, to be suppressed by Henry V in 1413.

1147

King Stephen moved against Pevensey Castle, now the property of Gilbert, Earl of Pembroke, to take it by force but due to the sea being close to three sides of the castle, an attacking army was limited in its approach. The Keep built against strong castle walls on two sides and with earthwork defences elsewhere, was to prove formidable.

The King, his attacks repulsed, was forced to set up a siege and his men guarded the landward side, while the sea and inland water round the rest of the castle enabled the King's ships to set up a blockade and complete the encirclement. Once again Pevensey Castle fell without assault.

c. 1163

In a charter of this time the monks of the great Cluniac Priory of St Pancras in Lewes were granted by Richard the Porter of Pevensey,

> . . . that the water of the sea may have free ebb and flow and passage to their mill at Langney through my marsh which is neighbouring to the mill . . .

The charter refers to a tide-mill in the area much later to be known as 'The Crumbles', an extensive coastal area with many water courses, in the region of half a mile west of Langney Priory.

As the charter also quotes,

> . . . the priory mill at Langney . . .

it is reasonably safe to assume that the mill was of Langney Priory, itself connected with the Cluniac Priory at Lewes. (*See* entry of 1624).

c. 1175

Otham Priory was founded by Ralph de Dene of a family linked with William the Conqueror's invasion and mentioned in the Domesday Book. The priory was built for Premonstratension canons (a reformed branch of the Augustinians) on land just two miles south of Hailsham and on the edge of the then tidal waters behind Pevensey, and many of the names on the foundation charter were descendants of knights who fought with the Conqueror.

The chapel built for the priory was dedicated to St Laurence and replaced an earlier chapel on the same site. (*See* entry of *c.* 1205 and appendix 'B').

The impressive old castle wall at Pevensey with a circumference of nearly half a mile, built by the Romans, was a valuable asset of which the Normans needed to make full use.

Against the inside of the eastern wall of the castle, the Normans built a tall Keep of stone from (east) Bourne. In protection of this stronghold, they also strengthened the existing protective ditch and palisade. Thus was created a formidable Norman castle at the eastern end of the former Roman castle. (*See* entry of *c.* 1248).

c. 1180

It was at this time that an early church at Lullington was known to exist. Barely 200 years later the church tower was demolished to be rebuilt in the 16th cent. The tower finally disappeared in *c.* 1775 after it collapsed.

1200   ### c. 1205

With prolonged winter flooding and acute discomfort from the damp and cold conditions, the Premonstratensian monks of Otham Priory were also suffering at times from near starvation due to the poor farming results on the scant land available to them. In such conditions, which repeated year after year, it was inevitable that the priory be abandoned and the monks settle elsewhere.

One of the greatest benefactors of Otham had been the De Brade family of Hellingly who took their name from 'The Broad' estate around the church. It was they who gave to the priory:

> . . . their peat moss of Langney, though wood was plenty . . . this combustible turf was of great use to give body and durability to fires while at the same time it was abundant and easy of access . . .

And at this desperate time, Tikeward de Brade offered permission for the abbey to move to his land at Hellingly, but the eventual decision was to move twenty miles north where Otham's Abbot settled at Bayham Abbey. Two monks remained at Otham to care for the chapel, that local people could continue to use it.

Nothing of the priory remains today above ground, except a few original stones that have been built into the walls of the present house on the site, called 'Otteham Court' on the outskirts of Polegate.

The chapel that survived after the monks left the priory was small, but it had been built with care and it was evident that, apart from local stone, the fine stone from Caen had been used where masons had added enrichment to the interior.

Among the features that can still be seen inside the chapel, are the small attractive pointed arch windows to the south and north sides each with bold cusps. Two very special pieces of work that have both been sadly damaged also remain; one is an excellent piscina in its usual place south of the altar, having a stone shelf used by the priest for storing vessels during Mass, and the other is a priest's sedilia now damaged and without its stone seat. Both of these features however, have the remains of excellent pointed stone canopies rising high on the wall above them.

Where the masons have created moulding and decoration in stone, the style is unusually advanced for such an early date as *c.* 1175, the date of the abbey's foundation. (*See* appendix 'B').

1207

King John granted Pevensey a Charter confirming the town as a Borough and a corporate (or limb) member of the Cinque Ports. As such a member, Pevensey was granted certain liberties and privileges, but in return, the port was committed to supporting the King's navy. In 1300 Pevensey was known to have supplied a ship to the King for a limited period.

1215

William de Fiennes of Herstmonceux supported the Barons in their resolve to curb the powers of the tyrannical King John. It was at Runnymede that the King yielded to pressure and set his seal to the Magna Carta.

1229

An Ordnance (or decree) was issued by Henry III dealing with shipping, and the duty of Cinque Ports to contribute towards the supply of ships and men in defence of England. Northeye was a very small port on the eastern side of the waters that extended inland beyond Pevensey at this time. Northeye was also important enough to have been a limb of the Cinque Port of Hastings.

On what we now know as Pevensey Marsh, with its rivers and dozens of minor watercourses, all under firm control, was once many centuries ago a vast marsh and waterway created by the fresh water of rivers flowing down to where the sea with its tides, came flooding inland past the broad coastal shingle. This volume of water created a natural harbour for Pevensey on its raised headland, where it was once capable of holding ships of the navy. Beyond the harbour was shallower water which allowed the passage of smaller boats taking cargo inland to Hooe, Herstmonceux, Boreham and almost to Hailsham.

The earliest references we have to the port of Northeye indicate a site on ground rising to one hundred feet called Barnhorn Hill. The site occupied the upper half of the hill but it is now split by the A259 road from Pevensey to Little Common.

Above the road on top of the hill, were traced during the last century, foundations that revealed the nave, chancel and west tower of the old chapel known to have been dedicated to St James and endowed by William de Northeye. There is little doubt that an entry in Domesday Book is linked with this chapel.

The lower half of the site situated below the A259 road was lower down

Part of Dill Hundred

HUNDRED OF FOXEARLE

HUNDRED OF NETHERFIELD

Penhurst

Ashburnham Furnace

Withersfield

Blackdown

Windmill

Harings

Cranl

Horsham

Cranl Furnace

Furnace

Cogers Cross

Winking hurst

North Street

Springham

Bucksteep

Ponts green

Parsonage

Ashburnham Park

Stevens C

Park Gate

Comb

Kitchingham

Standard hill

Foul Mile

Broadstreet green

Ashburnham

Calreech

Gardener's Street

Carters Corner

Brick house

Lime Cross

Windmill hill

Compost

Carters

Ruins of Boreham

Fishers green

Morr Hall

Nenfield

Venfield

Benham bridg

Inperha

Pass

North Street

Sharpers

Hellingley

Mugham Down

Park

Noibridge

Hurstmonceux

Colthnes

Boreham street

HUNDRED OF

DRED

Hooe Common

Nulls Cross

Hooe Courtledge

Horse bridg

Uppe

Ly cross

Michelham

Michelham bridg

Nate Wood

Hailsham

HUNDRED

OF

PEVENSEY

Warthing

Seavers bridg

Barnhorne

Ruins of Northy Chap

Couding Gr

Down Stream

Middle Point

MANXEY LEVEL

Sarland

Cotham

Rickney bridg

Glynley

Hankham

LIBERTY

Swines hill

Pool gate green

Peeling

Priesthams

Pevensey

Pevensey brook

Sluce houses

Sluce Haven

Walnut Street

Westham

Red house

Little Hatch

Longe Hatch

Pevensey Haven

Foul Ride Cross

WILLINGDON

LEVEL

Langney

Langney bridg

Pevensey Bay

Pevensy Cast a Large remain
of Roman building half a mile
in Circuit.

Willingdon

Nevington

HUNDRED OF

Patten

WILLINGDON

Crumble bridg

HUNDRED OF

Crumble Pond

E Bowne

BOURNE

Sea houses

Crumble Pond

Langney Point

EAST BOURNE

Bourn Place

Brown Hodes

Map of 1724 by
RICHARD BUDGEN
with an indication
of the marsh area

the hill and barely fifty feet above sea level. It was here that the old village of Northeye (some records refer to it as a town) once flourished as a cinque port.

The village site, for long known as 'Old Town Field' has the uneven surface of disturbed earth and in an exceptionally dry summer of 1859 the parched ground with its contrasting colours enabled the outlines of old buildings to be traced. These clear indications served to explain the reason there had existed as long as people could remember, evidence of past ancient buildings. The evidence took the form of isolated stones found about the large field, some still with shape and moulding and made from the fine textured Caen stone from France, so often used in the more important structures.

Not without significance is that even the complication and delay of using Caen stone, probably for parts of Northeye chapel, was found acceptable. The stone from across the Channel was of a clean appearance, cream in colour and could be worked to an extremely fine finish. The contrast of this stone with the readily available coarse grey/green stone from the nearby (east) Bourne quarry was extreme.

For centuries past the sea at Pevensey with its immense moving banks of shingle was a continual problem and it is the sea with its power and unpredictable action that is accepted as the reason for the demise and disappearance of this cinque port.

It would appear that in the ensuing years, through the influence of landowners and with the support of the Crown, a measure of control was exercised over the tidal waters. This safeguard was sufficient to allow a second Northeye to be built west of the abandoned 'Barnhorn' Northeye.

The site of this latter village was towards the centre of the marsh on a small area of rising ground destined to become known as Chapel Field, just 5 miles from Hailsham and but a mile inland from Normans Bay. Now, centuries on, the uneven ground of the field from which radiate a number of footpaths, the stone bridge of great age leading to an old road and the knowledge from research, have confirmed this second Northeye.

That there was a minister there in 1515 is known and the past existence of a chapel is acknowledged through nearly four hundred years of map making.

The early spelling 'Nordy' appears on John Norden's map of Sussex, drawn in 1595. In 1610 a map by Norden and Speed quotes 'Nordy Chapel' while in 1724 the map by Richard Budgen refers to the chapel field site as 'Ruins of Northy Chap'. Both of these deserted village sites are now acknowledged by the Archaeology branch of Ordnance Survey.

That two such villages, one at least seven hundred and fifty years old, should have existed by the inland waters of Pevensey and each with the same name is indeed intriguing and it can only be hoped that at some time a major archaeological investigation will reveal more of these two deserted medieval villages.

The same inland waterway, but this time at its western end, swept in from the sea past the port of Pevensey, and extended behind the high ground of Pevensey town until it covered the large area now known as Willingdon Levels. At the edge of these levels, barely four miles from Hailsham, was yet another small limb of the Cinque Port of Hastings with the name Hydeneye.

The site of this port with its chapel was on a small area of higher ground that sloped up from the water to a ridge over one hundred feet high where Willingdon village with its parish church overlooked the vast inland waterway. The old port, active many centuries ago but its water long gone due to reclaimed land, was on ground where now stands the community of Hampden Park.

Many acres of land where once stood the port had names linked to Hydeneye, i.e. Great Hydeneye, Green Hydeneye, Plough Hydeneye and Court Hydeneye etc. The use of the word 'eye' on the marsh indicates an island site as would Horseye for island of horses, Manxey for Monks, Hornseye for horned cattle, Langney for long island etc.

About 1750, inhabitants in the neighbourhood of Hydeneye spoke of, and were quoted as having remembered at that time, the walls of a few surviving buildings, once the Hydeneye of the distant past. But the stone of such remains were disappearing fast, being sought after and taken by anyone having a use for such sound material. It was a timeless habit that through the ages had reduced many abandoned stone structures. (*See* appendix 'C').

1229

Gilbert de Aquila, Lord of Pevensey Castle, whose grandfather was killed at the Battle of Hastings while fighting for the Conqueror, sought and was granted permission by Henry III to found a priory on his land at Michelham and to ensure its upkeep Gilbert de Aquila gave much of his land from neighbouring areas including Pevensey, Willingdon and Seaford.

The early buildings of the priory with a church, cloisters, chapter house, refectory and dormitory, were of various local stones but mostly of the sandstone from (east) Bourne which was transported to Michelham by sea and the River Cuckmere, a river that fed the priory moat and fish ponds.

To provide the first religious members, the Priory of Austin Canons at Hastings sent thirteen of their order (a prior and twelve canons reflecting Christ and his twelve apostles), and with this beginning Michelham Priory was established and began its work. Their day was hard and ordered to a rigid timetable, conducted mostly in silence. With cloaks of black they became known to the peasants as 'black monks' and were liked for the help they could provide.

With the need for offering charity to the poor and hospitality to the traveller, some of whom may well have been people of distinction to whom was given good food and comfort, Gilbert de Aquila enriched the priory with both Hailsham and Laughton parish churches, and the tithes they could provide.

During the ensuing years, further strengthening of resources came from land-owners who made various gifts of land to the priory. Most was nearby and within reach, but some of the land was outside the county.

Michelham Priory Gate

1234

The preservation and storage of food was of vital importance to the whole population, for it was salt that could keep both meat and fish in reasonable condition over long, hard periods.

For hundreds of years, salt making was an important activity spread over the estuaries and tide washed inland waters of Sussex, and Pevensey was known to produce quantities vast enough to be exported. It was in 1234 that the Abbey of Grestain in Normandy recorded their right to receive four hundred bushels of salt from the waters of Pevensey.

The summer occupation of making salt was a simple process of evaporating sea water until only salt was left, but at varying times and places the method employed often differed.

A common procedure was to skim up salt-impregnated sand or silt, wash it with water, which in passing through the sand, carried the salt with it into a metal container. The container, now full of brine, was heated with a fire usually in a salt-house, until complete evaporation isolated the salt.

A simpler method was to retain sea water from a receding tide in prepared ditches or trenches, from where it could be run into shallow clay-lined pans or salterns. It was then left to evaporate in the sun and the wind.

The Domesday Book recorded much salt-making along the tidal rivers and fringes of the inland waterways of Pevensey and more than thirty pans or salterns were in the neighbourhood of Hooe. Many salt-works were also busy along the course of the Pevensey Haven river, even as far inland as the Glynleigh stream. Other places mentioned as having salt pans and clearly once subject to a salt water tide were the Willingdon Inlet, Hailsham, Bowley (in Hailsham), Ashburnham and Wartling, while farther west there were as many as eight pans each at Ripe and Laughton from the waters of the river Ouse.

It is close to the tidal rivers inland from Pevensey that evidence remains today of an industry dating back a thousand years. And there can be found the now grass covered mounds many yards across and often over four feet high, some formed at least six hundred years ago of the sand and silt thrown aside after the extraction of salt.

This simple life-sparing activity dating back to the Saxons gave, at times, a prosperity to many coastal communities and the Domesday survey recorded more salt-works in Sussex than any other county.

c. 1240

The Benedictine Priory at Wilmington was built.

As a reward to his half brother after the Conquest, William the Conqueror granted Robert de Mortain extensive areas of land part of which was the Manor of Wilmington which Mortain, in turn, gave to the Benedictine Abbey founded by his father at Grestain in Normandy.

It was on land next to the simple parish church that the priory was built. Modest in size the nearby materials of chalk, flint and greensand stone from (east)

Bourne were used in the construction and surviving from that early time is an underground vaulted chamber with heavy diagonal ribs forming a series of crude stone arches overhead.

The 14th cent. north-east wing of the priory was built to within a few feet of the parish church wall and evidence indicates there was once a connecting passage of some sort to allow private entry into the church.

Additions to the priory were made through the centuries, the most impressive being the long hall of the 14th cent. of which the south front still stands. The flint and stone wall with a tall mullioned window is between two bold polygonal turrets rising up from the ground at each end. Robbed of its life as a priory and with the inevitable neglect of later tenants, the south front has suffered a loss of stonework but still there remains a dignity that recalls the prestige of early days.

With its site close to the coast and to Pevensey in particular, the priory was used by the Abbey of Gestain to supervise their estates and possessions in England. With such a task there was a regular communication between Gestain and Wilmington.

That Wilmington Priory was a French possession was in future years to cause repeated upheaval, for arising from England's long history of hostility with France was the confiscation of the priory and its land whenever the countries were in dispute or at war. On no fewer than five occasions of antagonism was the Wilmington establishment taken from the French, only for it to be handed back after varying periods of years, when a satisfactory relationship had been restored. During such periods of seizure by the Crown, the property was neglected and regarded solely as a source of income from a succession of tenants.

It was in the reign of Henry IV that Wilmington Priory,

> . . . in 1403, with other alien priories, was for the last time resumed into the King's hands . . .

Never again was Wilmington to be controlled by the French, for ten years later and but two years before his famous victory at Agincourt, Henry V granted both the priory and the manor to Chichester Cathedral in whose hands it remained until 1565, when it passed to Sir Richard Sackville. At this time it was but,

> . . . a manor house and farmhouse with accommodation for holding courts . . .

while part of the property was used as a vicarage.

From *c.* 1700 at which time Wilmington Priory was mainly used as a farmhouse, it was in turn owned by the Earl of Wilmington, the Cavendish family and the Duke of Devonshire who sold the farmland to Col. R. V. Gwynne, but retained the priory building and conveyed it to the Sussex Archaeological Society. It now has a museum of rural interests with an emphasis on Sussex agriculture. (*See* entries of 1413, 1538 and 1925).

c. 1248

Following the granting of Pevensey Castle to Peter of Savoy, Duke of Richmond, he concerned himself with improving the defence of the Norman Keep.

On its three unprotected sides, this descendant of a warrior who fought at Senlac Hill, built a huge stone curtain wall set with round towers. There was also a Gatehouse of great strength with twin towers and a drawbridge.

Much of this well-planned and solid defensive work, now of great age, still stands today.

1252

The Rights of a Market in Hailsham were granted to the royal favourite, Peter of Savoy, by Henry III

> . . . we have granted and by this our charter have confirmed to our dear and faithful Peter of Savoy that he and his heirs in perpetuity may have a market in his manor of Heylesham every week on Wednesday with all customs pertaining to such a market, so it be not to the detriment of neighbouring markets . . .

With the granting of such rights was that

> . . . a toll was to be collected in the market place each Wednesday market . . .

Peter of Savoy was an uncle to Eleanor of Provence who had married Henry III. Indeed, with Eleanor herself a sister of the Queen of France, the connection between the two royal families was close.

It was this stimulating affinity with French noblemen and their attractive culture, that proved a fatal inducement for the King to favour such men with high office in English affairs. Many such favours and appointments proved dangerous mistakes.

Among other past favours granted by the King to Peter of Savoy was that he be custodian of the castles at both Hastings and Lewes,

> . . . at length the patience of the Englifh nobility was exhaufted by the infults and injuries they received from thefe infolent ftrangers . . . deputed the earl marfhal to lay their grievances before the King. . . . the earl demanded an audience, which being granted, he informed Henry of the complaints of the people, he befought him not to continue lavifhing his favours on foreigners to the great neglect and injury of his natural fubjects . . .

(*See* entry of 1267).

1253

The Sheriff of Sussex was ordered to provide 30,000 horseshoes and 60,000 nails for the Royal army of Henry III.

The iron industry of the weald with its scattered and somewhat primitive early furnaces were concerned in this work.

At this time there were furnaces at Chiddingly, Cowbeech, Hellingly, Heathfield, Waldron and Warbleton.

c. 1260

A feudal document of considerable length set out in detail the

> ... services and customs of my men of Haylesham which should be rendered to their lord Robert Marmyun at Berewik (Berwick) ...

The document or charter, placed on record the wide range of obligations demanded of the villein cottager, who as tenant of a small parcel of land was completely subservient to his master.

In this case Robert Marmyun possessed huge areas of land in and around Hailsham, from which the tenant was required to provide food as well as labour and these duties would pass on to the heirs upon the death of the father.

> ... at Christmas to give 9 hens and a cock, at Easter to give 100 eggs, in summer one day with 4 strong men to mow meadows and in autumn one day with 4 men or women to reap crops ...

Other commitments of the villein was to find special payments to the Lord's family, in the event of a marriage of his son or daughter. A contribution was also to be made towards ransom money, should a knight of the family be taken prisoner in battle and a price put on his head.

From this document there emerges the illustration of how dominant in Sussex, were the families who owed their descent to the French Knights of the Conqueror's invading army two hundred years earlier.

Of the many witnesses who signed the document, the following had names of local significance:

> ... Peter de Haylesham, Simon de Hellingeleghe, Randulph de Brade (of the Broad estate, Hellingly), Walter de Aurringgeton, Simon de Hemstede and linked by name to the waters of Pevensey were: Nicholas de Horsye, Richard de Manekesey and Richard de Hydenhye.

1263

Entry in Sussex Assize Roll

> ... Gilbert son of Gilbert Godseb while bathing in the pond at Haylesham was drowned and Salomon son of John Russel who first found him is not suspected ...

1263

At Sussex Assize, Benedict the Jew, dwelling in 'Heylesham' was outlawed for clipping the King's coin. The offence of clipping the edges of coins for the value of the metal was widespread and extremely serious, and at times punishable by death.

1264

The Battle of Lewes was fought. King Henry III with his army set out from the old town of Winchelsea (now submerged by the sea), his destination the Castle in Lewes.

The march across East Sussex was to be one of atrocity, pillage and mutilation, a wild and vicious tendency not unknown in marching medieval armies. They camped a night at Herstmonceux and,

> . . . while his army were employing themselves in hunting and destroying the park,
> a certain nobleman, named Roger de Tourney, was killed by a chance blow of an
> arrow, which struck him in the throat . . .

then the army marched on through the outskirts of Hailsham to the coming battle at Lewes.

Following the King's defeat by Simon de Montfort, of those barons and knights who escaped from the battlefield, many fled past Hailsham to take refuge in Pevensey Castle.

Some of the Royalists sailed for France while others remained in the Castle, only to be overtaken by the son of Simon de Montfort who at once set up a siege.

The siege was succeeding, but it had to be lifted when de Montfort sent urgent word for his son and troops, to strengthen his own army, at that time on the Welsh border. From Pevensey, the son of de Montfort finally reached Kenilworth, where he was surprised and out-manoeuvred by an army led by Prince Edward, and suffered a heavy defeat. Without the reinforcements his son would have provided, Simon de Montfort was forced into battle against Prince Edward and the Earl of Gloucester at Evesham in 1265, where he lost both his cause and his life.

1266

To repair or rebuild the damaged stone walls of Lewes, the inhabitants were allowed to charge a one penny toll on all carts bringing iron items from Chiddingly, Heathfield and other furnaces in the weald for sale in the town.

The toll charge for a horse laden with ironware was a halfpenny.

1267

It was recorded that:

> . . . Peter of Savoy . . . unlawfully takes toll at the market on every day of the week
> to the great opression of the country . . .

The flagrant abuse of power with the injustices that followed had for many years caused widespread unrest.

Not until the wise and strong administrator Edward I came to the throne in 1272 were steps taken to curb the misuse of authority and it was he who introduced commissioners who, on behalf of the Crown, were sent to all parts of the country to seek and punish where deceit and corruption were practised.

The task was formidable and even as late as 1278, it was found that Walter de Endelenewick (named after a manor at that time near Ripe) was found guilty of illegal demands for he,

> . . . has levied stallage in the market of Haylesham from diverse men who should not

pay any custom . . .

The commissioners did much throughout the country to reduce blatant and illegal demands on trades peoples in the market places, and on more than one occasion heavy fines were inflicted in Hailsham for such fraudulent practice.

c. 1270

A map of Pevensey in this century indicated the presence of a Court House.

Whether any of this actual building has survived is open to doubt, but clearly the diminutive court house still to be seen in Pevensey today has parts of its structure of great age, as well as the alterations and repairs of later centuries.

The ground area of the court house is a mere nineteen feet by twenty-three feet with two cells and an exercise yard of only eight feet by six feet. At the top of a steep outside staircase is the court room of eighteen feet by fourteen feet into which are crowded narrow benches for the magistrate, jury, public and the clerk in addition to the prisoner's dock. It was this minute court that had the power to inflict the death penalty.

The building ceased to be used for public affairs in 1883 when it passed into the hands of the Pevensey Town Trust who have transformed the court room into a museum. Of special interest is the exhibit, the Seal of the Corporation, the oldest seal possessed by any of the Cinque Ports. It is of cast iron and dates from c. 1230.

c. 1274

At this date the free-trading or smuggling of wool out of Sussex, and Pevensey in particular, steadily increased due to the heavy tax Edward I imposed on its export.

1278

Simon, a merchant of 'Haylesham' was fined for selling false measures of cloth.

1278

An Assize Roll recorded that Thomas Alin was tried as a poacher and found guilty. This man was the Prior's manservant at Michelham Priory and as his activities were known to the Prior, his fine was paid by the priory.

1278

At the annual Priory Fair held at Fair Place, Otham for the sale of farm produce, cattle and general merchandise the canons were fined by the Queen's steward, Richard of Pevenes, for charging visiting merchants for the last four years, a toll which was illegal.

The fair, held on land but a few yards from the site of the old Otham Priory was held on the eve of, and on St Lawrence's Day. At this time the abbey building had become a farm, as indeed it was to continue, with repairs, alterations and different owners for some centuries to come.

1283

The Archbishop of Canterbury travelling from Battle Abbey was received at Michelham Priory, where he spent two nights in order to make local visits before moving on to Rochester.

On his return to Canterbury the Archbishop issued a complaint to the Arch-deacon of Lewes concerning the unsatisfactory state of the priory. This caused a fine and a warning to be inflicted on the priory.

1287

For many years the East Sussex coastline is known, due to its ever shifting shingle, to have been suffering from erosion, and an exceptionally bad storm in 1250 with very high tides caused the sea to break through on to the coastal levels of Winchelsea and Pevensey.

Thirty-seven years later it was another devastating storm that finally destroyed the already damaged town of Old Winchelsea. It was this same storm-swept high sea that surged inland over the wide expanse of Pevensey Levels, causing the smaller islands to be submerged.

One hundred and seventy-two sheep were marooned and drowned by the flooding. When found, the sheep were taken by boat to Pevensey Castle, where they were skinned and salted.

It has been recorded that between the years 1283–1294, for the value of their wool, up to six hundred sheep were kept on grazing land attached to the Castle.

1288

The ravages of time at this exposed coastal place and generations of neglect had left parts of Pevensey Castle in a state of ruin. Much of the stonework, by now nearly eight hundred years old, had collapsed or been eroded, while heavy timbers of great age had decayed.

With the need arising for the Castle to be saved, selected repairs and re-building, including a new drawbridge, were put in hand. The work lasted some three years and involved the use of local materials.

The stone came from the quarry along the coast at (east) Bourne, rafters came from Chiddingly, and scaffold poles were brought from Waldron. The lime came from Willingdon and sand from Bourne while regular supplies of bran came from the mill at Hailsham.

From the many accounts recorded by William Cropp who was in charge of the castle repair and rebuilding work we can read:

> ... wages of 3 men carrying stones and mortar on to the top of the gate (gate tower) on their backs for lack of windlasses being 8d a week each ...
> ... for iron bought for making hinges and straps for the bridge (drawbridge) ...

... for 50 sheaves of furze bought to put under windlass 18d ... for a cord of 27 strands bought to lift up stones, mortar and other things 15½d ... for mending and splicing the cord many times 4d ... for grease bought for windlass 1½d ... for carriage of timber for stairs from Clavrig (Clavering at Arlington) to Pevenes 4d ... ... for pugging (rough plastering) the pigeon house 6d ... wages of a carpenter mending the Queen's room and other buildings 2s 6d ... for pugging the Queen's room and chapel with mortar and for plastering the chapel 12d ... wages of a thatcher and thatching the Queen's chamber 12½d
... for obtaining reeds at Willendon for the thatching 6d ...
... wages of a carpenter putting new rafters in the south turret and mending the old rafters ...
... of bran (from the mill at Hailsham) for burnishing armour 12d ... grease for same 1d ...
... for a man cleaning and levelling the place where the chapel was built 4d ...

The heavy stone balls handled by men 'slingers' on the huge wooden catapult machines in defence of the castle were made of stone from the Bourne quarry as were the balls used in defence of the castle at Lewes.

c. 1289

Luke de la Gare, a '... Conservator of the Marsh of Pevensey ...' appointed by Edward I, ordered the building of an earth bank across the Haven river and the erection of a sluice near the sea. The work was intended to drain an area of waterway but there was serious miscalculation causing water to be obstructed on its way to the sea, with serious flooding inland.

The result of angry complaints to Edward I by landowners, including the Abbot of Battle and the Prior of Lewes, was a commission of enquiry to examine the problems of tides and complicated watercourses,

... to safeguard the defence of the lands of all persons, as well rich as poor ...

Among the decisions taken was to remove obstructions to the free flow of water and take steps to preserve land so often flooded in the past,

... to the peril of all persons dwelling in and around the same marsh ...

1291

The parish church at 'Alisham' was valued at £26 13s. 4d.

c. 1294

Walter de Pelham purchased land in and near Hailsham and later moved into Sussex from Hertfordshire. The family of Pelham was in future generations to be famous in Sussex and to earn great honour in battle.

1296

For many years bitter disputes and even legal battles, with varying results, had been waged between Bayham Abbey, under which came Hellingly church, and Michelham Priory whose monks insisted that Hailsham church belonged to them.

The quarrel was that Bayham demanded Hailsham church as their possession and even at one time caused its Rector to be violently ejected from his church.

Michelham Priory, however, strongly protested and after some twenty years of dispute it was agreed that the Archbishop of Canterbury would examine the complicated situation and give his personal opinion to be acted upon as a final judgement.

The decision of the Archbishop in 1296 was in favour of Bayham Abbey and given in a long and detailed award, which set out the obligations of Bayham as well as both the privileges and duties of Hailsham's parish church. The duties were to include providing rushes for the earth floor in winter, incense for 'censing' and wax for lights round the altar.

1298

Again it was a time of yet further repairs to the castle within a castle at Pevensey and with this renewed effort to strengthen the stone and wood structures, a decision was made to re-build the chapel that had, until now, stood inside the inner Norman walls.

The chapel was to be resited outside the Norman walls so that local people could freely attend and reach the chapel by passing into the castle through the gate in the ancient outer Roman wall.

A vast amount of timber was needed for new wooden structures and the accounts included:

> . . . cutting and squaring timber in the park at Mersefeud (Maresfield) for building the hall in the castle . . .

and

> . . . for 43 carts employed carrying the said timber from the park . . .

1300

1302

Edward I had stayed at the Priory in Lewes where thirty-eight years before, his father had suffered a crushing defeat by Simon de Montfort. Now, with his court entourage, the King progressed past Firle and by a circuitous route, probably through Alciston and Selmeston, reached Wick Street close to Michelham. It was at Michelham Priory that the King and his followers stayed the night of 14 September before continuing their journey the next day through Horsebridge and Boreham and on to Battle Abbey.

It was but a few years earlier than these visits to religious houses that the King, desperately in need of money after supporting large armies for his wars, had demanded taxes from the clergy. After protests he had appointed:

> . . . the heads of monastic houses who could provide strong-rooms for the proceeds of the tax; they were required to keep careful records, report regularly to the exchequer, and finally to submit their accounts for audit . . .

The King, now sixty-three years old and still undertaking arduous journeys over rough roads, was but within five years of his death and the end of a long reign of thirty-five years.

1304

A Deed from William de Hastings, Lord of Northeye, dealt with the drainage of Pevensey marsh land in the Manor of Bernehorne (Barnehorn).

The document concerned the Abbot of Battle wishing to drain certain of his land but it appears this could not be done without involving land called Grade, the property of the Lord of Northeye. The Deed allowed the drainage to proceed.

1315

The Heffle Fair began in Heathfield and remained an annual event for almost five hundred and fifty years. It was by tradition that each year on 14 April an old woman released from her basket the first cuckoo of spring.

c. 1318

In a castle so vast and complicated as that at Pevensey, with its outer walls nearly a thousand years old, repairs and replacements were a continuing problem. Indeed since its remote beginnings in history the castle had passed through the hands of many custodians and for long periods, with only parts of the castle being used, it suffered almost total neglect.

From this time it can be said the castle was never in complete repair again.

Such a weakness in defence on a coast so near France caused such concern that it prompted a full examination into the castle's condition. The result was that from 1329 men were engaged over a long period in limited repair work and Edward II paid John Ashburnham for sixty mature oak trees cut in Ashburnham Woods for use at Pevensey.

c. 1320

About this time, the Manor House at Alciston was built but a few yards from the west end of the parish church. It was an impressive house which, together with its extensive land, belonged to the Benedictine monks of Battle Abbey.

Being of the great Abbey of Battle, the status of the manor was considerable and a large number of permanent workers, apart from casual labourers, were engaged on the vast area of farmland. The land spread into many parishes surrounding Alciston, some of which were: Alfriston, Lullington, Hailsham, Arlington, Hellingly and Selmeston.

The main products of the manor were wheat and many thousands of sheep, three thousand alone were kept at Alciston, mainly for their wool which records indicate was higher in value than the wool in west Sussex.

The substantial manor house of stone and flint with fish ponds, a dovecot for hundreds of birds and rich farmlands was a flourishing establishment. Its interior still has massive oak beams dating back probably six hundred years and the stonework, where it remains undamaged, includes the narrow columns, carved caps and moulded arches of the Early English period. Such stonework even now reflects the original connection with a medieval religious centre.

Much of this work of nearly seven hundred years ago had a quality that was sometimes superior to the stonework of our local parish churches. Such work, where it can still be seen in the heart of the present house, provides a startling reminder of the distant past in spite of the alterations and additions of later centuries before it became the present Alciston Court farmhouse.

Built a little later to be part of Alciston Manor was the great Tithe Barn but a few yards away, a vast structure, the interior lit by two towering fifteen-foot high entries for farm carts loaded with hay. Of awesome size, immense timbers reach high up into the gloom of the roof, and create a majesty more in keeping with a cathedral.

Supported on sturdy walls of local flint nearly one hundred and seventy feet long, it has a roof thought to support nearly fifty thousand clay tiles. The barn is now part of the old Court House Farm, the property of the Gage family, who were awarded the manor of Alciston after the Dissolution of the Monasteries, in return for providing armed horsemen for the use of Henry VIII. (*See* entry of 1349).

1324

Edward II visited and stayed a few days at Pevensey, and in the following year the castle received and held special prisoners from Berkhamstead Castle.

1326

For the provisioning of the many armed men in Dover Castle considerable quantities of meat were needed to be purchased by Sheriffs of the south-eastern counties. In this year the Exchequer recorded the movement of:

> 21 Hogs from Hailsham, Hellingly and Eckington (a farmstead in Ripe) together with smaller quantities from Boreham and Berwick.

These carcasses were transported by pack-horse (not carts) to Seaford where a ship already carrying stores from Arundel and Shoreham, took them aboard and sailed on to Dover.

1341

It was at this time that a small chapel was in use on the island of Horseye, some twenty-eight feet above sea level on what is now Pevensey Marsh.

> . . . subject to the Chancellor of the Cathedral Church of Chichester . . .

This chapel, but two miles from Hailsham parish church, serves to illustrate how many chapels built by a patron to serve a mere sprinkling of local people, were in use until the improvement of tracks into roads made parish churches easier to reach.

It is recorded that the chapel was with a minister and in use in 1500.

1342

The small exposed village of Exceat was one of the settlements that suffered destruction during the raids along the south coast by the French. Such damage and loss of life worsened even the poverty already being felt in many parts of East Sussex.

It is recorded that just a little over a hundred years later the Exceat church was in ruins and with the extreme hardship and suffering of living at this place, Exceat became in time, a deserted village. (*See* entry of 1913).

c. 1343

The timbered house opposite the east gate of Pevensey Castle was built. Known as The Mint House it is possibly on the site of an early Pevensey Mint known to have minted coins when the Normans were in occupation of the castle.

Nearly two hundred years later in 1542 the Mint House was purchased by Andrew Boorde, a man of talent and strong personality, on occasions being known as Merry Andrew

> . . . on account of his drolleries . . .

Boorde was educated at Winchester and Oxford and became a Carthusian monk, during which time he was appointed to be a suffragan Bishop of Chichester. However the discipline of monastic life proved too arduous and he sought and obtained a dispensation from his religious vows.

Andrew Boorde was attracted to the study of medicine and travelled to many places overseas in search of knowledge.

> . . . then desiring to have a trewe cognuscyon of the practis of physycke he passed over the seas agayne, and dyd go to all the unyversities and scoles approbated and beynge within the precinct of chrystendome . . .

Study at his favourite university of Montpelier led him to become a member of the Royal College of Physicians and to practice as a doctor as well as to write several books including 'Dyetary of Health' on the subject of 'physycke'. He became known for his claim that '. . . water is not wholesome, sole by itself, for Englysshe men . . .'

In spite of his true ability and learned mind, he was known to have attended fairs and markets selling his own preparations with entertaining humour. At this time he would have known the market in Hailsham.

> . . . In spite of Boorde's sad slip at the end of his life, no one can read his racy writings without admiring and liking the cheery, frank, bright, helpful, and sensible fellow who penned them . . .

The harsh treatment of the monasteries at the Dissolution prompted personal appeals and protests to Thomas Cromwell that were strong enough to have him condemned to a period in the Tower. But in spite of his views he was, towards the end of Henry VIII's life, admitted to the Court as one of the King's physicians.

With the death of Henry VIII in 1547, his son, the boy King Edward VI, accepted the friendship of Boorde and stayed with him at the Mint House in the year of his coronation. Edward was destined to rule only six years before illness brought about his death in 1553.

Throughout his days, Andrew Boorde never settled for long but was known as a somewhat erratic wanderer. Towards the end of his life, Boorde was not always to prove a popular man and it is thought as a result of making enemies and causing offence at Court, he was destined to die in the Fleet Prison.

1349

The outbreak of the Black Death plague spread widely, especially among the undernourished with low resistance, and it was to bring about the death of at least a third of the population causing in its wake a catastrophic change in almost every phase of life.

In areas where the plague was at its deadliest, the effect on the population of some hamlets and communities was devastating; farms were abandoned and it was not unknown for entire communities to die. At Wartling twelve people died in March but by October a further sixty had become victims of the horrifying disease with many families decimated.

The plague struck hard at the area just five miles southwest of Hailsham for at Alciston few houses of age now remain, but below ground level, there is evidence of a past village of many people. At Berwick, again the church is now almost isolated but once it served a village of substantial size. Just half a mile north of Alfriston there was once a thriving community of Winton while across the Cuckmere there is the lone church of Lullington reduced in size to a mere incomplete chancel. A similar church without houses is at Beddingham and much thinking is inclined to regard Arlington as yet another shrunken village. Certainly the nearby priory at Michelham suffered severe losses among its Canons and workers.

A remarkable record of these times and the horror at Alciston is in the old Court Rolls of the Manor Court. It is a record of the proceedings at courts held during the first year of the plague, when widespread deaths on manor land in Alciston and the surrounding parishes were spoken of.

At a court of 14th April no fewer than twenty-four tenants were reported to have died and with increasing severity the plague claimed thirty-nine more deaths by 10th June. The court of 1st August added yet another fifteen, making a total of seventy-eight men struck down in barely six months. Of this number, the small village of Lullington lost twenty-five and Hellingly fifteen.

The figures recorded by the Manor Court referred only to tenants; mostly men who had worked small parcels of the Lord's land, but there can be no doubt that death also came to some of the wives and children, for it was not unusual for a family to be entirely wiped out. Where a family had all died or a survivor could not work the land, it passed back into possession of the Lord of the Manor and by August in this year of the plague, forty-four parcels or tenements of such land remained unclaimed.

By a custom of some age, the heir of a deceased tenant was obliged to give his Lord (the gift was called a heriot) the best beast of any owned by the dead man and at the August Court, no fewer than fifty-two heriots had passed to the Lord of the Manor who was no doubt subservient to Battle Abbey.

One of the effects on agricultural areas was the immediate shortage of workers, causing those that survived to be overworked in an effort to save cattle and crops. It was a desperate situation that caused acute unrest and workers, for long low paid, found a strength to demand higher wages for their now more valuable services. But nothing could prevent much of the land becoming idle and remaining untilled and wasted.

The changed times was a blow to landowners who were forced to accept their reduced circumstances and to plan for recovery, which was in time to come by turning unused fields into additional sheep pastures. This fundamental change in farming was to be the beginning of a great prosperity in wool and with ever increasing flocks came a surge of weaving and a flourishing export trade.

Inevitably, Hailsham was involved in the changing times and as sheep farming increased on every side, to be followed by the introduction of both import and export taxes, so too began the intensive pursuit of smuggling.

There was to be a prosperity Sussex had never known, and the avoidance of taxes encouraged a widespread and efficient smuggling organisation that was to bring good pay to hundreds of workers along the coast, and the inland routes that conveyed illicit goods many miles to the towns.

Over the years smuggling established itself as a very profitable activity and adapted to changing times and demands as they came along. In due course, the illegal and sometimes dangerous trade was to handle coinage, cloth, spirits, tea and even cannon and prisoners of war. It was a trade which by the 18th cent. was to reach international proportions involving men of considerable standing.

1356

The Pelham family came to England with William the Conqueror and had, in 1296, been granted vast acres of Sussex land including much that was in and around Hailsham.

The great fame of the family was to be sealed at the Battle of Poitiers in 1356 where Sir John Pelham fought the French with Edward III

> ... men of Sussex in thick of fray ... riding madly over dead and dying the Sussex contingent hacked their way through the main division of the enemy ... the French King John was captured by Sir John Pelham ... the French King gave Pelham the buckle of his sword belt ...

Sir John, the Sussex warrior of Poitiers and other continental battlefields, was honoured with burial in Canterbury Cathedral, where a stained glass window in the chapter house depicts him in armour.

The capture of King John and the incident that followed in this famous English victory, was the origin of the carvings of the famous Pelham Buckle, still to be seen in the stonework of churches at Laughton, Ripe, Chalvington, Chiddingly, East Hoathly, Wartling and Waldron.

Sir William Pelham (b 1486, d 1538) of a later generation, upon his return from the Field of the Cloth of Gold in France where he attended with Henry VIII, built in 1534, a grand moated house just two miles west of Ripe. The house had a chase or hunting ground that took in Chiddingly, East Hoathly, Hellingly and Warbleton.

Built in red and black brickwork with a tower over fifty feet high and walls three feet thick, it had unusual terracotta decoration. It was a unique structure that dominated the low lying ground of Laughton Level, fed and frequently flooded by the River Ouse. A mere fifty years later the Pelham family abandoned their impressive but damp abode in favour of a new mansion of great opulence built at Halland in 1595.

c. 1363

Edward III issued a proclamation that prohibited all sports on Sundays and Feast Days except that of archery and, in particular, the use of the formidable longbow.

> . . . that everyone strong in body . . . do use in their recreation, bows and arrows . . .
> to learn the art of shooting . . .

The most devastating English weapon of war was now the longbow, and there was an intense feeling for the need to maintain the superiority of this powerful weapon.

c. 1376

John Leem who lived in Willingdon, where he was a landowner and a man of authority, was made Prior of Michelham and in the thirty-nine years he was destined to hold this office he proved himself both invaluable and trustworthy.

In contrast to other priors of Michelham, some indifferent and some disreputable, his ability led to the acceptance of duties dealing with collecting local taxes, the responsibility as Commissioner for the repair and maintenance of Waterways on and around Pevensey Marsh, and from time to time ensuring that local forces could be raised to resist raids or invasions by French forces.

John Leem was prior during the Peasants' Revolt of 1381 much of which was directed against the exploitation of workers on the land by many religious houses, and it is thought probable that it was he who caused the formidable stone Michelham Gatehouse, at the entrance across the moat, to be built as a defence. This thinking would date the gatehouse as near 1390 and close to the time Hailsham church was being rebuilt.

In difficult times and with the priory urgently needing to increase its income, John Leem in 1398 appealed to the Bishop of Chichester and was allowed to take over the parish churches of Alfriston and Fletching, whose tithe incomes would help both the upkeep and the priory's work.

Under John Leem, Michelham was much respected and when the time came for him to leave, his character and years of sound guidance were to be sorely missed.

1381

The Peasants' Revolt was the eventual consequence of the terrible decimation of workers during the Black Death, resulting in the survivors' labour now being of much greater value than before the plague. Those workers who were free moved about and demanded the higher pay they were worth but Parliament attempted to prevent what they thought was a dangerous trend and passed the first Statute of Labourers law in 1349 which was an order that wages and prices were to be maintained with a special emphasis on building work. But the law had little or no effect except to inflame the feelings of those it attempted to control.

The lowly villein, however, who worked for and was entirely subject to a feudal lord or attached to a manor house, had no freedom and was forced to carry on working at his old pay in spite of much increased prices. The suffering this control of their lives created could only breed intense resentment, and attempts to achieve freedom were constantly frustrated by lawyers acting for landowners in local Sussex courts.

As time went on, the feeling against powerful church establishments and private landowners who upheld the widespread injustice, became a hatred that inevitably burst into the peasants' uprising, involving many men from in and near Hailsham.

In Pevensey there were disorders and with the damage to the town, the Manorial Records of the castle were destroyed.

The rising was initially successful and resulted in promises from the King for relief of the peasants which led to the revolt disbanding. The promises, however, were never intended to be kept and no measures were taken to correct the harsh suppression of villeins. The situation had not changed and the threat of another uprising remained.

1382

An annual payment of six pence was made by a John Janette as rent for an area of land on which to build a shop in the

> ... market place of Haylesham ...

It was almost certainly to have been in the vicinity of the now Market Square.

Many years later in 1510, records reveal the yearly rent to have been unchanged.

c. 1390

There is no record that would indicate the existence of an early church in Hailsham, but it is probable that a place of meeting or worship did exist in Saxon times on the higher land one hundred and nine feet above sea level where now stands the parish church of St Mary the Virgin.

The earliest reference to a Hailsham church was in 1229 when the founder of Michelham Priory, Gilbert de Aquila, was recorded as having an interest in and some control over the church in Hailsham. Such a church of this date was almost certain to have once been partly or wholly Norman, as a result of the intense church building activity the Conqueror's men put into effect over most of England.

No part of the church that stands today dates back to the church the Normans knew except possibly the lower part of the north aisle wall which reveals, especially in wet weather, the distinctive reddish sandstone with its iron content from quarries north of Hailsham.

The church of Hailsham after the Conquest was probably a small Saxon structure which the Normans had enlarged, or even replaced in their own style, but no evidence exists. The church was however rebuilt during the Perpendicular period of English architecture, an impressive period that extended for well over a century at a time of great church building. But, in spite of the numbers of men, and the time they worked on the now enlarged and more impressive church, vast and dominating in the Hailsham of those early days, there is no record that

HAILSHAM CHURCH SUSSEX.

1850

can reveal a positive building date. Only the nave and chancel arches remain untouched of this period and their simplicity in design and execution could suggest the date c. 1390.

The tower of the church however is very different, for the style is more advanced and with its chequer design and excellent flint work it could well have been built towards the end of the period at c. 1480.

The rebuilt church in a Hailsham of low population was indeed an impressive size due maybe to its nearness to the inland water of Pevensey, still a town and harbour of some importance. Though primarily intended for service to God there must still be the thought that the church might also have reflected the prestige of a patron.

With some of the rebuilding as early as say c. 1390 there can be little doubt that such a time was before a complete recovery had been made from the desolation of the Black Death plague. Death was widespread and no phase of life was spared, it touched labourers and craftsmen of every skill and so it was with those who worked in stone. With church building almost at a standstill and even repair work often abandoned, the need for stone-masons as with other skills, was everywhere a critical problem.

Many of the stone workers who had survived were attracted to the important religious centres for here was work with both status and high pay. Should the stone work on important buildings be delayed for a lack of skilled men, it was not unusual for such workers to be sought for miles around and when found, to be persuaded to move.

Where building was progressing under Royal patronage and the need was great, then extreme action could be taken by calling on Sheriffs of nearby counties to impress or force any masons of proven skill that could be found, to journey to the Royal work. Such journeymen were housed together in lodges on the site, often in unhealthy conditions, until the task was completed. At one period of near desperation, only a patron of significance and power could employ masons and carvers without the King's permission.

Thus it was that the church work in most parishes at this time could seldom claim workers of real skill and where the mediocre prevailed then the standard of workmanship was simple if not poor, and there is evidence in the Hailsham church to indicate the employment of stone masons with inferior if not poor ability.

The church nave with its two arcades each of four pointed arches are supported on octagonal columns all built of sandstone from the Upper Greensand layer, once quarried at (east) Bourne (see note at the end of this entry). Indeed it is the columns of the nave that have a rather unusual interest for they reveal in many areas, the low standard of workmanship common in many small churches of this time, for in a period renowned for its fine mouldings of curves and deep undercuts, the column bases, capitals and arches of the Hailsham arcades are quite devoid of such ornament. Particularly noticeable are the column bases, abandoned with their somewhat crude tooling as if merely in the rough preliminary state that one would expect prior to the final stage of producing clean mouldings.

Apart from some of the nave arch stones being unfinished due to having been cut from stone of inadequate size, generally the tooling to the arches and column caps, all of simple design, shows a rather greater care. The octagonal columns vary a great deal in the manner the medieval masons have carried out their work, and when one stands in front of a column and compares one stone with another, it can be seen how some stones with poor or even crude tooling can reveal the work of a bad or perhaps a young mason. In contrast, many other stones show the work of a good craftsman for not only is the tooling regular but care has been taken to create an unusual feature unseen in any other church within many miles of Hailsham.

On the face of many stones built into the eight-sided columns is an arrangement of chisel marks and as a guide for the mason to keep his marks regular and in the correct direction, sharp diagonal lines were scratched by a pointed steel tool across each stone face. The tooling pattern attempted, varies a great deal from stone to stone with the skill of the individual mason; many are reasonable, some uneven, but with some stones the tooling is poor.

A curious exception in this work however is that on one particular face of a nave column stone a mason has drawn the usual two diagonal lines across the stone with his sharp pointed steel scribe as a tooling guide, but the final stage of actual chiselling was not carried out and in spite of the stone with a mason's error being at eye level, it has survived precisely as it was when the column was built.

An intriguing factor arising from the difficult times following the Black Death was that as stone masons gradually increased in numbers, as indeed happened with other skills and trades, so too came a belated but widespread increase in the rebuilding of many long neglected churches. Almost all the new work was built in the Perpendicular style and in the area close to Hailsham almost all the stone used came from the Greensand quarry at (east) Bourne.

A serious problem for quarries in those times with poor roads and strong but simple wagons, was the need to transport huge blocks of stone away from the quarry to the place of building where masons would be working on cutting and shaping stones. But there is evidence indicating that on occasions, this task of moving massive blocks was made much easier.

There seems little doubt that while the Hailsham church nave was being rebuilt so too were the naves of other nearby parish churches, and the strong indication is that there were masons working in the quarry at Bourne, who shaped and finished many stones identical in size to allow their use on more than one church. In support of this theory, remarkable similarities have emerged when the stonework of some parish churches has been measured and compared.

Even allowing for the acceptable minor inaccuracies of medieval builders, spans across arches, the shape of arch stones and the sizes of stones built into columns coincide far too closely for it to be mere chance. Indeed there is a significance that points to a single mind controlling the work on several churches at one time.

In contrast to the rebuilt nave, the chancel of Hailsham parish church appears of greater age. The columns and pointed arches each side of the chancel are of several kinds of stone; very little is from the old quarry at Bourne but some, the fine textured Caen stone normally used in more important buildings, is from France. Indeed it is likely that this fine quality stone had been re-shaped and used again in the chancel after being taken from the ruins of an older structure elsewhere.

The long arched recess in the south wall of the chancel is a sedilia or priest's seat and its condition reflects a time in history when the church suffered abuse, for the front edge of the stone seat has long worn hollows having been used at some time as a sharpening stone for knives or tools or maybe even swords or arrowheads.

Through the arch in the south wall of the chancel is the Lady Chapel and built into the wall next to the altar is a special recess displaying a twin capital in sandstone that was dug up in the churchyard in the 19th cent. The caps are carved in the simple stiff leaf style of the Early English period and are considered unlikely to have ever been built into a parish church. It is possible the carving came from the destroyed Michelham Priory.

On the opposite side of the chancel an arch once opened on to a North Chapel. For a period in the 19th cent. the arch was sealed up and the chapel area used as a schoolroom, but when its need passed in 1876 the present vestry was built.

Clearly there were times when the church had a need for two side chapels as well as the main altar in the chancel for inevitably, close to each altar on its south wall was a stone piscina for the priest to cleanse the holy vessels after use. In those times the religion of the country was that of Rome.

Sadly, each of the three piscinas may well reflect the violent religious conflict of the distant past for they have all been subject to deliberate destruction. Their projecting bowls, now broken away from the wall leave only the still attractive cusped tracery recesses above. The corbel stones supporting the chancel roof trusses have also been damaged beyond recognition.

The font dates with the nave from the Perpendicular period and is octagonal, standing on a stem with each of its eight sides having a simple sunk panel with a tracery design. One of the panels however reveals that the mason's work was faulty and had to be completed without the two tracery cusps to be seen on the remaining panels. The stem of the Hailsham font is of the same stone and almost identical both in size and design to the fonts at Hellingly and Westham.

That there is but one outstanding memorial inside the church is perhaps surprising, but it is however impressive, being over twelve feet in height in a classical design with carving and all executed in white Sicilian marble. The memorial is to the old Luxford family with houses in the past in Hailsham, Robertsbridge, Framfield and Windmill Hill.

Through many generations much of their land has been in the old parish of Otham as well as Hailsham, an early reference being in 1679. In 1748 a Luxford was High Sheriff of Sussex and for many later years, the family were patrons of the church.

The 19th cent. saw the removal of much of the old woodwork in the church. Now gone is the rood-loft screen once across the chancel arch, the old three decker pulpit and the box pews in the nave. There was also at the west end of the church once a gallery possibly for minstrels or musicians. It would have been *c.* 1875 in a period of much Victorian rebuilding that the church lost its old stone floor with its many memorial slabs.

That most of the windows are now of clear glass is unfortunately due to a bomb in 1943 that destroyed all the stained glass except the 'Faith, Hope and Charity' window in the north aisle. Among the windows lost was a memorial to the men of Hailsham killed in the Great War. The superb new East Window illustrating the coming of the Wise Men dates only from 1954 when it was dedicated by the Bishop of Chichester.

At the west end of the church a tall impressive arch separates the nave from the interior of the tower. The arch, built in an attractive iron stained sandstone from the Sussex Weald, was for a time entirely sealed up by a timber framework covered with simple lathe and plaster, but in 1889 it was opened again. Built into the bottom of this arch is now a fine organ purchased from a Royal College for the Blind. It was first played in Hailsham by the organist of Canterbury Cathedral in 1955.

The Tower has three floors; above the organ is the ringing chamber with its bell ropes, the next floor is the clock chamber and at the top is the belfry. The approach to the upper floors of the tower is by a narrow winding stone staircase in a stair turret built up the outside of the tower. The bottom of these stairs is through an old oak door set in the tower wall and the stonework each side of the door has long worn areas, the result of having been much used for sharpening tools or weapons.

At the top of the tower, in the wall near the belfry door, a circular recess has been cut forming a small stone shelf that hundreds of years ago was a resting place probably for a shallow bowl holding a primitive naked light. Nearby, two of the wall stones have between them a gap wide enough for a hand. By squeezing a hand deep into the wall it is possible to feel the back of a stone with highly finished moulding. Clearly this stone, built into the tower nearly five hundred years ago, was once part of an even earlier building of great age and it is hardly likely to be the only such re-used stone in Hailsham's church tower.

Of the eight bells supported on massive timbers that make up the Hailsham peal, five are dated 1663 of which the tenor is nine and a quarter hundredweight. Their installation was soon after Charles II came to the throne when bell ringing was again, after the Commonwealth, being enjoyed. The three remaining bells were added in 1889.

Externally, Hailsham church indicates two distinct periods, the outside walls to the body of the church clearly show complete restoration during the Victorian era. And so it is inside the church where the nave, aisles and chapels have all received between the years 1869 and 1889 major restoration by the vigorous and well meaning Victorians. With however the strengthening and tidying up, much of historic and architectural interest has been sacrificed.

In contrast to the body of the church the tower is quite exceptional. Built in the Perpendicular style but later than the church nave, its refined proportions, its strength yet grace, and its commanding height of over seventy feet indicate a parish church tower of unusual quality.

The most interesting feature is the skilful use of local flints, knapped into flat surfaces and built into the tower with squared blocks of stone to form an effective chequer design over the entire height and even into the diagonal buttresses. The workmen of four hundred years ago, when building flints into the walls of the tower, would first strike a large flint boulder clean in half, thus creating two flat faced knapped flints. This age old working practice is clearly confirmed by the many pairs of flint faces in the tower walls, nearly or even next to each other, that are a perfect match both in outline, shape and the colour patterns on the flint faces.

An intriguing feature of the tower's south wall is an area of say eight feet above the ground where there are indications of the wall having been damaged by gunfire. On some of the square stones are small but deep depressions of some age, while many flints bear marks of having been struck with tremendous force leaving deep cracks radiating from a shattered centre. There is no recorded date of this violent damage (*see* entry of 1559).

At the base of the tower is the west door with its tracery window above, all enclosed in a high deep set but much restored arch of great dignity. At the top of the tower the four pinnacles are *c.* 1960 ribbed and taller replacements for those of old which had projecting crockets and together with a battlemented parapet, a low pyramidal tiled roof and five gilded weathervanes, the tower is outstanding and one of the finest of a parish church in Sussex.

Of similar design is the tower at Battle, but it lacks the flintwork or pinnacles; perhaps also comparable are the towers of All Saints at Hastings and St Mary's at Eastbourne.

Nearer at Westham, and of a little earlier date, the tower with its parapet, diagonal buttresses and minor flintwork has been said to be,

> . . . a sight of beauty and strength, gladdening the soul of the wayfarer, and even now it is impossible for a man to look at it without some sort of soul-stirring . . .

but in spite of this somewhat rhapsodical praise it fails utterly to compare with the tower at Hailsham.

The churchyard was reduced in size many centuries ago when houses were built over that part of the burial ground adjoining the main road through Hailsham. On its north side it once gave access into an area of church property called Vicarage Field. In the war of 1939–45 an underground shelter was built into it and twenty years later several mature oak trees were felled to allow the major building development of a shopping precinct.

As reminders of the past there are still 'grave stones' *c.* 1830 in cast iron and the unusual 'bed board' memorial in white painted wood to Francis Howlett, a schoolmaster and man of many talents.

The church records of christenings, marriages and burials were first entered in a register in 1558, some twenty years after Thomas Cromwell had issued his instruction that parish churches must henceforth keep a permanent register.

It is an interesting coincidence that the Hailsham register should have begun in the first year of the reign of Elizabeth I. (*See* entry of 1538).

Note: From the early centuries when the Romans built the immense walls of their Pevensey Castle, vast quantities of stone had been quarried at (east) Bourne to be used in building, not only many local parish churches but a considerable number of important houses of which several survive today.

The quarry from which so much stone was taken was certainly in the area of Devonshire Park, and that such stone still exists has been confirmed by the Upper Greensand bed being reached during deep excavation for some of the larger buildings in or near the park area.

Perhaps more satisfying however is when the sea at low tide reveals on that part of the shore between the pier and the bandstand, an outcrop of the same stone. While still wet from the receding tide, its characteristic greenish hue can match exactly the stone of local parish churches when soaked by rain.

1399

Richard II, who had deteriorated into a wild and tyrannical King, inflicted in the end such blatant injustices that the nation turned against him. It was inevitable that there should be a revolt and Henry, Duke of Lancaster, was the man who put forward his claim to the throne and led powerful forces against the King.

Away and supporting Henry in the north of England was Sir John Pelham (b *c.* 1355, d 1429) Constable of Pevensey Castle, and in the turmoil that ensued, the castle was attacked by royal troops led by William Fiennes and others who were opposed to Henry becoming King.

In the absence of her husband the defence of the castle, in poor condition from years of neglect, was in the hands of Lady Joan Pelham. Surrounded and without hope of support, she wrote a letter to Sir John that was smuggled away to reach her husband at Pontefract Castle where Richard II was to be a prisoner and die.

The letter told of the siege at Pevensey and of the dangers she faced, it told also at some length of her personal feelings. It was a remarkable letter for feudal times, of some three hundred words and the historian Henry Hallam, in later years wrote:

> . . . let no fair reader smile at the spelling of this letter or think lightly of its phrase-
> ology. It is the first letter ever written in the English language by a lady . . .

In due course, Henry of Lancaster became King Henry IV and in gratitude he bestowed on Sir John and Lady Pelham the Honour of Pevensey and its castle.

1400

1403

A party of French marauders came to Selmeston and carried off John Iford, servant of Robert Profoot.

Such an invasion by a party of armed Frenchmen seemed highly improbable, but in contrast, the French had the ability to attack with ferocity, then plunder and fire a town, as they frequently did along the Sussex coast during the 14th century and sometimes later. Revenge against the English was not without reason and Rye, Winchelsea and Hastings suffered badly, as did some lesser places along the coast.

As has been written:

> . . . it was now the turn of the English to suffer the terrors of enemy invasion . . .

and Winston Churchill of the early centuries has added that the English were the '. . . deeply hated foe . . .' of the French.

1406

Part of Pevensey Castle, where in 1394 Sir John Pelham had been appointed Constable and Custodian, was considered to be an impregnable State Prison. Two of the prisoners held there were the thirteen year old Prince James, confined for many years and later to become James I of Scotland and also Edward, Duke of York.

In 1419, Queen Joan of Navarre, widow of Henry IV was imprisoned by her stepson, Henry V, on a charge of witchcraft allegedly endangering the life of the King. She was accused of:

> . . . compassing the death of the King in the most horrible manner that could be devised . . .

The Queen was arrested in her castle at Leeds in Kent, together with suspected members of her household, due chiefly to information from her confessor John Randolf, a Franciscan Friar.

Confined first in Leeds Castle, where the Queen suffered the confiscation of her entire possessions, even to her bed and clothes, she was taken to '. . . the gloomy fortress of Pevensey . . .' where Sir John Pelham granted her essential servants and placed her in close confinement. Had Joan of Navarre been a woman without rank, a charge of witchcraft would have meant being burnt at the stake.

Henry V, back from his glorious successes in France, was soon to suspect his own early death and with a deep guilt, he made known in a written statement to his Bishops and Lords, his extreme remorse.

> . . . for the wrong and robbery of which he had been guilty towards his father's widow . . .

Freedom for Joan of Navarre was declared in 1422, after four years' imprisonment and many of her former possessions were returned. Of these was Leeds Castle, where she went after her ordeal in Pevensey.

Less than two months after his repentance, Henry V was to die free of guilt at the age of thirty-four. His ill-used stepmother was to live to an age of more than seventy years.

c. 1413

Warbleton Priory was founded by Sir John Pelham and called the 'New Priory of the Blessed Trinity of Hastings'. It was to replace the previous priory of Augustinian canons who abandoned their priory at Hastings, it is said, due to suffering from the action of the sea.

Built with much of the stone from the old priory, it was dedicated in 1417 by the Bishop of Durham, and in the course of time it was to possess considerable areas of land, some of which was in Willingdon, Westham, Herstmonceux and Wartling.

The second prior, a Stephen Lewes, proved in 1441 to be a poor custodian and following a visit from the Bishop of Chichester, he was fined a hundred shillings for serious negligence in his conduct of priory affairs. This man was not to be the only prior to fail in his duties for future years were again to see the condition of the buildings suffer serious deterioration.

Mostly destroyed at the Dissolution in 1536, what remained after much of its stone had been robbed for use elsewhere, is in pleasant secluded countryside on the Christians River just two miles east of Warbleton.

Around 1840, the part of the priory that had survived the centuries in reasonable condition was put into use as a farmhouse. Other buildings were also reclaimed, and their restoration carried out with the help of the abundance of stone still available from the ruins of the old priory chapel.

Again, with the passage of time and different owners, some of the buildings were to suffer, until in 1970 an intensive plan of restoration was put into effect. It was during landscape work on the surrounding fields that close to the farmhouse the complete outline of the five hundred and sixty year old priory chapel was revealed.

Now, in addition to what little stonework of the chapel survived above ground, are revealed the foundation lines of the nave, transepts, chapter house and cloister.

The old farmhouse with its priory remains now serves as a country hotel.

1413

With the death of Henry IV and the end of an unhappy and much troubled reign, the new King Henry V inherited a country made poor by intrigue, religious conflict and wars with Scotland and Wales.

But the new King was possessed of a tenacious resolve to recapture the rich provinces in France, once ruled by England.

> . . . Henry had, ever fince his acceffion to the throne, formed the defign of engaging in war with France, and from the confufed ftate of that Kingdom, determined now to make preparations for carrying it into execution . . .

With the dire need to find money for his impoverished treasury, Henry V, within months of his accession, suppressed the alien priories at Hooe and Wilmington, both of which were attached to abbeys in France.

The acquisition of valuable buildings and land became an immediate source of much needed revenue when leased to tenants. Wilmington Priory was granted to the Dean and Chapter of Chichester and the priory at Hooe eventually passed into the hands of Eton College.

It was the drastic change of use and many changes of ownership with varying prosperity that, over the years, allowed both buildings to deteriorate into ruins.

1415

Sir Thomas Hoo, an owner of much land in East Sussex, fought on St Crispin's Day with Henry V at Agincourt. He fought in the company of soldiers, all of whom came from Sussex, most being armed with the long bow.

1436

The manor of Horselunges passed into the possession of the Devenish family through John Devenish, who before he died in 1477 asked to be buried in the chancel of nearby Hellingly parish church.

In the chancel floor were once a pair of memorial brasses but now of one there is only the empty recessed space. The other brass, over five hundred years old and in a damaged condition, is of a lady in a costume of the 15th cent., which has encouraged the belief that below this spot lie the bodies of John Devenish and his wife Margaret.

In the Will of John Devenish money was left to the vicars of Hailsham, Chiddingly and Arlington, as well as money for building a south porch to Hellingly Church.

The son of the first Hellingly Devenish was another John Devenish, an M.P. for Sussex who fought with and was knighted by Henry VII at the last battle of the Wars of the Roses at Stoke in 1487. It was about this time, it is thought, that Sir John built the moated house called Horselunges.

A moat thirty feet wide and fed by the river Cuckmere surrounded Horselunges in defence of this heavily timbered house of magnificent proportions. With an interior of exceptional grandeur it had elaborate wood panelling and carving that reflected the status of the Devenish family.

Demonstrating the power at this time of a lord of the manor was the incident recorded in the proceedings of the Court of the Star Chamber in 1553 when:

> ...Richard Barnard of Hellingly feloniously as a felon did drown and destroy himself...

Barnard's goods and chattels were seized by Thomas Devenish as being his right as lord of the manor. After the accession of Queen Elizabeth the goods were claimed on behalf of the Crown who brought the complaint before the court stating Thomas Devenish (died *c.* 1560) of Hellingly and William Devenish:

> ...And other riotous persons came to the mansion and dwelling place of the said Richard Barnard, and broke and entered the same and took and carried away the said goods and chattels...

In 1567 William Devenish sold Horselunges to Herbert Pelham of Michelham Priory but the new property was to prove an expensive acquisition for Pelham was forced to sell Michelham Priory in 1601 due to heavy personal debts.

1441

The building of Herstmonceux Castle was begun by Sir Roger Fiennes, later to become Lord Dacre who was an Agincourt warrior.

> ...he took part in the glorious battle at Agincourt taking with him from Herst-monceux eight men-at-arms and twenty-four archers...

In connection with the choice of site upon which it was planned to build the castle it was recorded that permission had been granted to Sir Roger Fenys (Fiennes) to 'empark' (enclose) six hundred acres of his Herstmonceux land. In carrying out this action most of the families were forced to move away from the vicinity of the parish church causing the village to settle again nearly two miles to the north.

The extensive park was later used for hunting and a survey of 1570 recorded details both of deer and herons:

> ...the game of fallow deer in the same park by estimation two hundred, whereof are sixty deer of antler, at the taking of this survey... there is a Hernery in the same park called Hern-Wood, and they used to breed in divers parts of the park: the same hath yielded this year one hundred and fifty nest...

When the castle was built it proved to be a noble and impressive structure on which Flemish builders were employed, it was many years ahead in its planning and one of the first brick buildings of this magnitude in England.

1445

A visitation to Michelham by the Bishop of Chichester revealed a serious deterioration in the affairs of the Priory. Held responsible was Prior Lawrence who was proved to be both corrupt and indifferent to the daily life of his canons. Of the many charges listed against this man were:

> Selling oak trees from the Priory land for private gain, selling millstones from priory mills, thirty-eight oxen, six cows and twelve horses from priory farms and books and a silver goblet from the priory.
> The Prior had placed himself in personal control of all money transactions and it was established he failed to ensure sufficient food and drink for his canons.

Prior Lawrence was condemned for perjury and disobedience through the misuse of priory funds and property.

1450

With the French victories of Henry V now being reversed, and a further battle lost leaving only Calais in our possession, it all proved merely a background to the deep discontent actively voiced at home, over the hard times and genuine grievances suffered by the people under Henry VI.

Only a leader was lacking, and it was found in Jack Cade, formerly a servant of Sir Thomas Dacre of Heathfield. His promise to:

> ...correct public abuses and remove evil councillors...

brought a following of nearly twenty thousand supporters ready to act against the gentle but weak Henry VI and they came from all classes, including the Abbot of Battle, Prior of Lewes and the Bailiffs of Seaford and Pevensey together with many men from Hailsham.

The march on London by Jack Cade was a startling success and for a short while he could have ruled the city, but a lack of discipline was the weakness and his supporters ran riot.

The events that followed compelled Jack Cade to flee, but historians have disagreed on his destination. It is at Cade Street, Heathfield, however that the famous Cade Stone was erected with an inscription that reads:

> . . . rebel Jack Cade by Alexander Iden, Sheriff of Kent Ad 1450. His body was carried to London and his head fixed upon London Bridge. This is the success of all rebels and this fortune chanceth ever to traitors . . .

Certainly that he was struck down by Alexander Iden, Sheriff of Kent, is not in dispute but it has been suggested that the scene may have been in Kent. That his body was mutilated has never been in doubt, for his captors set out with their stricken victim on the road to London, but he died on the journey and upon arrival, his body was decapitated and quartered.

Note: With the men from Hailsham who supported Jack Cade were trades that reflected the importance of Hailsham's large Cattle market. The contingent from Hailsham included, John and William Osbern who were butchers, John Sherman and Michael Haryot both corvesers (shoemakers) and John Toby, Robert Bystrete and John Grent, who were all tanners.

Of a total of some four hundred other names from Sussex, there were only two butchers, three corvesers (one at Herstmonceux and two at Alfriston), and no other tanners at all.

1452

At this time the Hailsham market was busy and prosperous, and the large numbers of cattle being driven into the town created work enough to keep several tanners and leather workers busy. The tanning trade was important in the preparation of leather, and the exacting process, protected by law, was suited to Sussex due in part to the use of oak bark in tanning.

During the period 1540-1640 Hailsham was one of the chief centres, and much of the trade was retained until the decline of its market in later years.

1455-1479

It is known that during these years the records kept by the churchwardens of Arlington reveal in each year, many simply worded statements of payment for materials, and evidence of the wide range of tasks carried out by men both skilled and unskilled.

Sometimes the men were of Arlington and sometimes they came from other villages, but always the work concerned the church.

The wide variety of day to day activities so recorded are a remarkable reflection of life in Arlington over five hundred years ago, and could well be typical of many other villages in East Sussex with a church already old, and in parts, fragile and continually needing repair.

Each page of this churchwarden's book quotes how much was paid for every item of work carried out; some tasks were infrequent but many were repeated and indicate the presence of structural problems the church continually faced. Both the tower and the roof were troublesome and much money was spent on purchasing timber, nails from Alfriston, lead from Michelham, lime from Willingdon, tiles and, on occasions, large quantities of wood shingles from Dicker.

In the bell tower, as the upper floor was known, a peal of three bells (10 cwt, 15 cwt and the 'great bell' 1 ton) were clearly much used, for items of repair or replacement are often recorded. Several times the words clappers, wheels, collars and baldricks appear as well as leather for parts that took so much wear. In particular, during the period of these records, no fewer than fourteen bell ropes were bought, including 2d paid to a man for carriage of a great bell rope from Lewes to Arlington.

Of vital importance to the church, as indeed it was to others when a room needed light, was a continual supply of wax. The main source was from nearly thirty cows the church owned; these were hired out in return for an annual payment of wax.

> ... 72 pounds of wax from the farm of 18 other cows so farmed out these two years, each cow at 2 lbs of wax ...

With regular supplies of 'wick yarn' the wax was melted into shallow hollows of pottery or metal to set into a light. When finally burnt down, the wax remains would be scraped out and saved until, with enough 'ends and gutterings', and new wicks, the endless task,

> ... and 8d paid to the sacrist for collecting the wax of the lights and the melting of the same for 2 years ...

would produce yet more lights.

For church services, purchases were made of incense, frankincense, candles and wine, while less often money was spent on linen for making vestments, replacement keys, washing and repairing surplices and,

> ... 3d paid to the sacrist for cleaning the church from various defilements ...

A stone mason was paid for repairing the font and holy water stoup and a carpenter for repairs to the church door and pulpit. A large payment in 1476 was for the

> ... expenses of carpenters making the upper floor in the bell tower and hanging two bells, in a lump sum by contract made with the wardens £4-0-5, ... and paid for their board £1-0-6 ...

and in the churchyard there was the making of a new stile, the 'cutting of brambles and other weeds', frequent repairs to fencing and

> ... 8d paid to John Clerk for filling up the lime pits ...

In every year there appears evidence of 'visitations' to the churches of other villages when money was given to help the travellers.

> ... and 3d paid for the expenses of Lawrence Mabbe toiling (possibly through mud) over to Lewes because of a visitation ...

and

> . . . at (east) Bourne at the time of a visitation before the Bishop, who was then there . . .

and at another time,

> . . . 15d paid for the trouble and expenses of various parishioners at Ripe for the visitation there . . .

Other villages so visited were Willingdon, Hailsham, Alfriston and the chapel at Otham, once part of the Priory. (*See* entry *c*.1175).

Of particular interest was a reference in 1469 to a chapel in Arlington churchyard

> . . . and 11d paid for lights in the chapel of the Blessed Mary in the churchyard . . .

But centuries later all trace of the building had gone except, it was recorded in 1911, for the foundations which could still be traced.

The pages of these churchwarden records were written in Latin on coarse paper over five hundred years ago and are all still legible in spite of the once dark ink having now faded to a light brown. These seventeen pages (each 305 mm x 210 mm), some damaged in the past due to damp and one page with a portion missing, having been torn away, are now in the care of the Department of Manuscripts at the British Library.

c. 1468

King Edward IV ordered by law that every parish should have land set aside for archery practice, and it should be decreed that if an archer accidentally killed a man while practising, it should not be considered a crime.

For many years the English had been supreme in battle due to their skill with the powerful long bow, its reputation established long ago. Victories at Falkirk and later in France at Crecy, Poitiers and Agincourt, often when greatly outnumbered, established this English weapon as unassailable.

> . . . the stout yeoman of England were acknowledged the finest infantry in Europe . . . these skilled archers with yew long-bows of five feet could shoot accurately up to three hundred yards and their arrows of three feet with tips of steel could penetrate a four inch thick oak door . . .

. . . and as the historian Dr George M. Trevelyan has written:

> . . . for men shall never shoot well unless they be brought up in it . . . the art of the long bow was so difficult that foreigners never learnt the knack that would send an arrow through armour . . . the longbow was the master weapon in Europe and remained an English monopoly . . .

On what was once Hailsham common land, there is now an area of housing called the Butts Estate and one of its roads is Archery Walk. Similarly a terrace of old houses in Station Road, near the Common Pond, are on what was originally called Buttsfield Place.

There can be little doubt but that Hailsham provided its share of archers who had travelled to foreign battlefields.

1472

An Act of Parliament lamented that archery was:

> ... great discontinued because of the scarcity of bowstaves ... merchants bringing goods from abroad were ordered to bring four bowstaves for every tun weight of his ship ...

English Yew had been proved the best wood for bowstaves but with the intense practise of archery a serious shortage had developed and yew was continually sought from overseas.

1478

A further visitation to Michelham Priory from Chichester resulted in the Prior and Brethren being charged with religious laxity and loose living involving a woman. Punishments and penances were inflicted and the Priory was placed under new supervision.

This state of affairs had, through the years, become typical of many smaller monasteries and priories, for they were slipshod in religious matters and often dishonest in the administration of the establishment.

1481

The Rolls (records written on vellum) of the Manor Courts of Ripe for the period 1481 to 1505 may, with permission, still be examined in the British Museum.

The courts could well have been held in the Manor House of Ripe, a medieval timbered structure, most of which still stands. The house, however, was greatly enlarged in 1686 when extra rooms and a new south front with two porches and gables was added in red brickwork.

The early Manor House would have had a large hall extending upwards to the heavy roof rafters (now divided into upper and lower rooms) and it would probably have been in this hall, that twice in each year the courts would have been held. Here, prisoners would be heard and sentenced unless charged with a more serious crime when they would be taken to the assizes probably at Horsham.

1484

A man '... John at Mill ...' lived in a small cottage in Market Square next to the entrance to the churchyard. In later years it became a tavern called *Jolly Sailor* and later again it was renamed *The Good Intent*. It is now a baker's shop with rooms used as a small restaurant named 'The Homely Maid'.

1500

1525

Born in 1470 Thomas (a name much used by the family) Lord Dacre of Herstmonceux had at an early age fought for Henry VII and in 1493 was made Constable of Calais. With wealth and power, and favoured by the King, it is both inexplicable and baffling how in his fifty-fifth year he could bring disgrace upon his family.

Clearly recorded and beyond doubt a document dated 7th February 1525 states:

    ...The Lord Dacre hathe this day knowledged and confesste the bearinge of theuves, and his remysnes and negligence in ponyshement of them, and also his famylyer and conversaunte being with them, knowing them to have com'ytted felonye and dyvers other his misdoings, in manner and forme as ys expressed in his confessyon and submyssyon, subscribed with his owne hande, whereupon he ys com'ytted to y keapinge of the warden of the Fleate, and his recognisaunce taken and knowledged the 30th day of Januarye last past, as well for himself as for his sureties ys decreed by the saide most reverende father to be utterlye voide frustrate and cancelled...'

As a result of being charged with receiving and harbouring suspected felons, Lord Dacre was to spend some time as a prisoner in the notorious Fleet Prison. Just three years before he died in 1533, his Will requested:

    ...My body to be buried in the parish church of Hurst Monceaux, on the north side of the high altar. I will that a tomb be there made for placing the sepulchre of our Lord... and that a tomb be set over my grave...

and it is in the small brick built Dacre chapel of Herstmonceux parish church that the stately monument was built of fine Caen stone from France and Purbeck marble from Dorset. Acknowledged as an exceptional tomb worthy of a cathedral, it has tracery panels and a massive carved stone roof sweeping in a curve high over two stone effigies, as clad in armour they lay side by side each with their hands together in prayer.

One is the figure of Lord Dacre (1470-1533) once of Calais and later of the Fleet Prison and the other, his son, Sir Thomas Fiennes, who died before his father.

It was perhaps ominous that the next Lord Dacre, having lost his father when very young, surely suffered from the:

    ...corrupting nature of the atmosphere which he breathed at Herstmonceux, and the evil influences with which his boyhood was surrounded...

Certainly, the young Dacre was at Herstmonceux when his grandfather kept disreputable company at the castle and it was the same young man who was hanged before he could grow to maturity. (*See* entry of 1541).

1536

The Parliament of Henry VIII passed the Act for the Dissolution of the Monasteries and in spite of having income from land and property in much of the surrounding area including:

    ...Laughton, Alfrston, Arlyngton, Flecchyng, Downashe, Haylesham, Helynglye, Westham, Wyllyngdon, Pevensey, Mafeld, Sefford, Yevyngton and Borne...

the Priory at Michelham was still to prove too poor to survive the relentless decision that as a lesser priory, it must be suppressed and destroyed.

The Act was supervised by Thomas Cromwell, the King's Vicar-General, and introduced as a church reform made necessary by the manner in which most of the smaller religious houses had declined in their christian way of life. With the Act passed however, charges were made with flagrant severity and it was put forward that some were

> ...dens of vice, dishonest and lax...with manifest sin, loose with abominable living...

On occasions these virulent charges were not without a degree of truth for there was indiscipline and frequent mishandling of abbey or priory affairs, and a loss of respect from the community indicated such places had outlived their usefulness.

With the Act in force no time was lost in examining the affairs of the lesser establishments and the attitudes and methods adopted by the visiting royal commissioners, assisted in Sussex by Sir John Gage of Firle, revealed less concern with reform than with the acquisition of land, property and valuables to provide urgently needed wealth. Money had become vital to the Crown, now almost bankrupt with extravagance and wars.

Any abbey or priory with an income of less than £200 per year was listed for suppression and it was calculated that Michelham had an income value at £191 19s. 4d. There was no survival and in 1537 the priory was plundered of its contents and the structure robbed of any building material likely to be of use elsewhere. With many of the buildings left open to the weather Michelham Priory was abandoned to begin its fall into a ruin.

Among the items of value sold to benefit the King's Exchequer were church ornaments, furniture except the Prior's bed which was given to him by the King's Commissioners of the King's Charity, pictures, silver vessels and the five large priory bells weighing forty hundredweights sold to John Ettonbury of Maidstone for melting down. Even the lead, much of it stripped from the roof and amounting to thirteen wagon loads was taken away and kept by Anthony Pelham and John Fawkenor.

> ...to be kept safe for the use of the King...

and as L. F. Salzman put it

> ...The King flung the remains to his faithful jackal, Thomas Cromwell...

Having ended the life of the priory the Crown took care to avoid former members of the household being left completely destitute when the people's anger could be provoked. Most of the servants and outdoor labourers

> ...were paid one quarter's wages when they did leave their work...

while the canons were pensioned and in most cases helped towards church priesthoods. One of the canons, Edmund Pelham, became a priest at Otham chapel near Pevensey Marsh and upon his death was buried in Hailsham.

1538

Thomas Cromwell, the Vicar-General to Henry VIII, introduced in September, an order that every parish church must henceforth keep a register for recording the baptisms, marriages and burials within its parish. The initial reaction of the people to this far reaching instruction was a considerable hostility, for there arose the strong suspicion that its purpose would be yet another fee or tax for the King's exchequer. Such feeling could have been well founded, but in the event the instruction came into effect without a charge.

In the State Paper of Cromwell's order were the words:

> ...shall for every church kepe one boke or registere wherein ye shall write the day and yere of every weddyng christenyng and buryeng made within yor parishe... and for the sauff kepinge of the same boke the parishe shalbe bonde to provide of these comen charges one sure coffer with twoo lockes and keys whereof the one of remayne with you, and the other with the said wardens...

As a result of concern due to the registers of some churches being ill-kept and written on poor materials, an instruction was issued in 1598 that all registers must be sturdy and made of parchment and those on other material should be rewritten to ensure a safe and permanent record.

In 1644, during the Civil War, registers were not kept regularly and in 1653 the new Commonwealth Government instructed that registers were to be kept by laymen. At the Restoration in 1660, Charles II directed that the clergy again be made responsible for keeping registers.

The Hailsham parish church register is made up of several books, the first of which commenced in 1558, the first year in the reign of Queen Elizabeth I, the last entry being made in 1638.

This book, in use for eighty years is strong and heavy, having been made with care of a cream coloured skin (usually from a calf), which when prepared is known as vellum. In the fairly stiff leaves are a number of small oval holes, probably due to skin punctures on the living animal which enlarged when stretched during the preparation. The leaves are joined together with thonging.

In spite of occasional stains, again due to skin blemishes, the writing is seldom faded but in the early years of the register, translation is necessary.

The first baptism recorded in the register was of Tomsyne Drew, daughter of Christopher on 28 March (the mother had either died or deserted). The first burial was of Alice Russell, daughter of John on 28 March (again no mother mentioned) and the first marriage, on 8 May, was between Richard Ellyate and Elizabeth Putland.

1538

Chalvington parish church register begins.

A small church and as are others near Hailsham, a simple church of very great age. The typical example of Norman zig-zag moulding above the north door is of the church built nearly nine hundred years ago, while the immensely heavy main door is probably over seven hundred years old.

Of special interest is a window in the north side of the nave having a fragment of 13th cent. stained glass bearing it is thought, a portrait of Saint Thomas of Canterbury.

1538

Herstmonceux parish church register begins.

Sited over one and a half miles from its present village, this church is near the northern edge of the marsh once the inland water of Pevensey Harbour. It is an area that was within sight of William the Conqueror's landing and destined to be influenced by the army and followers of the Conqueror for many years after his great victory at Battle.

The victorious knights with wealth, power and vast grants of land, planned the building of castles, religious houses and many churches, and Herstmonceux church was one in particular that enjoyed Norman patronage. Indeed its first seven rectors were of Norman descent.

The church is small and the interior has a charm that reflects much sensitive design and workmanship, and possibly due to an irregular plan there is a seemingly gentle atmosphere in pleasant contrast to what might have been, had mathematical accuracy prevailed.

There is evidence of care in its early design, especially in the large column caps of the nave which have carvings of early English leafwork in fine textured Caen stone from France. This no doubt reflected the influence on the church of the De Monceux family who were descended from the Conqueror whose Domesday Book recorded a Saxon chapel on this site.

The chancel floor has an impressive Brass of 1402, that has survived in immaculate condition, to Sir William Fiennes whose son was christened in the church and grew up to become Sir Roger Fiennes of Herstmonceux Castle.

Two outstanding features of the church are the Dacre Chapel with its brickwork almost the earliest for church work in England, and the beautifully carved Caen stone canopied monument with its painted effigies. These effigies were referred to in 1826 by Dr. Gideon-Mantell, surgeon and diarist as

> ... very superb but being cruelly daubed by the parish painter by order of the churchwardens ...

These two painted effigies of men in armour have now been painted with great skill and would surely be outstanding in a cathedral.

Around the churchyard there are still a very few lengths of fencing of great age, on the top rail of which can be deciphered the numbers in Roman numerals of farmers once committed to keeping that length of fence in good repair. Elsewhere on several of the older gravestones are examples of Jonathon Harmer's terracotta floral and cherub plaques (see entry of 1806), and as a reminder of the great Sussex iron industry, there is on another grave, a huge cast iron ornamental urn. It is of impressive design with ornate handles and a square base, all of considerable weight and over three feet high.

1538

Ripe parish church register begins.

The Tower is of the 15th cent. The chancel windows are earlier being of the Early English Decorated period in the 14th cent., and the east window of excellent

Curvilinear design, with its typically graceful and flowing lines has in it fragments of yellow and green glass probably over six hundred years old.

Cut into the door of the tower is a carved 'Pelham Buckle' denoting a church connection with the Pelham family. It is an emblem now famous and visible on churches and houses once associated with the Pelhams.

Ripe church is sited barely half a mile from Chalvington church and both are at junctions of roads in an area that is quite unique in Sussex, for these two villages are in the centre of a remarkable system of roads that are both straight and at right-angles to each other, as if they had been planned on a grid system. This would appear to be confirmed by the hedge lines again being mainly straight, thus creating fields of rectangular shape. This small area is in striking contrast to the more usual meandering Sussex lanes and somewhat shapeless fields.

With the remains of Roman roads in the near vicinity, it becomes apparent that the layout surrounding Ripe was based on a centuriation system of survey carried out possibly one thousand two hundred years ago or even longer, that used a Roman measurement linked with a hundred units, having no relationship with English measurement.

A modern survey of this area only four miles from Hailsham revealed the remarkable similarity to a road and field lay-out existing today at Padua near Venice, in Italy. (*See* appendix 'A').

1538

Wartling parish church register begins.

Situated high on the tip of the peninsula jutting out into Pevensey Marsh, the church dates from the 13th cent. and has the stonework of additions of other centuries as it slowly enlarged from the original chancel, once a chapel. This small church still has its entire seating in tall box pews enclosed with doors. It also has a small square boarded bell-turret finished with a low wooden spire.

Still surviving is the north porch with its roof of heavy stone slabs as were used on many roofs in medieval times.

1538

Wilmington parish church register begins.

Standing as it does next to the remains of the 13th cent. Benedictine Priory, it is not difficult to imagine the early days of this church when it was connected to the priory by the paving of probably what was a simple stone cloister. At this time the chancel with its Norman walls of massive thickness and the unusual remains of the stone seating against those walls, was almost certainly used by the Benedictine Monks of the Priory.

There can still be seen preserved in the nave an example of wall painting indicating how once the walls were coloured with such work, before being covered with plaster over three hundred years ago. The oak pulpit is of considerable interest being in an early Jacobean design complete with its large suspended sounding board.

Alfriston parish church

The brick paved nave has on the south side a short but impressive arcade of two pointed arches, probably of the 14th cent., rising up from the usual flat-sided columns. They are all light in colour and a gentle scraping of the surface will reveal the dead white colour of chalk from the Downs. It was also in the Downs that the flint was dug to build so much of the church walling.

Outside this church there are two outstanding features. One is the small neat white-boarded belfry, supported by huge beams that span the nave at the west end.

The other feature is the giant yew tree of twenty-three feet girth, bound by heavy chains that through the years have bitten deep into the ancient branches. To support the enormous weight, stout wooden props are now needed by a tree that could have been planted in the time of King Edward I over six hundred years ago. It was this King who ordered yew trees to be planted in churchyards for the protection of the churches.

1538

Alfriston parish church register begins.

There also exists a record of 1504-5 showing a few entries of marriages at that time.

Built *c.* 1360 on a cruciform plan with above its centre an impressive tower, the church stands on a large circular mound which was almost certainly a burial place centuries before the present church was erected.

The exterior consists of immense areas of knapped flint, which the builders of six hundred years ago would have found so readily on the nearby Downs, and where the ground had been flint mined hundreds of years before even the Alfriston church we know. The great care taken in shaping the thousands of flints in the church walls clearly indicates a church of rare significance.

The interior of somewhat grand proportions has unusually graceful columns of considerable height, supporting arches at the crossing of the transepts with the nave and instead of the normal flat sides as in octagonal columns, the sides are wide shallow hollows.

There are excellent windows, some with the flowing tracery of the Decorated period and others with the dominant vertical lines of the Perpendicular period. The chancel, unusually enriched for a village church with stone carving, has on its south wall a highly ornate three seater sedilia complete with small columns separating the seating spaces, while next to it is a handsome piscina to match. Exactly opposite on the north wall and again unusual in a village church, is an Easter Sepulchre, a recess used in medieval days where the host and altar cross were placed on Good Friday to be watched over night and day until they were moved to the high altar on Easter Sunday.

This fine church, for many years known as the Cathedral of the Downs, is in the company of tall trees and stands on high ground overlooking common land known as the Tye which serves as a village green. Backing on to the green that has seen the history of centuries is the unique Alfriston village of which has been said,

... on no part of the South Downs is there more exquisite entertainment for the antiquary ...

1540

Anne of Cleves, to become the fourth wife of Henry VIII, travelled from Dusseldorf through Bruges to Calais, where her embarkation for England was delayed by high winds and rough seas.

On 27th December ... attended by a Royal convoy of fifty ships ... she sailed to Deal from where she was conducted to Dover Castle. It was on the final stage of her journey to the City of London and the King, that of her escort was Thomas Lord Dacre of Herstmonceux ... clad in a coat of velvet with chains of gold ...

The honour of being among the peers chosen to serve the King on this colourful day was in tragic contrast to his trial and execution but a year later.

1540

The Vicar-General to Henry VIII, Thomas Cromwell, was executed on Tower Hill. During his years of office he was responsible for many reforms and statutes including those that enabled the religious break with Roman and the widespread destruction of religious establishments during the Dissolution.

As King's secretary he was concerned with much of the private life of Henry VIII, a privileged position that brought enemies and a court intrigue resulting in his death on a charge of treason.

1541

While staying at Herstmonceux Castle as guests of Thomas, Lord Dacre, plans were made for a day's hunting and on 30th April a party of men rode out and at some time during the day, while on the land of Nicholas Pelham of Laughton, there was a violent encounter with some of Pelham's keepers. As a result of the argument and eventual fight, a keeper died two days later.

The affray between Lord Dacre and his friends with the keepers occurred in a field called Pickhay, on Broad Farm. The field is on the bank of the River Cuckmere, barely five hundred yards south of Hellingly parish church.

The arrest of Lord Dacre, together with some of his friends followed and on 27th June, at a Court of the Lord High Steward and Peers before the Lord Chancellor, Thomas Lord Dacre was tried and found guilty of murder by killing John Busebridge, a keeper, when he attempted to prevent the poaching of deer on land owned by Nicholas Pelham.

> ... had Lord Dacre been an ordinary offender he would have been disposed of summarily. Both he and his friends were favourites ... the Privy Council hesitated long before resolved on a prosecution. They repaired to the Court to intercede for his pardon ... Henry VIII remained (on this occasion) true to his principles of equal justice ... thoughtlessness was not an adequate excuse because the offender was a peer ...

Lord Dacre was hanged at Tyburn in London and buried in St Sepulchre's Church, Newgate, where Tyburn bodies were often buried. His companions were tried in a lower court and three were found guilty and executed at St Thomas Waterings, a place of execution for Sussex and Surrey, situated on the Old Kent Road. It was named after a stream where pilgrims to Canterbury could stop and water their horses.

With his duty as Constable of the Tower, Sir John Gage of Firle had the task of officiating in bringing Dacre to justice and finally his death. It was a sad and difficult responsibility since he knew the young Dacre well.

Thomas, Lord Dacre came to the title and wealth when only sixteen years of age. His father had died when he was but eleven years and his mother a year later. His grandfather, an acknowledged bad character, left him the title, the castle and wealth only five years later.

Such were his young years that, in spite of marriage to a daughter of the powerful Lord Abergavenny, owner of much land in east Sussex, Dacre's reckless free-spending nature and bad friends, all seemed the inevitable factors in an unnecessary murder.

Two sons were left fatherless: Thomas died at the age of fourteen years and Gregory lived until he was about fifty-four, but there were no surviving children.

c. 1542

Referring to local Wills about this time, Mark Anthony Lower, when speaking at a meeting in Herstmonceux in 1851, drew attention to the frequent use of 'pious phraseology' and remembrance of the poor as an indication of christian belief.

Such Wills often list with care many simple possessions of the deceased, each chosen for passing to a friend or neighbour. Even on occasions to the owner of the land on which they had lived, as when Nicholas Willard left his 'best chamlett jackett' to Anthony Devenish of Horselunges in Hellingly.

The following extracts are typical of the husbandmen who lived a life of 'honest toil' on land surrounding Hailsham.

Nicholas Willard of Hailsham in 1543, made a request for prayers at both a month and a year after burial. He also desired that

> ... a steer to be killed of the value of 12s.–0 to be distributed and given to poor people, to pray for his soul, with meat and drink convenient ...

Robert Fuller of Herstmonceux in 1542, wrote in his Will,

> ... bequeath my sawle to Almighty God, unto whose image it was created ... and my body to the erth from which it came, to be buryed in Crystyan buryal, and all my goods to the world in which I dyd geat them ...

John Collbrond of Bodyllstrete in 1540 bequeathed 12d to the high altar for the

> ... recompence of his conscience, 2d to the mother church at Chichester and directed that three masses be said at his funeral with 20d given to the poor ...

William Longeley of Herstmonceux in 1543 bequeathed his,

> ... sowle into the hands of Almighty God the Father, to our Lady St Mary and to all the glorious company of hevyn ... it was also his wish that ... at my buryeng,

one barell of bere and a bushell of whete to be bake in brede and one fat shepe to
be bake in pies to refreshe the povyrte of the parish . . .

John Honwyne of Herstmonceux in 1544 directed in his Will that his body be
buried in the 'churcherthe'. He desired four masses at his burial and gave 10s–0 to
the high altar and 12d each to the parishes of Wartling and Hailsham for the
honest people.

With particular reference to names in such Wills, M. A. Lower wrote of the
remarkable tenacity with which families of the 'humbler rank' chose to remain
in the same localities. An example was a small parcel of land in Hellingly parish
of c. 1300 with the name Akehurst. Two hundred years later a Thomas Akehurst
lived on the same land and in 1851 the name had remained common in Hellingly.

In 1982, nearly seven hundred years after the name's appearance, a house on
the land is still called Akehurst and many families so named can be found in the
Hailsham area of east Sussex.

1543

In this year at Buxted, just ten miles from Hailsham, the technique of gun casting
which came to Sussex from France was to result, with the assistance of Peter
Baude, an experienced French brass founder, in the first iron cannon being cast
in England. In the years that followed many Frenchmen were to work at Buxted.

The technique introduced proved to be of immense importance. The Weald
had always been rich in easily dug iron ore with unlimited timber for fuel and the
combination had bred small iron-making furnaces in almost every village. The old
process had been crude but with the new skills great progress was made and with
it a prosperity for many years in iron-making villages, some close to Hailsham.

1544

With the increasing danger of war with France, denization lists were drawn up
which served to control and allow aliens to stay in England. It was recorded that
eight of the wealden iron-works were employing Frenchmen who were expert
and sought after where casting needed to be of high quality.

1545

An attack on Seaford by the French was beaten off by the men of Sir William
Pelham.

c. 1545

The substantial gable-ended building, known in its earlier days to have been the
Fleur-de-Lys Inn, was built adjoining the Market Square. It was an impressive
structure of immense timbers as were other buildings in the main road through
Hailsham, and it was to survive and play a significant part in the life of the town
for over four hundred years.

In the centre of the High Street on its west side is another timbered structure
of this period that has survived, albeit with some alterations, for part of it is

now serving as a chemist's shop. Still intact are the great oak timbers of the original roof, some of which bear evidence of even previous use as ship timbers.

Probably the oldest house in Hailsham is 'The Stone' in Vicarage Road, a heavily timbered structure of the Wealden Hall type. A deed dealing with the property 'Le Stone' together with land in Hailsham still survives dated 1535. The house is on an important site, being just a hundred yards from the parish church and on the road which once led from the Market Square direct (along what is now Marshfoot Lane) to the tidal waters that flowed inland past Pevensey.

1546

John Thatcher was given permission to take seventy-seven cartloads of stone from the ruins of Pevensey Castle to improve his house at Priesthawes. But it was not always with permission that materials were taken from buildings falling into decay, for at this time quantities of lead were also taken from the old castle for use at Priesthawes, provoking the issue of a stern warning from Whitehall.

The house was, and much of it still remains, just two miles from Hailsham on the road to Stone Cross that in later years was to become the turnpike road to (east) Bourne.

With the completion of the new work, this large house, originally 'E' shaped on plan, was three floors high and built of stone, with bricks similar to those used at Herstmonceux Castle. The workmanship was impressive and it had gardens, a bowling alley, and an enclosed courtyard, enabling it to rank as one of the finer mansions in Sussex.

Today, this famous house, once associated with the powerful landowners and statesmen of England, is now but a shadow of its past.

Approached along the winding road from Hailsham the house can be seen on the left half hidden by trees on the brow of a low hill, with a line of ragged Scotch pines leading down to the road. When closer, the old pines can be seen forming and aged and uneven row each side of the rough drive up to the house.

From the road the eye notices the massive high brick and stone wall with its enormous retaining buttresses that surround the site where once was a tudor garden. About the year 1855, with the house then suffering from great age, additional rooms were built on in the Victorian Gothic style, while some old walls were repaired with a cement covering.

But still there is evidence of the original building, for a high gable end wall, scarred with rough repairs in brick and flint, shows the great age of the stone from Pevensey Castle, as also do the two mullioned windows high up in the old wall and now long last past their intended use.

In a survey of 1620 Priesthawes was described as,

> . . . fair and sumptuous . . . having a stately Bedchamber with stone carving . . .

Salzman the historian claims Priesthawes was originally a monastic house but no evidence has been found to support this.

Part of the paving to the stone entrance porch was a slab of Sussex marble, just half of what was once a long memorial slab, inlaid with a brass figure of a

Priesthawes

Bishop surrounded by a decorative border. The sunken outline of the brass inlay is still clear on the surface of this heavy slab, and it serves to indicate that the building from which it came almost certainly had a religious connection. This heavy marble slab was removed from the floor of a derelict stone building of great age only four hundred yards to the east of Priesthawes and referred to as 'The Old Place'. It was a John Webber of Hankham about 1873 who supervised the removal of the slab, for he was at that time in charge of some thirty men engaged by the then owner of the nearby house 'Glynleigh'.

The men were dismantling the stonework of 'The Old Place' and carting it away for re-working and use on the extensions, including new front turrets to Glynleigh. But when the old site had been almost entirely robbed of stone, even down to some of the foundations, the work was suddenly abandoned, for during the digging an old burial ground was revealed.

For over one hundred and seventy years generations of the Thatcher family were to live at Priesthawes and, with little deviation, they were to prove ardent Catholics. The short reign of Mary, when the Catholic religion was forced upon England with a cruel frenzy (*see* entry of 1555–57), was followed by Elizabeth I who revived the Protestant religion and, largely from a sense of fear, created forces with power to stamp out the religion from Rome wherever it could be found. But there were fervent Catholic families, often with wealth, who could not accept this suppression and such was their brave devotion that there emerged a secret resistance aimed at keeping alive the religion in which they believed.

A descendant of the builder of Priesthawes, a devout Catholic also named John Thatcher, died in 1649 and left a long and complicated Will that had been drawn up with friends. In it were a series of instructions to be carried out by the trustees of the Will and one of the instructions was to ensure that money was to be provided from his estate to pay for selected youths to come to England from the Continent to study the Catholic faith.

There can be little doubt that Priesthawes, the home of the Thatcher family, within sight of both Hailsham and the low lying ground of Pevensey Marsh, was once an important Catholic refuge. There was a need for such sanctuaries through the county and to ensure the private chapel in Priesthawes continued to be used by both visitors from France as well as Catholic friends, John Thatcher arranged that money would be available after his death, both for the care of the chapel and to provide for a priest to sing mass.

Due to the harsh intolerance of Catholics and to conceal the real reason for the presence of these youths, they were to be called apprentices. They were each to be granted an annual payment, and their study in seclusion was with the intention that they may one day be able to assist in the restoration of the Catholic faith in England.

> ... when it shall please God to restore the catholic religion into England ...

(*See* appendix 'D').

1548

Pressure from those active in the export of Sussex timber, much of which had been crucial to the extensive French gun foundries of Henry VIII at Calais and

Boulogne, prompted a coastal survey by the King's Commissioners to record, for those who favoured their closure, all iron furnaces nearer to the English Channel coast than ten miles. It was a drastic and calculated proposal and a somewhat inaccurate report referring to Chiddingly that was recorded:

> . . . the iron hammer of Chiddingly within four miles of salt water . . .

This foundry of consequence, was at one time owned by the ironmaster John French whose nearby house was called 'Streame'. Indeed in this area the soil had yielded iron ore even back in Roman times.

Other early and smaller furnaces were also active at various times in East Hoathly, Waldron, Cowbeech, Rushlake Green and Marle Green in Horam as well as Cinderford and Grove Hill in Hellingly.

A great variety of castings would have been made through the years at these places including cannon balls, blades, bolts, tools and grave slabs, as well as countless items for domestic use from small pots and kettles to the attractive and treasured firebacks with coats of arms or decorative panels in relief.

Legacies of the ironworking times are surely the old inns *The Six Bells* at Chiddingly and *The Gun* at Horam.

1555

A victim of religious intolerance was Richard Hooke of Alfriston who was condemned at Chichester in the reign of Queen Mary.

> . . . of devilish iniquity, on account of his manifest wicked errors, detestible heresies, and damnable opinions opposed, and contrary and repugnant to the Catholic Faith . . . Since Holy Mother Church can do nothing further against such a putrid member, we have handed over to your Royal Highnesses . . . the said Richard Hooke as a heretic to be punished and broken . . .

Also about this time Thomas Chatfeld the younger of Chetinglegh (Chiddingly), Joan Thomset of Esthothlegh (East Hoathly), and William Fayrwaye of Haylsham were protestants who refused to respond to questioning and were excommunicated. This was a preliminary to further action phrased as

> . . . the civil arm is now invoked . . .

but their fate is not recorded.

1555–57

The burning of Protestant martyrs in High Street, Lewes was on 20th June 1556 when Thomas Mills of Hellingly and Thomas Wood, both protestant ministers were burnt to death. Richard Woodman, an ironmaster and farmer employing over one hundred people at Warbleton, had for many months openly resisted with argument and example, the religion of the Papists.

The powerful Gage family were ardent Catholics and active in seeking out those who preached anti-popery and it was Sir Edward, the local magistrate and High Sheriff of Sussex, one of the most influential men in the county who had Richard Woodman arrested for the second and last time.

A churchwarden in Warbleton parish church, Woodman had been imprisoned a few years earlier for publicly accusing his priest of changing his religious outlook. The arrest on this final occasion arose out of being tragically betrayed for continuing to preach his simple faith. A spirited man in his thirties, he had for long, evaded and outwitted his pursuers until finally he was captured in the secret room of his house. Bound helpless, he was taken from Warbleton to the Gage home at Firle and from there to prison in London.

Woodman was finally brought to trial in St Mary's in Southwark. A man of wealth and an accomplished speaker on religion, his defence was both fearless and spirited.

> ... throughout Woodman proved himself a real student of God's Word. Again and again he confounded his accusers by his ready and powerful arguments from Scripture. His fearless manner and his charges of unfair treatment, of deliberate perjury, and of evil living on the part of some of those who examined him only made them the more determined to have his life ...

The verdict was never in doubt and Woodman was taken to Marshalsea Prison where he was

> ... otherwile lying on the ground, sometime sitting in the stocks ... sometimes bound with cords that all my body had been swollen, much like to be overcome for the pain ...

On 22nd June, Richard Woodman, together with James Morris with his mother, Margery, of Heathfield, were with other men and women from Lewes, Rotherfield and Mayfield all burnt to death in Lewes. Only Woodman and Mills had been put on trial.

The High Sheriff, Sir Edward Gage, was present and gave the order for the execution of these brave men and women. Over the many years since their burning, they have become known as the Sussex Martyrs. An accomplished writer, Woodman left after his death a remarkable record of his experiences in prison, his faith and conversations with his accusers.

There were two hundred and twenty seven victims of persecutions in Sussex between 1555 and 1557 of which thirty-three were burnt at the stake including seventeen in Lewes. This county and East Sussex in particular suffered more than any other from the religious oppression, for the resistance of the individual was stronger here. It is thought that the heavily wooded areas and the poor roads, often impassable, caused many Wealden villages to live with a degree of isolation. It was a condition that brought little interference and encouraged a self-reliance that perhaps strengthened their Protestant faith.

Protestant martyrs were condemned to be burnt in different towns spread throughout the county, with the object of striking a general fear into people and Hailsham as well as the surrounding villages suffered greatly from this disquiet and unrest, for the patron of the Hailsham church living was the Catholic Sir Edward Gage of Firle. Nearly two hundred years later in 1730, his descendant Sir William Gage conformed to the Anglican church.

1558

Queen Mary, the rejected child of Henry VIII, grew up into a staunch Catholic as was her mother Catherine of Aragon, but with failing health she died on 17th November. The terrible religious persecution and cruelty of her reign, when the most fierce measures were taken against Protestants in her passion to revive

Catholicism, had earned her the name 'Bloody Mary'.

1558

Hailsham parish church register begins. (*See* entries of *c.* 1390 and 1538).

1559

It was but a few weeks since the end of the virulent oppression, a time not helped by Sir Edward Gage of Firle, having in 1554 installed John Oldfield as a Roman Catholic priest in Hailsham, that a

> . . . heynous dissorder . . .

was committed by the inhabitants of the town.

In response to a report on this violent eruption, the Privy Council at Westminster on 29th March, 1559 recorded the minute:

> . . . A letter to Thomas Bushopp and John Thatcher Justyces of Pease in Sussex, aunswerynge a letter of theirs unto Sir Richard Sackevyle Knight, wherein they are wylled for the better punisshement of an heynous dissorder lately committed by the inhabitaunts of the towne of Halisleham, of the said county, in spoyling the parishe churche there, to call for thassistence of Sir Nicholas Pelham and Sir Edward Gage and other Justices dwelling nighe unto them, and having founde oute who were thauctors and ringeleaders of that matter to committ them to warde, and to putt them to suche fynes for their offences as by their discretions shalbe thought most mete and agreeable to the lawes . . .

Note: While Thomas Geering has expressed the opinion that the damage to flints in the church tower was caused by firearms (*see* entry of *c.* 1390), others have written linking the occasion with the disorder of 1558. But this assumption must be subject to the gravest doubt for at this time handguns were extremely rare and valuable, having only late in the reign of Henry VIII, been introduced into England from Europe.

1559

East Hoathly parish church register begins.

The tower of this church was built in *c.* 1445 and is typical of many in east Sussex but the remainder of the church is of a later date. The chancel was shortened by ten feet in 1726 after which the church generally seems to have been badly neglected, until in 1801, a report drew attention to an urgent need for repairs causing the Lord Bishop of the Diocese to require extensive and drastic work with the trust that,

> . . . churchwardens may be able to conscientiously report on oath, that all things . . . are in proper order . . .

but in 1856 the church was finally beyond repair and entirely demolished except for the tower.

During demolition, workmen unearthed a unique carved Norman pillar piscina now to be seen in the new chancel. Clearly the piscina relates to the period of the first Rector Robert de Terring of 1287 and is quite remarkable.

Another exceptional feature is the vast area of the East wall brilliantly decorated in mosaic, tiles and alabaster where the figures are strongly reminiscent of the Pre-Raphaelite, Sir Edward Burne-Jones.

Of special interest outside the church, apart from the tower, is the lavishly carved tablet on the chancel wall that the Duke of Newcastle had erected in 1742 in memory of Samuel Atkins who was his head gardener.

1559

Queen Elizabeth I introduced the Act of Supremacy. It was designed to establish by law the supreme power of the Crown and the Protestant religion, and the rejection of worship in the Catholic faith. Henceforth clergy were on oath, to convert to the new faith or be charged with high treason.

To persist in attending Mass was also a crime,

> . . . whosoever shall at any time hereafter say mass, or procure mass to be said, or willingly suffer it to be said in his house, . . . shall be judged in law a felon and shall suffer the pains of death . . .

The Act was not universally popular and much of the country was confused and divided in its religious thinking. It was a condition that was to cause the nation terrible upheavals in the future, even to it being a factor in the disastrous division of opinion that was to culminate eighty-three years hence in the Civil War. But most of the clergy gave way to the Act and conformed to the protestant faith.

The Catholic John Oldfield was in 1554 installed by Thomas Gage as the Hailsham priest, but in 1559 he changed his allegiance from the Pope to that of Queen Elizabeth and remained a priest in Hailsham until he died in 1581.

1559

Warbleton parish church register begins.

Upon entering, there is a sense of history and great age and of the many features of this church the most dominating is the huge wooden structure filling the centre of the north aisle.

It is the Squire's Pew or Galleried Manorial Pew built in 1722 with twelve wide stairs to take up to where, seated aloft, the Squire's family from almost the top of the pointed nave arches, looked down on the congregation. It is a private enclosure with a desk and upholstered seats, and separated by a low partition with its own door is the smaller space for servants. This handsome enclosure once for the elite has panelled sides and, secure in its isolation, it all stands on four tall columns.

There is a frail but elegant pulpit, a heavy aged wood chest bound with iron straps and fittings for at least six padlocks. The chancel floor has a fine canopied Brass over five hundred years old set in marble and protected by low iron posts with red silken rope. In the north chapel a grand and well cared for monument to Sir John Cade has a sculpture by the famous John Rysbrack.

In the tower staircase is the impregnable door in wood, leather and iron to seal off intruders, which is probably the work of the ill-fated churchwarden and prosperous ironfounder who once had a house next to the church. He was Richard Woodman the martyr who was burnt at the stake in Lewes. (*See* entry of 1555–57).

Perfectly situated on a raised mound and seen against the sky, this old church

is quite exceptional.

In future years, a workhouse was built opposite the parish church but when conditions became intolerable even for paupers, it was converted into the row of cottages still standing today. Those to the right of the row are from the oldest part of the structure.

1560

Willingdon parish church register begins.

Built on ground rising out of Willingdon Level which was once the western area of water entered from Pevensey, the ground rises steeply behind the church to form downland.

The Early English tower is almost detached from the church at its north-west corner. The church interior is early 14th cent., and of good design with monuments of 1617 in alabaster. A gallery at the west end is an addition in the Renaissance style of Sir Christopher Wren.

An early Chiddingly Place was rebuilt by Sir John Jefferay and even from what is left today, it surely once stood serene and impressive. Chiddingly born Mark Antony Lower, long ago saw a more complete house, and was of the opinion that it must have been one of the finest Elizabethan houses in the county.

The fame of Sir John after his long experience in Parliament and as a Judge, was in his final elevation by Elizabeth to Lord Chief Baron of the Exchequer. Sadly but a year later in 1575 he died. At such a time he was with few equals, but a man of a similar name who lived later was to cause unpleasant confusion. The man was the notorious Judge Jeffreys, whose dreaded deportation and death sentences prompted his west country courts to be named the 'bloody assizes'.

Undoubtedly the splendid Chiddingly Place, of a size demanding countless hands and an abundant supply of money, could not for ever stave off the deterioration that age must bring. Thus over hundreds of years the structure has suffered the usual relentless change leaving what is there today, an abode no longer as it was, for it is now a working farm, with the machinery and stores one would expect spread about the age old structure of brick and ochre coloured stonework.

In many places there are unused moulded stone windows and doorways, some in vast brick walls; there is a huge solid brick barn once called chapel barn, which long ago was a two-storied wing of many rooms. But the centre of the old mansion is still used as a house, having mullioned windows and a charming entrance with columns and cornice. All well set behind an open space of grass and fine trees, it is still of some dignity.

1560

Folkington parish church register begins.

The church, much of which is in flint from the Downs that rise close behind it, is both small and simple with a weatherboarded bell-turret containing a single bell.

Much of the church is still of great age being in the Early English style of *c.* 1230 while the interior seems almost humble with its plain box pews and the lack of a chancel arch. The floor has unusual panels of black marble in which are set coats of arms in wrought iron.

1561

Laughton parish church register begins.

Built at the edge of Laughton Level barely twenty-five feet above sea level and a little over a mile from the ruins of Laughton Place, the early home of the Pelhams (*see* entry of 1356) with whom this church is so securely linked.

Laughton has in the past been called the village of the Buckle reflecting the very special significance the place has for the Pelham family. As with many local churches, there is a Pelham buckle carved on the arch over the west door of the tower.

This small church built by Gilbert de Aquila, who also built Michelham Priory, clearly has architectural features and workmanship from unusually skilled masons, that sets it apart from many other churches.

Perhaps the greatest interest is in the outside of the chancel walls where the priest's doorway has an exceptionally attractive curved arch and rising high above both corners of the east wall are highly decorative pinnacles that at once lift the church above the normal.

A further unusual feature is the outside walling of the chancel still in immaculate condition due to it being made of flint and beach boulders. Both flints and boulders have been individually positioned into the walling with the greatest possible care and each row has rounded boulders and square knapped flints placed alternately so that on an entire wall is made a precise but subtle chequer pattern of square and rounded shapes.

It is the chancel of this church, rebuilt with great care between 1790 and 1801, that holds for the Pelhams the closest possible meaning since below the stone floor is a large vault almost as large as the entire chancel itself. In this unique burial chamber, resting in stone recesses are thirty-one coffins, containing members of the Pelham family, among whom were Earls, Dukes and Prime Ministers. This burial place was finally sealed in 1886 with simple stone slabs that now form part of the chancel floor.

A reminder of the link with history are two helmets that rest on the old beam that spans the chancel arch. Both are Pelham helmets, one dating from *c.* 1520.

1563

The first Poor Law Act of Elizabeth was passed as a result of the suppression of the monasteries and other religious houses. With the abolition of these centres was destroyed a means by which those in acute poverty could call and hope for food and help.

In an attempt to alleviate this new hardship, the Act compelled each parish to appoint two Collectors of

> . . . charitable alms of all the residue of the people inhabiting in the parish . . .

Quite often the collectors would be church wardens and the Act gave powers to compel as well as encourage generosity. The collectors were required to account to the parish meeting every quarter.

1565

Pevensey parish church register was commenced in 1565 but the first leaf with entries from 1565 to 1569 was lost. The register was written on paper as were most others at this time, and when in 1597 an instruction was issued that registers must now be written on vellum, the Pevensey vicar did not obey. In spite of this neglect however, the second book of entries was not only on vellum but it was bound in leather as indeed were the third and fourth books, all of which had on their covers, tooled ornamental patterns.

A parish church, built eight hundred years ago, would normally have been built in a dominant position, both overlooking and seen by its people, but in Pevensey it is to be found in a quiet narrow back lane away from the main street.

An explanation could be the extreme age of this small but ancient town. It is surely probable that when the Normans erected the church, a small part of which survives today, the centre of the town was already occupied with Saxon dwellings, some probably with stonework still standing from the Roman occupation. Indeed the Romans left with us inescapable evidence of the place in history they gave to Pevensey, for they were here, and built an almost indestructible castle over seven hundred years before the Normans invaded.

The chancel, almost as long as the nave, dates back to the reign of King John and has in it fine examples of Early English stonework, including column caps with beautifully carved leaf-work. It is a chancel of great dignity.

The nave, much of which was built in stone from the old quarry at (east) Bourne, is of a later period with columns having much more enrichment than many local churches. The simple font in the much earlier Norman style could be the oldest stonework in the church and nearly nine hundred years old.

The church dedication is to St Nicholas the Patron Saint of Sailors and a reminder of the great part shipping has played in the history of Pevensey is the monument to John Wheatley who died in 1616, a parishioner who gave much money towards England's defence against the powerful Spanish Armada.

With gradual recession of the sea that once came inland and lapped Pevensey on three sides, the harbour, of great age, slowly began to lose its shipping until, as the water became more shallow, the decline finally ended in the total loss of the port for sea-going ships.

Once busy and prosperous, the town lost much of its importance and suffered in many ways. The poorer times were reflected in the sad neglect of a once fine church until, in the 16th cent., the unhappy decision was made to build a wall across the chancel cutting it off from the nave. Thus was created a much reduced church more suitable for the hard times.

Walled up and now discarded the chancel fell into such disrepair that for a long time it was used for cattle and at a later date for storing contraband.

Most of the outside walls appear unusually clean and neat due to them being built of selected boulders from the nearby beach and carefully laid into the walls in courses straight and level. The builders of this early church were exceptionally skilled.

1568

During a survey carried out at Pevensey Castle, it was discovered that quantities of lead were being taken without permission and being delivered to Lord Dacre of Herstmonceux Castle. It was also found that John Thatcher had accepted deliveries of stone from the castle and had confessed that it was for further work on his new house 'Priesthawes'.

The castle was suffering the fate of all such neglected or abandoned structures by being systematically robbed of its building materials and, if it was by a man of means and power, then the operation could be so much easier and on a more ambitious scale. There can today be but few buildings in the surrounding country-side still surviving from this time that have not been assisted in their survival by the stone of Pevensey Castle.

1572

Magistrates were enabled to deal with inhabitants who consistently refused to give alms. The office of 'Overseer of the Poor' was created and appointed by the Vestry. It supervised charitable funds, collected fines and later assessed inhabitants for a poor rate.

1573

Following a period when several of the buildings in Pevensey Castle had suffered serious dilapidations an inventory revealed that much was now impossible to repair.

The immense size of the castle with its vast length of walling and the huge Keep, all year by year deteriorating beyond recall, was all too easily robbed of its loose stone. Such was the condition of the castle by 1588 that the State Commissioners finally issued the instruction for its demolition.

In spite of many men being put to work on the destruction the task proved beyond their power for the Roman walls yielded little to their efforts. Today, some four hundred years later, the outer walls of Pevensey still stand, having survived sixteen hundred years since they were built by the Romans.

1575

Alciston parish church register begins.

To reach this simple church is to travel in the only direction possible, along a narrow quiet road almost as far as the slope of the Downs. A turn off along a fenced footpath takes the worshipper to the small parish church built by the Normans.

The interior has a chancel, shortened since it was first built, and there still exists a very early window confirming the church's Norman beginning. This simple church was to 'suffer' restoration in 1853.

The thick walls of flint from the Downs merge with the landscape and are in harmony with the ruins of a large flint dovecot but a few yards away and part of the old Alciston Court. It has all been there with flint and tile farm buildings, in a compact and historic group, since the 12th cent.

1576

Westham parish church register begins.

Possibly only a mile from the momentous landing of William the Conqueror and within a few yards of the castle built by his victorious Normans, this large and impressive church once stood in the midst of great activity.

Many men were concerned with boats both in the harbour and anchored off shore, and there were hundreds of Norman soldiers and their leaders in this area of Sussex of which the castle and the church were the centre.

It was a time of consolidation and the movement of armed battalions intent on establishing the communications that were to spread Norman influence throughout England.

The Norman church was built cruciform in shape and of immense strength. The south wall of the nave facing fields to the sea has typically narrow Norman windows, on the outside little more than slits but splayed wide inside through the thick Norman walls to let the light in. The windows are high in the air as if positioned for defence and this massive wall with its windows is still standing today.

In a quiet but somewhat misleading backwater, the peaceful church we now find has a Priesthawes Chapel dedicated to the Thatcher family who built the elaborate house 'Priesthawes' just two miles from Hailsham and on the road to Stone Cross (where there once was a stone cross) and Westham. In the chapel is an altar stone once used with the religion from Rome but probably defaced, as so many were in the time of Elizabeth I. Its fate, was to be used in 1602 as a gravestone for a vicar's wife until it was restored to its rightful place a few years ago.

The interior stonework, much of which was from the quarry at (east) Bourne, is mainly of the Perpendicular period of the 15th cent., as are many interiors of our local churches, but the stone mouldings are clearly more ornate as may well be expected in so significant a church. Also of fine workmanship is the oak rood screen spanning the chancel opening, now somewhat rescued by repairs but actually made five hundred years ago.

Externally, the church again has stone enrichment of a high quality and of special interest is the knapped flint work in certain areas of walling where large squared stones alternate with sets of knapped flints grouped together in similar squares to form with the stonework an effective chequer pattern, but with age, much of it shows evidence of rough repair work.

Built into the outside of the wall by the west door of the tower is a medieval stone holy water stoup very low in position and tending to indicate that the ground has risen over the centuries as much as twenty inches since the stoup was first in use.

The tower dominates the church with both its size and weight; and the decorative use of flint, the solid diagonal buttresses and, at the top, the embattlemented parapet, all combine to convey a great dignity in this quiet place, once alive with events affecting the whole of England.

1581

Heathfield parish church register begins.

With a shift of population over the centuries this church is now in what is known as Old Heathfield.

Built of chalk and local sandstone only the tower has survived in anything like its original state dating as it does from the 13th cent. The oldest stonework however, is in the vestry where some of the original Norman church can still be seen.

Of the rest of the church much was renewed in the Victorian era.

The churchyard has several small cast iron 'gravestones' with shaped outlines of very ornate floral designs. They were cast locally and are shaped at the bottom to a point for driving into the ground. (*See* entry of 1607).

1581

The Manor of 'Haylesham' was granted to Gregory, Lord Dacre of Herstmonceux.

The manor, through the centuries, was to be held by many people and in the sixty years until 1640 it was in the hands of William, Lord Burghley, Robert, Earl of Leicester and Sir Thomas Gage of Firle. When the manor passed to Sir Thomas, the Indenture (document of sale) quoted the place name Earsham (on other occasions Ershams) instead of Haylesham.

1581

An agreement was made by purveyors appointed at Winchelsea that they would supply grain at the prices ruling in Hailsham. This important decision confirms the wide influence enjoyed by Hailsham's market at this time.

Later the market was able to conduct business using its own standard measure for corn.

1587

The first private owner of Michelham Priory after its suppression was Herbert Pelham who, as he intended to make the priory his home, put in hand extensive repairs and even rebuilding where it was necessary, since the site and remains had been in ruins, robbed of stone and overgrown for many years.

1588

This was the year of the Spanish Armada and the time preceding its defeat was one of great concern and preparation.

It was but a few years since a Commissioner's report had claimed that Pevensey Castle was far beyond repair having been deserted and for many years robbed of its loose stone. But in this time of danger to England, surveyors were ordered by Elizabeth:

> . . . to call on such persons as they think requisite and skilful to consider the state of the castle in timberwork and stones; to report whether it be worth repairing and if so what costs will be required . . .

The decision caused only minor defence work to be carried out and with the defeat of the Spaniards and the country free from attack, Pevensey was once again abandoned and dismissed as beyond further use.

When on future occasions the castle attracted official attention it was usually to assess the value of what wood and stone might be available for use elsewhere.

c. 1590

About this time there stood but a few yards north of Eastbourne parish church a substantial structure in stone and flint which almost certainly served the church as a rectory manor and parsonage.

Today, linked with the parish church by a short cloister, it is used as a vestry and church hall and known as The Old Parsonage.

Nearly four hundred years ago a very similar stone building was built at Hailsham in the same style as the Parsonage at Eastbourne. The site of this structure was a few yards from the rough cart track now called Marshfoot Lane that led from the Market Square in Hailsham down to the edge of Pevensey Marsh. This ancient track was along a narrow ridge and the old building in brick with stone from the quarry at (east) Bourne was situated as if to be as near the marsh as possible for it was at the end of the ridge where it began to slope down towards sea level. It is likely that this once important spot where the ridge ended, was the reason for it being named Marshfoot, i.e. foot of the marsh, for barely a further mile towards the marsh we know today, the ground is little above sea level. At the time the stone building was built, just four hundred years ago, the ground level would have been even lower and the building much nearer the tidal water.

This isolated building of some dignity was of two storeys and nearly seventy feet long with many mullioned windows and doorways with low curved arches. It was described by a Hailsham man over a hundred years ago as:

> ...made of red brick and hewn grey stone, with walls two feet thick, solid deep foundations and dungeon-like cellars ...

there were also

> ...tomb-like stones that once partly covered a kitchen floor now hidden by boards ...

With Hailsham but a small village, this structure was impressive and of some importance for there appears little doubt that it was built for an ecclesiastical purpose, probably with monks, and linked before the Dissolution, with the Priory at Michelham. (*See* John Hollamby's poems in appendix 'M').

Some two hundred years ago neglect and exposure to the weather had sadly affected the condition of the building at Marshfoot, and it is known that by 1860 it had been divided into four somewhat primitive homes for labourers' families. It was barely forty years later when further deterioration to a sad ruinous condition brought about its demolition by 1902.

The destruction of Marshfoot House, as in the end it was called, released much material for use elsewhere and it was a discerning mind that appreciated what remained of the stonework, for it has been recorded that it was

> ... bought and taken down by an American gentleman ...

who was to use it for building a house at Clayton, another source records that the old stone was used on a house called 'Clayton Holt'

... in a scooped out part of the Downs ...

Today, there is a house at Clayton of this name which was built in 1907 amid trees (the name 'Holt' is Anglo-Saxon and associated with trees) on the north side of the Downs by an American named Leland H. de Langley who returned to America in 1914.

In Hailsham, the man-made pond of centuries ago is still to be found near the old cart track which even today at that place is an unmade country lane. But no trace exists of the 16th cent. stone building except evidence a few feet below ground level of its brick-lined cellar, once so vital for the storage of food.

Also at this place was an old well some sixty feet deep and on protective brick stilts, there was a boarded granary with a tiled roof. Still standing today however is a sturdy brick and flint barn of considerable age, with sandstone foundations from the quarry at (east) Bourne as was the stone of the medieval building, which once stood but a few feet away and was so important in the life of Hailsham.

1597

During the greater part of the century now drawing to a close, the sadness and suffering created by poverty had been steadily increasing. And where victims were helpless and often without hope, so lawlessness increased in the effort to sustain life.

Such suffering had for long been widespread and there was a concern that prompted increasing efforts to help those who were desperate.

It was just six years before the death of Queen Elizabeth that the Act of 1597 introduced a Poor Law, that enabled a fund to be collected for poor relief financed from rates levied on those able to pay.

In rural areas the worsening poverty owed much to an increasing population and drastic changes in farming where growing wheat and root crops had largely given way to the rearing of sheep. Vast flocks were to be found in the coastal areas of east Sussex. In particular, the Downland and the rich pastures inland behind Pevensey, now reclaimed from the sea, were ideal but few men were needed for the care of such flocks.

This early Poor Law Act now combined the post of Collector of parish alms with that of Overseer of the Poor. It was an Act that through the centuries that followed, was subject to many additions and amendments, all intended to relieve the plight of the poor in ever changing social conditions.

1600

1601

This early Poor Law Act made every parish in England responsible for its own poor and was to be the basis of progress through other Poor Laws for many future generations. The Act instructed Overseers of the Poor to be selected from churchwardens and landowners, while local taxes aided paupers and where possible, set them to work. Persistent vagrants who drifted about from district to district and had no intention of working could be, and often were, deported from the town to reduce the burden on the ratepayers.

It was also at this time that there arose an increasing urgency to control the growing numbers of idle vagrants; men who travelled the countryside choosing to live by their wits, they were the small fry rogues, absconding servants and disorderly men and women, all of whom would readily live on charity wherever it could be found.

Such lawlessness prompted in each county, Houses of Correction aimed at restraining and '. . . correcting the idle poor . . .'. These abodes, the responsibility of the local justices, were often little short of prisons and controlled to the advantage of the keeper in charge.

1601

Michelham Priory was sold by Herbert Pelham to a favourite of Queen Elizabeth, Thomas Sackville, Earl of Dorset, later to be Lord Buckhurst.

The priory was to remain in the Sackville family for nearly three hundred years, during which time it was mostly let out to tenant farmers until in 1897, it was sold to J. E. A. Gwynne of Folkington.

c. 1602

The brick and stone house to be lived in by Samuel Barton was built at Cowbeech and became known as 'Barton House', due to its occupation by the family over many generations. It is known that Samuel Barton was allowed to hold Presbyterian services on his property, and at this time he was also a churchwarden at Hellingly parish church. (*See* entry of 1672).

Barton House, eventually to be known as Carters Corner Place, became in 1917 the home of the statesman, the first Lord Hailsham, Lord Chancellor in 1928–29 and Secretary of War from 1931 to 1935 who was to die in 1950. The second Lord Hailsham was also to live in this house with his family but he gave up possession in 1964 when he was the Minister for Education and Science and Lord President of the Council.

The second Lord Hailsham has offered the personal reminder that by tradition Samuel Barton assisted the escape of Charles II from Cromwell's forces. He has also offered the opinion that the Presbyterian services of 1672 were probably held in the large barn demolished in 1923 but which was then but a few yards from the house being probably that shown in a Carters Corner Place drawing of 1785 by Samuel H. Grimm.

1603

With the death of Queen Elizabeth after her momentous reign of forty-five years, the rarity of a new king was an event of such magnitude that it was surely the reason news of the King from Scotland was written into the Hailsham church register.

Lines drawn across the vellum page both above and below the announcement separated it from the baptism entries that filled the rest of the page. Written in were the words:

... The XXX day of Marche James the sixth Kynge of Scotland wast proclaymed
Kynge of England in the town of Haylyham ...

Such a proclamation was probably made from the market cross in the Market
Square.

1604

Brickmaking was carried out at several small sites in and around Hailsham. One
such brickfield and kiln was situated a mere three hundred and eighty yards from
the Market Square, it was a site much later to have the bungalows of the present
Old Orchard Place built upon it.

c. 1606

With furnaces for smelting iron as close as Chiddingly, Horam, Waldron, Heathfield, Warbleton and East Hoathly, all of which had been operating for many
years, the steady destruction of forest land for fuel was now causing much concern and it was recorded that Dicker Common had lost seven thousand oaks, of
which six hundred were mature.

The devastation of trees was widespread and so serious that parliament had, on
several occasions, passed Acts with restrictions aimed at controlling the damage.
But often these Acts in turn reacted against even the simple life of the peasant
for he frequently lost grazing land when the use of woodland was forbidden to
him, or land was cut off by its enclosure to encourage the growth of young trees.

Timber, and especially oak, was needed by the towns and for export but
most important,

... the navy wanted Sussex oaks for the 'wooden walls of England' indeed con-
tracts for building the King's ships stipulated Sussex oak before any other kind ...

1607

John Norden, the map maker, wrote in his book, *Surveyor's Dialogue*:

... He that well observes it, and hath known the Weald of Sussex, the grand nursery
of oak and beech, shall find an alteration within Less than thirty years as may well
strike a fear lest few years more as pestilent as the former will leave few good trees
standing ... such a heat issueth out of the many Forges and Furnaces for the
making of iron, as hath devoured many famous woods ...

1607

Arlington parish church register begins.

On a Roman site the beginning of this church was a humble Saxon structure
nearly one thousand years ago of which isolated parts still remain, as does the
chapel the Normans added late in the 12th century. The rest of the church has
examples of other early periods and in spite of Cromwellian damage and whitewash, the faint remains of several remarkable wall paintings can still be seen.
There appears little doubt that the church was regularly visited by pilgrims, who
followed the old Roman road after leaving Lewes on their way to Canterbury.

A small and simple church of some beauty that has long lost its village but
retained an atmosphere of great age, it is a church rare indeed for the stonework

that can be seen from the labours of countless masons through many centuries. These men, inevitably journeymen travelling to wherever such work offered itself, have each cut, tooled and sometimes carved the countless stones that form the structure of Arlington parish church. Each stone bears witness to the style of its time and to the ability of the mason, whether good or poor. Certainly these varied stones survive from periods throughout almost the entire span of English history.

Some hundred years ago this simple, yet remarkable parish church was described as:

> ... being in a state of dirt, decay and ruin and bare of almost every decent requisite of worship ...

but after the long sustained efforts of the Reverend Thomas Bunston (1889-1918), an appreciation recorded with some truth that:

> ... the whole church presents a complete history from the earliest time of christianity in England, and well deserves attention from all lovers of archaeology ...

A remarkable possession in the chapel and now protected by a glass case, is a storage jar, probably for food, discovered in 1891 embedded in gravel and sand under the flooring during the restoration of the tower. This find was rare indeed, for it has been established as nearly seven hundred and fifty years old and without equal in the British Museum.

Still surviving in the church are early stone coffin lids, a massive rough boarded chest with two locks and a double lid possibly eight hundred years old, and an ancient iron font cover made locally where there was once a forge.

The three bells of this fine village church are exceptional; two bells being nearly four hundred years old, while the tenor bell was cast by William Hull at Bell Banks in Hailsham, as long ago as 1677, and weighs one ton.

Due however to the extreme age of the tower and until certain repairs can be attended to, these heavy bells are not fully rung. Nevertheless they are still being heard by the ropes being pulled just enough for the clapper to tap against each bell.

1607

The Rev. Robert Hunt, vicar of Heathfield parish church since 1602 sailed as chaplain with an expedition, sanctioned by James I to the New World. The ship finally anchored at the end of its journey at what was to becomes Jamestown in Virginia:

> ... the settlers built a fort and a church as well as a storehouse and a row of huts ... they were determined to found a lasting colony ... but against their worst enemy they could offer no effective resistance ... men were destroyed with cruel diseases ... but for the most part they died of famine ...

In 1612, five years after their landing, the colonists struggled to produce a first crop of tobacco which was sold in England at a considerable profit.

It was in 1962 that the actress Dame Margaret Rutherford unveiled a stained glass window in Heathfield parish church showing a scene recording in history, the Rev. Hunt with companions in the dress of the period, celebrating Communion in Virginia.

1609

Hooe parish church register begins.

Today, the small church of St Oswald stands on a dominating site with ground sloping down on three sides to the rich pastures of Pevensey Marsh, once long ago a huge expanse of inland water. In such distant times the church was the centre of homes and village life, but now, the scene is somewhat lonely with the church isolated among fields and away from roads.

Over a thousand years ago there was a small Saxon church on this site but with the invasion by the Normans, Hooe became a place of some local importance and was given as a reward by William the Conqueror to his supporter the Earl of Eu. Under Norman influence a new stone church was built to be followed by a priory sited nearby, but now long gone.

Standing alone, this small church is of considerable interest with an exceptional east window, a font of Sussex marble dating from Saxon times as also does a remarkable muniment chest (for documents). Above the pulpit hangs a sounding board made about 1690 with fine inlay work, no doubt reflecting the wealthy patronage the church enjoyed in the distant past.

During the restoration work in 1891 there were clearly seen through the flaking limewash, traces of medieval frescoes on the walls of the nave. In 1905 the Rev. Cuthbert Routh recorded:

> ... more than one rude figure discovered at the restoration in 1891, with other decorations and texts. Walls re-plastered and paintings destroyed ...

In the porch there still survives a holy water stoup, a reminder of the days when the church was Catholic.

As with nearby Wartling, the church overlooks the valley through which flows the Wallers Haven river, a valley that once saw navigable water flowing past and almost up to the village of Boreham.

The old village of Hooe with houses and abodes reaching down almost to tidal water, suffered on occasions from heavy seas that came inland past the coast. A medieval record confirms:

> ... it suffered considerably from inundation of the sea and fresh-water streams. Between 1291 and 1340, four hundred acres in Hooe had been rendered useless for cultivation from this cause. In the latter year one third of the demesne lands (*see* note at end of this entry) were untilled owing to the poverty of the inhabitants, all of whom lived by agriculture ... '. (*Note:* Demesne land was at the time, land of the Lord of the Manor on which villain tenants in return for the use of land, had to work certain periods of the year without payment.

1610

A mace of silver gilt was made as the symbol of office held by the Pevensey Bailiff. It was the duty of the bailiff to preside in the Court House when the court, having the power to hear cases and pass sentences, was in session.

The Court House, a very small building dating from the 16th cent., and still existing in Pevensey, comprises two cells for prisoners and a minute exercise yard behind a high spiked wall. On the floor above is a robing chamber, with a court room measuring only eighteen by fourteen feet into which is crowded a magistrate's bench and desk, prisoner's dock, jury bench, clerk's table, public bench and the bailiff's mace. (*See* appendix 'E').

1611

Berwick parish church register begins.

This small and simple church on raised ground overloooking the beautiful Cuckmere valley and the Downs beyond, was mainly built in the 12th cent. to replace a small Saxon church.

A reminder of this earlier church is the massive and somewhat crude font, almost completely lacking in decoration and of great age. Built into the face of the west wall, it is a part of the church that could well be nine hundred years old.

Within feet of the font is a carved box dating from Henry VIII when a church bible needed to be cared for and protected. Above this spot, the stone wall reveals deep scars where arrows were sharpened in medieval times.

With the neglect from generations of a small community and damage to the tower by lightning in 1774, a long sad decline was finally halted in 1837 when E. Boys Ellman came to Berwick as a curate. By that time the spire had been destroyed, and the four bells, two of them broken, lay dismantled on the ground. The chancel had been shortened and was barely protected by a poor thatched roof while a derelict north aisle had been bricked up.

Boys Ellman became Rector in 1843 and within fourteen years and with increasing support from the villagers, his devoted and inspiring efforts had restored the church from its past desolation.

With the stained glass windows blown out by a bomb during the 1939–45 war, the new windows are now clear, creating a bright interior from which can be seen the surrounding countryside. Being unusually light, the church interior is now transformed and alive with colour from the recently painted panels in the chancel, and the many vast and fine murals that dominate the nave. (*See* entry of 1943).

In the churchyard is an unusual steep mound thought to be an ancient burial site.

c. 1617

The Act Book of the Archdeaconry Court of Lewes constantly recorded items of offence to the strong religious zeal of the Puritans, who in some parts of south east England had sufficient strength and influence to uphold their principles.

Entries in the Act Book about this time were:

William Fox of Hailsham for being '. . . a notorious breaker of the Sabboth day running matches in the tyme of divyne service . . .'

Hellingly church

Carter's Corner Place

Ralph Brooke of Arlington for '. . . wearing a great payre of hornes uppon his head in the churchyard when henry hall and his wife were going to be married, shewing thereby that the sayd hall was lyke to be a cuckold . . .'

John Abington for '. . . killing of a porker upon Sonday . . . which he sold the next day at Selmeston fayre . . .'

Elizabeth Collins of Chalvington for '. . . washing clothes upon Easter day . . .'

Edward Kingswell of Wartling for '. . . harbouring of women that had children begotten out of lawful wedlock and suffering them to depart without penance . . .'

Henry Elliott of Warbleton for '. . . unreasonable ringing, excessive drinking, brutish abusing of the church in the most beastly manner . . .'

Stephen Weekes of Pevensey for '. . . carrying of iron to a boat uppon the Sabbath day . . .'

But there was a disillusionment with the amount of Catholic doctrine still permitted by King James causing many Puritans who desired a simpler and 'more pure' Anglican church to feel threatened and the need to find a new life with freedom of worship. The Puritans urge to seek the 'New World' was with the knowledge of the King and '. . . they had to content themselves with his promise not to molest them provided they kept the peace . . .'.

On 6th September 1620 a hundred and four men, women and children, afterwards to be called the 'Pilgrim Fathers', sailed from Plymouth in the *Mayflower* to settle sixty-eight days later in what is now Plymouth, Massachusetts.

1618

Hellingly parish church register begins.

Founded *c.* 1180 the church, set in one of the very rare circular churchyards, was once cruciform on plan and now survives with several medieval architectural periods in evidence.

The nave has an excellent Early English arcade with carved column caps, while the chancel is remarkable for its fine Norman stonework including two windows on the north side.

The chancel is not a straight continuation of the nave but noticeably inclines to the south in sympathy it is said, with the inclination of Christ's head upon the Cross.

On the chancel floor is a Brass of a lady in 15th cent. costume. A brass panel by the south door recognises in 1923, the service as a churchwarden of Walter Holford Pitcher, one of a family that has lived in Hellingly without a break since *c.* 1650. Many descendants of the family are still in Hellingly and Hailsham.

In 1802 the church was known to have a modest weatherboarded bell turret with a shingled spire, but in 1836, building work commenced on the stonework of a sturdy square battlemented tower.

1618

A Proclamation was read in Hailsham church by order of James I which allowed sport to be played on Sunday when Divine services were over. It was a relaxation in custom that was not welcomed by many Puritans.

c. 1620

Puritan names reflected the intense religious feeling of the times and the following were among those recorded in the registers of Hailsham and nearby parishes:

> ...Muchmercy, Sindenie, Zealos, Rejoice, Helpless, Lament, Mortifie, Freegift, Bethankful, Fearenot, Kill-sin, Humilitie, Faithful, Be-stedfast ...

The presence and frequency of such names in church registers can now help to indicate the strength of Puritanism in specific areas.

1621

Chiddingly parish church register begins.

As with most Sussex parishes the conquering Normans were concerned in Chiddingly with church building, for evidence of such a period has been uncovered. Its dedication unknown, the church reveals the changes and additions of several centuries, having a nave, precisely square on plan and built as early as *c.* 1310, while the chancel was rebuilt as recently as 1864.

But it is perhaps best known for its tower and spire, possibly over five hundred years old and rising to a height of a hundred and twenty-eight feet. The stone spire is one of only five in Sussex; a structure of great weight, it was strengthened in 1897 by the addition of a heavy retaining chain fixed round its base.

Dominating the interior of the church is the spectacular monument to the Jefferay family (*see* entry of *c.* 1560). Unexpected in both size and workmanship, and demanding attention even behind its heavy railings, it is lavish in architectural detail with much carving and sculpture. Of marble and the much weaker alabaster, its unfortunate damage reflects the years that have passed.

When this huge and costly monument was built into the church it must surely have been a sight at which to wonder, and now, even as a shadow of its former beauty, it still impresses as no doubt was always intended.

As the church memorials will confirm there were once near the church, many houses lived in by men of consequence and it was recorded that,

> ... during the residence of Sir William Pelham and other well known families in the area a total of fourteen coaches could be seen outside Chiddingly church during the main Sunday service ...

Chiddingly is one of several East Sussex churches having a 'Pelham Buckle' carved in its stonework, this example being by the door of the Tower. In the churchyard there are still round its boundary, the wooden posts and rails, varying lengths of which were once kept in repair by local farmers. The particular rails to be looked after by a farmer were marked with his initials and called 'church marks'.

There were times as now, when Chiddingly church was well cared for but in 1686, Timothy Parker the rector of East Hoathly was asked to inspect certain local churches and of Chiddingly he wrote:

> ... the windows of the Chancell want glasing. The church wants new whiteliming. A carpet wanting to ye Communion Table. The churchwarden hath engaged to have what's wanting provided, and what's decay'd repaired ...

The south wall of the old Otham Priory Chapel when in use as a farm building. Drawn by Mark Anthony Lower, c. 1860

The chapel of old Langney Priory in 1785 from the drawing by Samuel Grimm

1624

The owner of Langney Priory, Sir Thomas Dyke, granted to Thomas Thungar, a lease for the further use of the priory as a farmhouse with its extensive land between Pevensey and (east) Bourne.

The priory was situated but a few yards from the wide shingle beach of the Crumbles and at the end of the track that led south from Stone Cross. Built on land barely twenty-five feet above sea level the priory, in a direct line, was less than six miles from Hailsham.

The simple chapel of the priory with its hall above, was built of local stone in the 12th cent. on land given by William the Conqueror to his half brother the Count of Mortain. This Norman warrior was at the time, also concerned with the building of Wilmington Priory and probably others, for his land spread over vast areas of East Sussex.

Other such powerful Norman noblemen with both wealth and land, were to introduce their superior building methods and cause to be erected many small and much needed religious establishments, where monks could support themselves on their land.

The chapel built at Langney, with its hall for the monks, was connected with the great Cluniac Priory of St Pancras in Lewes. A magnificent building, it had a church larger than Chichester Cathedral, but it suffered ruthless destruction in the Dissolution. And it was the Dissolution that also destroyed the daily life of the monks at Langney, as indeed it did at Michelham and Warbleton.

Built by the Normans, barely fifty years after the Conqueror's victory, the chapel was a simple structure of narrow deep set windows in walls of immense thickness. But some three hundred and fifty years later, the chapel and its hall were rebuilt using stone from two miles along the coast at (east) Bourne.

The new building reflected a more advanced architectural period, the original somewhat crude Norman windows were replaced by those surviving today with simple tracery heads. Above the altar a mutilated mullioned window faces north-east while just a few feet away, the stone wall bears signs where a priest's small piscina has been savagely broken away, a reminder of religious hostility in the distant past.

It is however the surfaces of the outside walls and buttresses, built *c.* 1460, that still compel attention. Stone and groups of flint have been used in alternate spaces but the flints are projecting boldly in front of the stonework, now badly eroded through coastal exposure. However there can still be seen a similarity in design to the superb tower at Hailsham, indeed the work at both places proceeded at much the same time.

But the walls of this remarkable, yet small isolated chapel at Langney, rebuilt over five hundred years ago, still display signs of flintwork equal to any in East Sussex, the sides of each flint being knapped straight with great skill enabling groups of flints to be set in the wall tight against each other. Clearly these walls were built by men with an ability to match the demands of a discerning mind in control of the work.

Today, the priory chapel and hall above with its enormous king-post roof timbers are seen to have been joined on the north and east sides by a number of domestic extensions and additions. These date from the medieval period to the late 18th cent. by which time the property had for many years served as a farmhouse, with the former chapel a mere farm outbuilding.

Situated close to the junction of the B 2191 road with the coast road A 259, this structure is now a family home surrounded by houses of the Langney Village estate built in 1953.

It was however in 1950 that the priory with its remarkable chapel was saved from demolition for at a public enquiry, held in the face of a compulsory purchase order from the Eastbourne Borough Council who were in need of land, the Minister for Local Government and Planning, spoke successfully in favour of preservation.

1625

A certificate of instruction was sent out by the deputy lieutenants of the county to those responsible for raising men for musters, which read:

> ... we have mett this day and have given directions for the calleing of all captaynes with the trayned bands both of horse and foot before us within the Rapes of Pevensey and Hasteing at Hayllesham Comon on Wednesday 21 September ... and have given orders for the Beacons to be p'sently repayred and well watched along such places the sea coste as are leaste defensible and likest to invite an enemy to land ...

1626

In this year the family of Calverley were recorded as living in Hellingly; they were descended from the Lords of Calverley in Yorkshire during the reign of King Henry I. Thomas Calverley built 'The Broad' in 1753, an impressive Georgian house standing but four hundred yards west of Hellingly church and now known as Broad Farm.

Some years later in 1649 Edmund Calverley a descendant, was summoned to the Michaelmas sitting at the Quarter Sessions Court at Lewes and charged with neglecting to repair certain roads in the parish:

> ... wheras Edmund Calverley of Hellingly is presented by the Surveyors for the highwayes in the parish of Hailsham for this present yeare for his default in not finding and sending at the days appoynted for the amending of the highways two waynes of Carts furnished ... whereupon the penalty of Six pounds is estreated against him ... '

At this time the sum of six pounds would have been a considerable amount, but he was allowed the opportunity of reclaiming his money if,

> ... he shall doe such porcion of worke ... as the sayd Surveyors shall appoint him ...

1626

The vicar of Hailsham, Brian Duppa, was also vicar of Westham and regularly in the company of Charles I during his imprisonment while awaiting trial.

He later became tutor to the young Prince Charles who, in the distant future was to ascend the throne as Charles II.

The religious belief of Brian Duppa was one of high church and he was thought well of by Charles I. Upon being made Bishop of Chichester in 1638 Duppa was shocked at the condition of most Sussex parish churches and he undertook to raise their standards.

As a preliminary to visiting his parishes a 'Visitation Article' was sent. This document was a lengthy list of questions enquiring into the condition of the church and was intended to encourage improvement. Among the questions listed were:

1. Are the walls of your church whited?
   (There was a widespread use of whitewash at this time for it had been used to cover the colourful paintings of the pre-Reformation period.)
2. What manner pews are built? Are they decent and uniform, or have not some built them so much higher than others as may hinder their neighbours from hearing Divine Service?
3. Is your Chancel severed with a partition from the body of the Church? Is it decently kept, not encumbered with pews or other lumber?
4. Is your Communion Table or altar strong, fair, and decent? Is it set, according to the practice of the ancient Church, upon an ascent at the east end of the Chancel, with the ends north and south? Is it compassed in with a handrail to keep it from profanation?

Many churches were uncared for and some had sunk to an appalling level with a dire need for cleaning and repairs. Windows were broken, pews and floors unkempt, fonts unusable. There was defilement by pigeons and dogs and even concern about shallow graves. It was recorded about this time that at some services there would be those who were guilty of talking, spewing, playing cards, singing rudely and on one occasion a man beat his wife.

Even the church in Hailsham, some forty years after Brian Duppa left, was still badly neglected for there was no poor box, repairs were needed to the roof and pews, and the floor was uneven with gravestones and nothing but damp earth in some places.

Those who favoured a high church wanted reform, but they were not helped by the churchwardens, who, frequently aggressive, were sometimes unable to read. Brian Duppa constantly tried to persuade that chancels must reflect a beauty and be clean and orderly.

In 1638, questioned about the altar position the puritan churchwardens of Chiddingly said:

> . . . Our communion table stands in the midst of the chancell and without rales . . .

and such a reply could well have been typical, for the puritan belief in East Sussex was both strong and obstinate, which is why the ambitious visitations of Duppa met with little success.

After three years at Chichester Cathedral, Brian Duppa transferred to Salisbury, where during the Civil War he was deprives of his position by the Puritan government. It was not until the Restoration of Charles II in 1660 that he became

Bishop of Winchester and his death in 1662 was followed by burial in Westminster Abbey.

1629

A map of Arlington village.

> ...A Perfect and Exact Survaye of the Glebe land belonginge to the Parsonage of Erlington ... made by Edward Gyer dated September 1629 ... scale 3½ inches = 40 (unspecified units) ...

shows the parish church with several buildings nearby that are not in existence today. In the same area is also shown a substantial house named as a parsonage.

With the evidence of considerable past ground disturbance visible in the same fields of today, it becomes clear the church once stood among many more houses than are now standing. There is also a trace of a medieval fish pond.

The field boundaries shown on this three hundred and fifty year old map probably belong it is felt, to a very much earlier date but in some cases the field outlines on the map are exactly as they exist today.

1632

Nicholas Stonestreet, a yeoman, bequeathed to his brother Henry,

> ... the Crowne in Haylesham ...

together with land at Whitedyke on the marsh and a meadow called 'Kerbycroft' (this name still survives as the title of property in what is now North Street in Hailsham).

At this time there was a *Crowne* Inn on a site facing the market square (*see* entry of 1806) which was converted to other uses in *c.* 1770.

The other *Crowne* Inn, situated in Hailsham's High Street and now known as the *Crown* Hotel is an establishment of unknown age. The severe and unadorned style of this hotel, as well as perhaps its size, suggests having been built between 1775 and 1800 when it could offer space at the rear for wagons and coaches, and extensive stabling for the many horses used at a time when, with the roads generally improving, people were travelling more with each year that passed.

The Corn Exchange building at the rear yet linked with the *Crown* Hotel is again entirely of brick, but with its tall Gothic windows and patterned brickwork, a later building date is suggested.

1634

From early times and up to an Act of 1529, the death of a man of certain means meant that his second best beast or possibly a chattel, was given to the church; a tradition intended as a gesture to compensate for any tithe payment that may have, in the past, been overlooked. This offering was known as a 'mortuary' or 'Corpse-present'. The dead man's best beast (called from Saxon times a 'heriot') was once given to the Lord of the Manor.

Since 1529, such mortuaries given to the church, and often abused, were restricted and replaced by a varying yet reasonable sum of money, but this profitable tradition was slow to die and certainly the Act of Henry VIII's reign was still abused as late as 1634. At this time, a small village, ill served by roads and little seen by travellers, could create an isolation that tended to soften and blur the very existence of some laws. Thus it was that with complete indifference, and choosing to profit rather than conform, the Rector of Ripe made the following entries in his church register

> ... William Wade who died as a stranger, for whose mortuary, I, John Goffe, parson of Rype, has his upper garment which was an olde coate, and I received for the same, 6s ...   [William died in 1632].

and

> ... I buried Alice Whitesides Feb 22 who being but one weeke in the parish of Rype, died as a stranger, for whose mortuary, I, John Goffe, had a gowne of Elizabeth her daughter, price 10s ...   [Alice died in 1635].

1634

At the East Sussex Assizes in March following a long period of heavy rainfall, the court heard that such was the deplorable condition of the roads around Hailsham that it was considered dangerous for people to set out for the market.

1635

For ships with cargo sailing the English Channel there was always a risk. In bad weather a gale and heavy sea could drive a ship ashore or even off course, where the rocky headlands of Seaford or Beachy Head would bring destruction. At other times, a boat could suffer attack and be plundered by a 'foreigner' to be left drifting helplessly. Indeed for hundreds of years, ships have been driven ashore by winter storms along the East Sussex coast and such disasters, often with loss of life, quickly attracted the hardened locals who knew the weather and the results it might bring.

With long experience and regardless of danger, men and women would carry away whatever was there for the taking, and at times, the risks and rewards came even to be regarded as a coastal industry.

Any ship wrecked on the coast was said to be the property of the Lord High Admiral whose local agents were ever watchful for such events. But there was often complication, for east of Seaford Head the Wardens of the Cinque Ports were known to make their own claim, as also were prominent landowners on whose shore a wreck may have been driven.

In 1635, for Sir Thomas Pelham the year showed a vast profit, when from ships driven ashore at Bishopstone, Pevensey and further east, there was the salvage of assorted cargo that included wine and even an anchor with its chain which had its value.

On such occasions, there was the need to act with all speed and a tenant or agent looking after his landowner's rights could do a rewarding service. But should there be delay in reaching the unhappy boat, then the watchful local families would plunder and carry away, regardless of conditions, whatever cargo was within reach. It was in places a tradition which yielded a heaven-sent profit to the daring.

At such times, when wrecked cargo could bring much needed money to coastal families, men could be hard, and, if a legal minded agent chose to confront or oppose, then the solution could be violence. One such occasion was when the son of Thomas Chown, the JP living at Frog Firle, Alfriston, rode to Seaford beach in the hope of using his father's authority, but the looters were in force and brutally swept him aside leaving him to return to Alfriston with his injuries.

1636

A comment on the activities and pastimes of the age read,

> ... These recreations are the meetest to be used, which give the best refreshment to the bodie ... Stoolball and the like are rather to be chosen than diceing and carding ...

Said to have been played in farmyards and churchyards, a book of 1767 illustrated Stoolball being played using a stool. Much later and in contrast, the game was, in 1917, played at Lords, no doubt by kind permission of the M.C.C.

1638

On the map of Sussex produced by John Norden, Hailsham was indicated as a market town but its market was not always to prosper for during the next century it slowly declined.

1639

Stephen Goffe became Rector of Herstmonceux parish church. He was also Chaplain to Charles I.

1642

In August of this year Charles I raised his standard at Nottingham and heralded the start of a Civil War that saw bitter fighting all over England until 1651.

With growing anger the people had long suffered from both the arrogance and lack of understanding the King had displayed towards them.

> ... he evinced throughout the whole tenor of his conduct, principles diametrically repugnant to the true interest, welfare, and happiness of his subjects ...

His attitude to Parliament, which was opposed to almost everything he stood for, was one of scorn which led him to dissolve the House in 1629. It was a course of action that, together with his belief that he had a divine right to rule, provoked between men many years of bitter enmity until a long Civil War brought the King's tragic end.

To a Parliament with strong Puritan principles the marriage of Charles, already sympathetic to the Catholic faith, to a French Catholic princess encouraged a powerful minority to show harsh intolerance towards people of a more simple faith.

> ... religious persecution began to break out with such violence, that a number of protestants, and particularly those of the sect of Puritans, emigrated to America ...

Following an eight day seige in this first year of the Civil War, the parliamentary forces on 29th December broke through and captured Chichester from the royalists. It was Colonel Herbert Morley with

> ... three troops of horse and two companies of Dragoneers ...

who played a prominent part in the victory, an action to be followed later in the war by his success in defeating royalist forces in their advance on Lewes.

The home of Colonel Morley was Glynde Place, an Elizabethan house built by his grandfather in 1569, some of whose family were Wealdon ironmasters. Fiercely opposed to any form of 'popery', this man of simple beliefs was to play a distinguished and influential part in the course of the war and among his East Sussex friends who opposed the King were: Sir Thomas Pelham of Laughton, Herbert Hay of Glyndebourne, Sir Thomas Parker of Ratton in Willingdon, the Swingate family of Broyle Place, near Ringmer, and Anthony Stapley of Framfield and Patcham. Among the King's followers were John Ashburnham and Sir Thomas Gage of Firle.

As the years of the war dragged on, with East Sussex almost entirely for Cromwell and the west divided between Parliament and Charles I, so it became necessary to impress men into the army, a brutal procedure which provoked violence and brought hardship to countless families robbed of their bread-winner. At times, the reluctant Sussex soldier was to be feared for his wild behaviour, as when complaints were voiced in the Commons in 1645 about outrageous behaviour, including rape.

The war, when even families could be split, brought many injustices for, apart from widespread religious prejudice and property confiscation, even simple country people were force to accommodate soldiers at an expense that could never be recovered, and such hardships lasted many years.

1642

Surrounded by an area of Sussex where the vast majority were for Parliament in the struggle against the King, one man in the village of Arlington, spoke often and fearlessly in defence of the King. Foolhardy but insistent, he proclaimed that:

> ... whatsoever the King commands, we are all bound to obey, whether it be good or evill ...

This reckless man with dangerous opinions was John Wilson, the parish priest, and in these times such a man could not in the end, be tolerated. Indeed, with the need that he be silenced, he was indicted by the justices at the mid-summer sessions and condemned as a common barrator. Despised for spreading his persistent Royalist beliefs, John Wilson was yet to be further castigated and banished from his Arlington church.

Determined to expose both priests, who were unworthy, and the church episcopacy, who had ordained such men, the House of Commons ordered the publication in November 1643, of a book to be entitled:

The First Century of Scandalous, Malignant Priests

The book, written by John White, member of parliament for Southwark, was not entirely without a political motive for it revealed in a brutal tirade the weakness and sins of a hundred priests who in due course would probably be replaced by Puritan preachers.

In a somewhat long and depressing introduction, the reader is warned with some force of the low morals and ignorance of men entrusted to preach the word of God.

> ... thou maist by perusall of this booke clearly see what manner of persons those Cleargie-men be, that favour the present course of his Majestie against his Parliament and people ...

and in a few words the writer expresses a dangerous hate:

> ... scandalous of corrupt mindes, and ill effected to the Peace and Safety of the Kingdome, men unfit to preach to, or live among Christians, their wickedness being so great, as that they are condemned by Heathens ...

The first preacher to be named in the book was John Wilson of Arlington, who had recently been sequestered (deprived of his church living) and of whom was written:

> ... the Benefice of John Wilson Vicar of Arlington in the County of Sussex, is sequestred, for that he in most beastly manner, divers times attempted to commit buggery with Nathaniel ..., Samuel ... and Robert ... his Parishioners, and by perswasions and voilence, laboured to draw them to that obhominable sinne ...

The denunciation went on to say that he, at the baptising of a bastard child blasphemously said openly in church:

> ... that our Saviour as he was in the flesh, was a bastard ... that baptisme utterly taketh away origonall sinne ...

and in his sermons, the book accuses Wilson of having:

> ... much commended Images in Churches, as good for edification, and that men should pray with Beades and hath openly said, that the Parliament were Rebels, and endeavoured to starve the King ...

To complete the destruction of this Royalist priest, the long and bitter attack finally added that he was

> ... a usuall frequenter of Ale-houses and a great drinker ...

Such was the impact of this 'First Century' book that a proposed 'Second Century' was never published, for the writer, John White,

> ... was persuaded by his own Bretheren from putting out a second Century for fear it should prove scandalous, and bring an impeachment on the whole Body of the Clergy ...

The Royalist John Wilson, an M.A. of Oxford University and vicar of Arlington from 1629 to 1643, died in 1649 and was buried in Fletching churchyard.

1643

At this time of Civil War most of East Sussex showed support for the Parliamentary forces of Oliver Cromwell and in the beginning, with the need to organise against the King's men, small meetings were held in manor houses. An active figure in such affairs was Thomas Jefferay who lived at the impressive Chiddingly Place, where painted on the wall of a room was the Puritan quotation:

> . . . Have minde of Deathe and fear to sinne . . .

To put into effect the many new measures now regarded as essential for the support of Cromwell's effort, on July 18th the Commons:

> . . . ordered that forty men shall be Committees for disposing of the affairs of Sussex . . .

Among the wide powers given to these men of whom Thomas Jefferay was one, was the right to seize and confiscate, to raise money for the struggle and to find men who would fight for Cromwell.

1643

As the war developed and opinions hardened so unlike most ennobled families with great wealth and extensive estates, the attendance of Lord Dacre of Herstmonceux Castle at the House of Lords became less frequent.

In the early years of the King's reign Dacre, as would be expected was for the King, but as the obstinate King forced his will against the interest of England and its people so his opinion wavered until finally he held back from open support.

On the 22nd January 1643 he was glad to use the hard winter as an excuse not to be involved when he wrote to the deputy-speaker of the House:

> . . . On Wednesday night last I received your Lordship's of the ninth of this month, and would have most gladly obeyed the commands of the House of Peers, by coming presently away to wait on the affairs of the kingdom on the 22nd, had not the ways ever since been so extremely clogged by a very deep snow, that men pass not without much difficulty and danger: I beseech your lordship to add to this reason the weakness of my own health, not being able to endure the rigour of the journeying on horseback in such exceeding cold weather, as now it is; and to represent this to their lordships' favourable constructions; not that I intend to make long use of any way to excuse myself from that duty, which I shall ever owe to the commonwealth, but very shortly shall give my attendance on their lordships with all willingness and readiness. And so I rest.
>   Your lordship's
>   Most humble servant,
>   Francis Dacre

It was said he preferred the peace of his Pevensey marsh and he was not alone in seeking to avoid the embarrassment of debate, for some of his friends with wealthy estates hoped to remain neutral. Indeed at this time Lord Dacre was content to enjoy life at Herstmonceux and regularly entertained prominent men of the county, regardless of their political allegiance.

Of those who stayed at the castle were: anti-Royalist soldier Sir William Waller, Sir Thomas Pelham of Halland, John Busbridge of Etchingham, Viscount Montague of Cowdray near Midhurst, Sir Nicholas Selwyn of Preston near Brighton, Sir Selwyn Parker of East Bourne and Lady Campion, the Royalist daughter of Sir Thomas Parker of Willingdon while Sir Isaac Sedley and Sir Philip Stapleton were of the Parliamentarians from Kent.

These and many more knew Dacre well for he was a popular host; yet while he spread his favours wide, he remembered to include in his circle the lesser names of neighbours who lived but a few miles away.

But events slowly moved to a crisis and on the 2nd January 1648 a Bill from the House of Commons decreed that:

> . . . a high court of justice for the trial of the king be erected . . .

and on this crucial occasion Lord Dacre attended and showing considerable courage and rare loyalty voted with a small number of other peers in support of the King. Such an action at this time aroused a noisy demand for their arrest as enemies of the people, but they survived.

The Dacre family, of Herstmonceux was known as 'Dacre of the south' and before Francis Dacre died in 1662 he inherited several lordships of great value in Cumberland and Westmorland; This was due to another branch of the family 'Dacre of the north', long ago warriors of the English victory at Flodden and other border battles, having failed to produce an heir.

The son of Francis Dacre was Thomas '. . . the last descendant of the ancient families of Herst and Monceux . . .' and he, by his appointment as Lord of the Bedchamber,

> . . . had the misfortune to come very young to the dissapated court of Charles II . . .

Influenced by the freedom of Restoration Court, Thomas Dacre gambled heavily and embarked on wild extravagances involving structural alterations to his castle with much new furnishing and carving by Grinling Gibbons. Such was his spending on living in the grand manner that his huge debts could in the end, only be recovered by the sale of a number of the family estates.

1645

Payment '. . . was made at Hailsham . . .' to improve the sea water entry at Pevensey Haven which had silted up for many years. This work much improved the passage of boats that took goods to and from Herstmonceux. From the accounts of Lord Dacre of Herstmonceux Castle:

> . . . paid Burton for his horse and cart to bring goods out of the warehouse at Pemsie to the waterside for bring them thence to Herstmonceux in his boat 4s. 0d. . . .
> . . . paid for 12 li of pitch to cauke the boat to carry corn to Pemsie . . .
> . . . paid for help of waggon 3 daies helping home the hay and fetching 1 load of chalk and 2 loads of stone from Pemsie Castle £1. 5s. 0d. . . .
> . . . paid halfe yeares rent for my Lords warehouse at Pemsie . . .

c. 1647

The first meetings of the Society of Friends were held at this time. Such meetings became frequent in East Sussex, small in the beginning, they were of brave people with strong principles whose spiritual thinking was extreme in its simplicity with no need of a church. Such honest thinking often provoked abuse, hence Quakers, 'those who quake at the word of God'.

In the early days of the Society, Alfriston grew as a strong centre for Quakers and many meetings were held in the houses of surrounding villages including Hailsham.

As more followers joined the Quakers and their outspoken criticism continued, so through the years they attracted attention until such meetings became both forbidden and dangerous.

There can be little doubt that the courageous George Fox, founder of the Society of Friends, when leaving Lewes in 1655,

> . . . from thence eastwards to Warbleton and them parts . . .

preached in the area of parishes that included Hailsham.

1649

The Death Warrant of Charles I that followed his trial:

> '. . . to be putt to death by the severinge of his head from his body of which sentence execucon yet remaineth to be done . . . require you to see the said sentence executed in the open streete before Whitehall uppon the morrowe . . .

was signed and sealed by fifty-nine Cromwellian supporters, forty-four at once and another fifteen after persuasion.

The majority of Sussex was staunch for Parliament and one of the nominated commissioners at the trial was Colonel Herbert Morley of Glynde who in spite of being the most prominent and active of Cromwell supporters, was conspicuous by refraining from signing the warrant that permitted the ultimate violence.

In spite of the conflicts and hard fought battles of the Civil War with Englishmen killing their own countrymen, often a curious and chivalrous relationship survived as when Cromwell's soldier and confidant Colonel Morley of Glynde maintained an old friendship with his close neighbours, the Royalist Gage family of Firle.

Of the seven Sussex men who signed away the King's life two were Antony Stapley, a relation by marriage to the Thatchers of Priesthawes and Peregrine Pelham, a descendant of Sir William Pelham of Laughton.

At the time of the King's execution in Whitehall on Tuesday 30th January, John Ashburnham was suffering imprisonment for what the Parliamentarians regarded as a most serious crime, namely the complete devotion and unwavering loyalty to the King shown by this man to become known as the Cavalier.

Ashburnham had shared many dangers of the Civil War with the King and on those occasions when he chose to attend Westminster, it was of help to the King in the early years of his quarrel with parliament, to be advised of the opinions and tendencies being discussed by his enemies.

In 1646 the King in a letter to his wife said:

> ... The necessity of my affairs hath made me send Jack (his name for John) Ashburnham to thee; who at this moment is the most (and with the greatest injustice) persecuted of all my servants, and merely for his fidelity to me ...

John Ashburnham the Cavalier died in 1671 and in his Will he referred to a gold watch given to him by Charles I before he died. In his Will he bequeathed the watch to his grandson with the words:

> ... my watch with an inamel'd case of imagery which was given mee by my late deare Master kind Charles the First of ever blessed memory and a case of gold I made to preserve the same and my desire is that after his death the said watch may descend unto and bee perpetually enjoyed and possessed by those persons to whom the Manor of Ashburnham descend or come to as an heirloome ...

The King's watch with a single hand and winding key is of exquisite workmanship with its centre, a circular panel of richly coloured enamels depicting an arrangement of flowers in which feature a chrysanthemum, a tulip and a magnolia blossom.

This remarkable and beautiful Relic of nearly three hundred and fifty years ago has been passed through the generations of the Ashburnham family and is now kept with the closest security.

Also surviving from the King's last days are the garments he wore after his own clothes were taken from him. Still cared for by the descendants of John Ashburnham and secure against harm, is a long coarse linen shirt with a wide collar over the shoulders and a series of 'gathers' around the waist and cuffs, also two heavy linen garters and a pair of dull cream coloured drawers in knitted silk. With these simple garments is a heavy linen sheet on which is embroidered in red thread a monogram of CR with a crown.

Following the death of James, the son of Bertram Ashburnham in 1774, his Will bequeathed

> ... the sheet on which the body of His Majesty was laid after his demise and the drawers worn by the said King at the time of his demise ...

Thus these Relics were placed with the shirt and watch already in the care of the Ashburnham family.

Up to 1830 the clothing Relics were kept in Ashburnham church, largely rebuilt by the Ashburnham family, for it was said that to touch the dead King's clothing would effect a cure of the then scrofula (a tubercular condition), commonly known as the King's Evil.

To these historic possession was added a small locket, for in 1815 the King's coffin was opened at Windsor in the presence of the Prince Regent and a piece of his hair was removed. The hair, now sealed in the locket, is kept in safety with the King's garments.

The King's sole attendant in his final days of captivity was Sir Thomas Herbert, and the execution was to be in the cold air of a January morning when the King's doublet would have to be removed before he knelt over the block. The King spoke of his concern that exposure to such weather could well cause him to shiver, and convey the impression that he was afraid, and it was for this reason that he wore two shirts at his death.

After the execution it was Sir Thomas Herbert who took care to record some words the King had spoken:

> ...let me have a shirt on more than ordinary by reason the season is so sharp as probably may make me shake, which some observers will imagine proceeds from fear. I would have no such imputation. I fear not death! Death is not terrible to me ...

These words have been personally confirmed by Sir Robin Mackworth-Young at Windsor Castle, and he has also explained that the extra garment worn on that fateful day was of fine holland material with drawn thread work round the neck, sleeves and hem, and with coloured ribbons on the sleeves.

The garment was for many years cared for by the strong royalist family of Lord Coventry of Aylesborough, Lord Keeper of the Great Seal and friend to Charles I. Not until 1909 did an opportunity present itself for King Edward VII to purchase, and have it kept secure in Windsor Castle where it now remains.

1649

A Survey of Pevensey Rape has as its object to set out the '... Yearly Value of Lands, Rents and Tithes ...' applicable to each village and town, when interesting comparisons were recorded:

Arlington	£2,298	0	0	Alfriston	£594	0	0
Laughton	1,206	0	0	Berwicke	422	10	0
Chiddingly	929	7	0	Chalvington	298	13	4
Hellingly	1,427	6	6	Ripe	790	10	0
Haylsham	2,266	17	6	Selmeston	748	18	0
Eastborn	960	11	8	Pevensey	2,702	8	4
Willingdon	1,124	10	0	Westham	1,349	7	8
Wilmington	435	10	0				

1651

John Lulham, bellfounder, cast at Chiddingly six bells for St Mary's parish church at (east) Bourne.

An entry in an old (east) Bourne parish book reads,

> Paid to ye bell founder John Lulham for casting ye bells by composition £7. 0. 0.
> To John Lulham for additions of bell metal and 6 days labour about ye bells
> £2. 5. 0.

John Lulham also cast bells for the church of St Thomas at Cliffe in Lewes.

1652

A 'churchale' was arranged in the churchyard of Herstmonceux parish church for a Sunday in July.

This event primarily involved the sale of ale ostensibly intended to commemorate the dedication and to raise funds for the church, but there could be a tendency for too much drinking with even a degree of abandon, unthinkable to the Puritan mind.

There had in several counties been strong puritan condemnation of churchales for the abuse, drunkenness and even fornication that was known to happen and many had been cancelled.

Concerned to prevent a '...profanation of the Sabboth...' by abusive behaviour on this day at Herstmonceux, a serious warning was issued from the local magistrates.

1653

Commissioners of the new Commonwealth of Oliver Cromwell visited Hailsham to survey and value lands which were to be seized or subject to a financial settlement with the new government, for there was much land around the town owned by men who had fought with Charles I. Sir Thomas Gage, Lord of the Manor of Hailsham was one such King's Man.

Among the Hailsham properties owned by the King before his execution were the houses from Market Square along that part of the High Street that backed on to the churchyard.

1653

The Puritan Parliament held the view that a marriage ceremony with its degree of display, was less concerned with religion than being a civil contract with a possible association with property. In pursuit of this outlook, a ban was placed on all marriages in churches.

The responsibility was now placed with magistrates and JPs and Colonel Herbert Morley, the ardent Puritan of Glynde Place just eight miles from Hailsham, soon encouraged the election of a local registrar who carried out his duty for couples that came from the surrounding villages. But with many, this harsh denial of traditional ritual was far from popular.

Opposed to this extreme puritanical attitude was Robert Baker (1652–1677), vicar of Chiddingly who was brave enough to persist in conducting weddings when in three years, he married nearly seventy couples instead of the more normal two or three in a year.

Such couples, grateful to be married in a church, travelled by horse or even by farm waggon if the mud-churned winter roads were not impassable. They came from nearby villages and from: Rotherfield, Brighton, Fletching, Lewes, Willingdon and Mayfield, while some entries in the church register even recorded couples from Godstone in Surrey and Cranbrook and Faversham in Kent.

Such blatant disregard of the law brought about a threat of his appearance at the next court sessions but this he escaped, for the ban was lifted in 1657.

To conduct civil marriages when weddings in church were forbidden, each parish elected a man to act as registrar and in Hailsham, instead of in the church, the banns were read from the market cross in Market Square. Of particular interest, are some of the East Sussex church registers that recorded the births, marriages and burials. During the years of the ban the registers of Arlington, Berwick, East Hoathly, Pevensey and Ripe are all without mention of marriages.

Only the Hailsham church register showed continuing entries of marriages for written across a page in 1653, the year of the ban, was the heading . . . 'Publications and marriages' . . . and underneath were written the names of couples who had been married by the registrar. Surprisingly, most records of civil marriages were written into the register with more detail than in normal times, an improvement that may well have reflected the influence of the newly elected registrar. In addition to the names of each couple together with their occupations, the names of the villages from which they came were also recorded.

The vicar at this time in Hailsham was John Lover from a yeoman family in Glynde and being a Puritan he was 'ejected' in the year of the Restoration of Charles II. At this time in 1660 the Anglican church once again had authority, but it was to meet a great deal of opposition from the puritanism of Cromwellian days.

Four years after his ejection (*see* entry of 1664) Lover was brought before the Quarter Sessions at Lewes for . . . not going to Church and hearing Common Prayer . . . and he was fined £20, a month . . . till Submission and Conformity . . .

A Year later in 1665, still true to his simple beliefs and persisting in Nonconformity he was arrested while praying at a forbidden conventicle (clandestine religious meeting) in a house at Cranbrook, Kent. Under arrest by a mounted Justice of the Peace, he was forced to walk the rough road alongside the horse several miles to Maidstone where he was sentenced with others to two months imprisonment.

Released from jail, John Lover returned to Hailsham and when in 1672 (*see* entry of 1672) there was a somewhat short-lived period of permission for Nonconformist meetings, he was granted a licence and preached in his Hailsham house. Lover died in 1682 and was buried in the parish churchyard.

1657

The acute need for a coin of smaller value had been apparent for many years but with dangerous political unrest at this time, followed by civil war, the problem was overshadowed and no decisions ever taken.

From increasing frustration, came as it must an answer, and private Traders' Tokens appeared with immediate success. The tokens were struck and issued by traders as change and received back when another purchase was made. These small tokens or coins were mostly of copper but some were brass and a few were in lead.

The first tokens issued in Sussex were by an inn keeper of East Grinstead in 1650. Later, two Hailsham traders issued their own farthings; those of Samuel Giles, a mercer (cloth merchant) were dated 1657. William Hartnup's farthings were undated but attractive with his initials and 'Hailsham in Sussex' on one side, while the obverse side displayed his name and the simple heraldic design for a grocer.

The token system worked well but with the death of Oliver Cromwell in 1658 and more settled times coming with Charles II, parliament strongly opposed the unofficial coinage although it was not until 1672 that a proclamation by the King actually forbade the use of tokens:

> . . . those culpable therein shall be severely punished . . .

and an official issue of a well-made half-penny coin was made and welcomed.

A halfpenny token was issued by Richard Page at Hellingly in 1669 having on its obverse side a crowned King's Head, but it was farthings that were in great demand and these were issued in several villages including Alfriston, Pevensey, Waldron and Boreham.

1658

Just seven months after the Lord Protector, Oliver Cromwell, had with both suspicion and anger, dissolved what had become a much improved parliament he . . . was attacked with a fever . . . and died. As a soldier Cromwell had been brilliant but his rules for living often proved extreme and widely unacceptable. With some truth, it was said he was

> . . . a tyrant without vices . . .

or equally

> . . . a prince without virtues . . .

Cromwell's son Richard took his place but within a mere four months he was deposed by the army, an event that heralded a number of overtures that gradually brought together, albeit uneasily, men who once fought each other.

There were many who had fought for Cromwell, some had fled and some were punished. Colonel Herbert Morley of Glynde Place had in recent years become increasingly disillusioned.

> . . . the rule of Cromwell manifested itself in the form of numberless and miserable petty tyrannies, and thus became hated as no government has ever been hated in England before or since . . .

Morley had always been a firm supporter of human rights but the extreme measures being inflicted on the people served to reinforce a growing distaste. There was need for moderation and tolerance and he was known to speak for justice.

To become accepted at a time of change, Morley was advised and helped by royalist John Evelyn, later to achieve fame as a diarist, for he had been a friend since their school-days together at the grammar school in Southover, Lewes.

Not without some concern Morley applied for his pardon, and no doubt helped by the knowledge that his humanitarian principle in refusing to sign the late King's death warrant together with his changed outlook and recent appointment as Lieutenant of the Tower, it was granted subject to the payment of a heavy fine of a thousand pounds.

The long awaited free parliament followed on the 25th May 1660 and the new King Charles II, having been escorted across the Channel by the English Fleet, stepped ashore at Dover.

1659

On the map of Sussex by the Dutch cartographer Joannes Janssen and published in Amsterdam, a chapel was indicated in Boreham. It was shown in the centre of the village and on the north side of the main road.

1660

In spite of a degree of religious tolerance at the Restoration of Charles II, and there was a genuine desire by the King himself for more unity, the Parliament of the day was unyielding in its dislike of the Puritans who were determined,

> . . . to oppose the reintroduction of the Book of Common Prayer with the various obnoxious customs . . . wearing of the surplus, kneeling at the holy communion, bowing at the name of Jesus, making the sign of the cross in baptism . . .

Indeed in the years that followed, Parliament was dedicated to establishing the Church of England and was severe in its hostility to any dissenting sect. Towards Puritans and Roman Catholics there was both bigotry and acts of persecution.

1663

Five bells were cast at Bellbanks, a road near the Common Pond in Hailsham for St Mary's parish church. The bells each carried the inscription:

> John Hodson made mee.

John Hodson was at that time a famous London bell-founder, but it was his foreman, a William Hull, who was at Bellbanks for the casting. Later in 1676 William Hull set up his own business in South Malling, Lewes, and again visited Bellbanks to cast a bell for Ninfield Church. Eventually he was also to cast bells for the churches at Pevensey, Arlington, Wilmington, Ringmer and Herstmonceux.

1664

The Conventicle Act came into force, and was effective in dividing the country into those who conformed to the Church of England and those who chose to be Nonconformists. The Act arose out of fear, and was aimed at controlling the now disturbing growth of non-conformist sects.

A vindictive albeit short-lived measure, it had great power for among other things, it forbade any Nonconformist assembly of over five persons apart from those of a household, and later, there came a crippling limit to the distance a minister could travel. For a time these vicious restrictions, enforced with troops and paid informers, made even simple worship a perilous risk.

It was in this year that Moses French, the Quaker, was taken from Alfriston and imprisoned in Horsham Gaol for eight years. Two years later several other Quakers from Alfriston were arrested and imprisoned.

In spite of the dangers to Nonconformists however there were enough Baptist, Congregationalists, Presbyterians, Anabaptists and Quakers with firm resolution in Hailsham and its surrounding parishes to continually meet in a safe house, barn or cellar.

1667

Selmeston parish church register begins.

In this village there was a church long before the Normans conquered England and its site saw human activity over two thousand years before Christ. (*See* entry of 1933).

Of the church in early days little now remains for it was largely rebuilt in 1867. An extremely rare feature that survived the new work is the arcade of three pointed arches in the nave. Supported on octagonal columns with carved capitals, it is all of Sussex oak and probably dates from *c.* 1370.

The porch still retains a medieval holy water stoup and the churchyard is one of the few in Sussex to be circular.

With much of the ancient structure beyond repair, the drastic rebuilding in Victorian times was guided by the Reverend William Douglas Parish, vicar of Selmeston for forty-one years. An exceptional man, it was he who in 1875 wrote the remarkable *Dictionary of the Sussex Dialect.*

He was said to have had, by the late Sussex writer Esther Meynell:

> ...chin adorned with side-whiskers, square hat, front-buttoning waistcoat decked with looped watch-chain; the whole man was square and broad, with more than a touch of the historic John Bull in the dogged face and set of the shoulders ...

and to have been:

> ...a man that any shepherd and ploughman and hedger and ditcher and thatcher, any flint-breaking roadman would recognise as one of their own breed ...

Of his dictionary, the Reverend Parish wrote:

> ...every page of this dictionary will show how distinctly the British, Roman, Saxon, and Norman elements are to be traced in words in everyday use among our labouring people, who retain among them many of the oldest forms of old words which although they have long ago become obsolete among their superiors in education are nevertheless still worthy of our respect and affection ...

1669

The status of Hailsham as a market town, in spite of the serious decline in agriculture, was the reason it was served by a horse Post Coach from Rye. This long journey through East Sussex was more frequent in the summer months, for in bad winter weather many roads were often impassable.

Two years later and whenever conditions allowed, Hailsham was served from Lewes by a foot post and a little later, in 1673, the town was confirmed in some degree of importance by it being listed as Post Town with its surrounding villages dependent upon it for their postal communication.

Hailsham was soon to lose its market and, with it, much of the work and trade it brought to the town.

1669

Many East Sussex Nonconformist meetings were carefully recorded in this year and of the villages listed were Heathfield, Wartling, Hertsmonceux, Warbleton and

Alfriston. Of those known to have been held in Hailsham, the house of John Lower was listed with forty in the congregation with those present being of the,

> . . . most meanest sort of people . . .

With the descriptive details of other meeting places were people described as,

> . . . poore, ordinary, mean, some middle sort, tradesmen and labourers and inferior . . .

and of a meeting at Wartling those present were listed as,

> . . . many persons of considerable estate . . .

At this time Quakers were meeting regularly in Hailsham as their own surviving monthly meeting books, for the years 1669 to 1682 confirm.

1672

In an effort to ease the hardship suffered by Nonconformist religious sects, unflinching in their worship independent of the Anglican Church, Charles II, at a time of Parliamentary recess, introduced his controversial 'Declaration of Indulgence'. An extract read:

> . . . we shall from time to time allow a sufficient number of places as shall be desired in all parts of our Kingdom for the use of such as do not conform to the Church of England to meet and assemble in, in order to their public Worship and Devotion . . .

The King's Declaration was immediately followed by many applications that licences be granted for assemblies to meet and worship without hindrance. Twenty-six such requests came from Sussex, one of which was from a Samuel Barton desiring Presbyterian worship in his home known as 'Barton House' in Cowbeech. (*See* entry of *c.* 1602).

An extract from the licence granted to him read:

> . . . Charles by the Grace of God, King of England . . . Defender of the Faith . . . To all Mayors, Bayliffs, Constables . . . and Military, whom it may concern . . . we do hereby allow of 'a Roome or Roomes in the house of Samuell Barton of Hallingly in Sussex to be a place for the Use of Such as do not conform to the Church of England, who are of the Perswasion commonly called 'presbyterian' to meet and assemble in, in order to their publick Worship and Devotion . . . whom it may concern, are to take due notice thereof . . . and to protect them in their said meeting.
> Given at our Court at Whitehall, the '9th' day of 'December' 1672.
> By His Majesties Command . . .

The King's tactic to evade his Parliament proved to be an error of judgement for in the following year it was Parliament that condemned his declaration and,

> . . . drove him to yield, and he broke the seal of his declaration with his own hands and recalled the licences issued under it . . .

1673

Hailsham was listed as a Post Town, it being linked with a route from Rye.

In 1785 the horse post from London was to Tunbridge Wells and then on to Hailsham when the roads were in good enough condition, for in the bad winter weather . . . narrow clay ditches that passed as roads . . . many Sussex roads were impassable due to deep mud.

Hailsham was the local centre for posts over a large area of surrounding countryside and the postal addresses for East Bourne and Meads were 'near Haylesham'. The mail for Pevensey had to be collected from Hailsham.

1675

A document of this date revealed that,

> . . . On 15th December in the 15th year of the reign of Charles II . . . Ellinor Walnett was put out and bound as an Apprentice by Thomas Caine, Churchwarden of Berwick and Edward Carle and Thomas Ranger, Overseers to the poore . . . to William Dobson of Berwick, yeoman, with the assent of Sir William Wilson J.P. . . . from this date until the age of 21 or marriage if sooner . . . shall serve her master faithfully, obediently, behave herself honestly and orderly as becomes a servant . . .

Ellinor Walnett was just nine years old.

c. 1677

In an upper room overlooking Hailsham High Street, of a property extending back to the churchyard, a large wall painting can be seen behind a protective glass panel.

The work, still in good condition, is on plaster panels between oak wall timbers of the 16th cent. Expert opinion has advised that the particular Royal Coat of Arms in the painting could possibly date back to the reign of James I, but certain other features in the decoration suggest the reign of Charles II.

Of particular interest is the painting being in a room with exposed wall timbers at least four hundred years old, which serves to indicate that in more recent years this old building has at some time had its ancient timbered front removed and replaced by brickwork. Viewed from the High Street the building with its shops below now gives no hint of an ancient interior.

In the first panel of the painting are the lines of a verse of which the last line is unaccountably incomplete:

> The peace of God,
> A Quiet lyfe, A content
> mynde An honest wyfe
> A good report, A frend in
> store what neede a man with . . .

The second and third panels have a bold and talented painting of a Royal Coat of Arms with the lion and unicorn, and around them are drawn the simple outlines of leaves and flowers among which the tulip is featured. At this time the flower was highly fashionable and such bulbs were much prized throughout Europe. It was a period of enthusiasm that prompted the expression 'Tulipomania'.

Wall painting has been cut away to make an opening for a new door

2'-10"
Above floor

— WALL PAINTING 8'·4" LONG —

Painted verse has been damaged by plaster repairs

The peace of God, A quiet life, Content An honeſt mynde, A good report, A frend in ſtore that needſ a man with

WALL PAINTING at N° 16 HIGH STREET · HAILSHAM

(THE BUILDING BACKS ON TO THE CHURCHYARD AND THE ROOM IS ON THE FIRST FLOOR OVERLOOKING THE HIGH STREET)

(·A·R·)

The third panel in which the unicorn is painted has at some time in the past been partly cut away to allow a door to be inserted in the wall.

The style and content of the existing three wall panels has prompted the Department of Prints and Drawings of the Victoria and Albert Museum to offer the opinion that there was once a fourth panel wherein the verse was completed. Thus the original wall decoration would have been of a panel with verse each side of two centre panels with flowers and heraldic emblems.

Such a secular wall painting as this particular example is considered rare in England.

1677

In June, the Treasurer to the Earl of Sussex recorded that he paid the Earl the sum of £3 before setting out from Herstmonceux Castle on a journey to Dicker.

> . . . paid to my Lord when his Lordship went to the crekitt match at ye Dicker £3-00-00 . . .

It is claimed that this cricket match played at Dicker has so far proved to be the second oldest match to have been recorded.

1678

The Burial in Wool Act was enforced:

> . . . that no corpse of any person except those that die of the plague shall be buried in any shirt, shift, sheet or shroud or anything whatever made or mingled with flax, hemp, silk, hair, gold or silver or in any stuff or thing other than what is made of sheep's wool only . . .

In the particular volume of the vellum covered Hailsham church register starting in 1678, the first page was headed

> . . . A Register of the Affidavits according to the late Act of Parliament for buringe in Woollon . . .

It was laid down that a witness was required to sign the register within eight days of burial to confirm that wool was used to wrap the corpse. It should be remembered that at this time it was still rare that a body be buried in a coffin, certainly of a person without rank or wealth.

On the page covering January 1699 to April 1700, the untidy writing listed six burials, four were marked S.P. for smallpox of whom three were children. Of these burials five were initialled to indicate the use of 'woollon' and while the last entry lacked initials written in, was a note saying that 'woollon' material had been used.

The Act was introduced to encourage prosperity in the wool trade. It was repealed in 1814 by which time it had almost fallen into disuse.

Parish church registers can provide simple evidence that for generations past 'uncoffined' burials were normal among the poor, and such burials continued even into the 18th century, albeit much less frequently. A register entry in 1638 revealed the charges made for coffins as an addition to the grave and the tolling of a bell:

```
... for a coffin  . . . . . . . . . .    1s-0d
     for a man without a coffin. . . . . . .    8d.
     for an infant without a coffin. . . . . .    6d.
```

1680

Ten miles east of Hailsham at Crowhurst parish church the vicar, Matthew Wing, witnessed the brilliant display in the sky of a comet, to be known in future years as Halley's Comet. The sighting was recorded in the parish register at the time:

> ... A Blaesing stare appeared in this Kingdom in the yeare 1680. it did First shew if selfe 10th of December that year 80 which Did streame from the south-west to the Middle of the heaven broader than a Raine-Bow by farre — And continued till the Latter end of February ...

It was this comet that was seen by Sir Isaac Newton and Dr Edmond Halley.

Note: This historic sighting has, in many books on Sussex including the *History of the County of Sussex* by Horsfield, Vol. 1, been mistakenly attributed to the register of the parish church at Old Heathfield.

1688

James II, the Roman Catholic King, offered concessions of religious tolerance and civic equality to Nonconformists. The object was to gain support for the unpopular Catholics against whom certain laws enforced degrees of suppression.

The King's offer, a blatant bribe, was rejected and he responded by openly and aggressively attacking the clergy, then finally demanding that all clergy read from their pulpits an illegal 'Declaration of Indulgence' suspending laws against the Catholics.

The King was totally mistrusted and the Anglicans resisted his demand. Seven Bishops, headed by the Archbishop of Canterbury, submitted to the King a petition protesting against his outrageous decree, whereupon they were charged with seditious libel and to the mounting anger of the people, imprisoned in the Tower to await their trial.

On 30th June a jury declared the seven men 'not guilty' and it is recorded that the bells of Hailsham parish church were rung in celebration of the King's humiliating defeat. It was a defeat that sent James II to France, where he died in exile.

1689

The first real step towards religious tolerance in England came but a few months after the protestant Prince of Orange from Holland became William III.

In this year the Toleration Act reduced the Church of England's domination by conceding a religious freedom that allowed dissenting sects to worship openly. Caution however still forbade meetings that were clandestine.

The Act was never intended to grant a religious equality, but it was a merciful progress from the days of brutal suppression. For the many Nonconformists in and around Hailsham, tension and persecution were much reduced.

1693

John Fuller, an M.P., acquired land near Heathfield on which he built his most important furnace and forge to add to his other iron-making activities in East Sussex.

Due to the excellent iron content of its soil and the ample and readily available timber for furnaces, the Weald, and Heathfield in particular, enjoyed a tremendous prosperity. It has been written:

> ...in Heathfield for example, almost every field has been dug over at some time for its iron ...

The Heathfield site was to develop into one of the greatest gun-founding businesses in England, and over many generations it was one of the largest suppliers of guns to successive Kings through their Boards of Ordnance. Other countries also sought cannons from Heathfield and many were sent to Italy and Sardinia. For over two hundred years there can have been few battlefields on which Fuller guns were not fired.

The cannons from Heathfield ranged from the small Falconet of 3 ft. 9 in. long and weighing five hundred pounds, to the huge Cannon Royal of 8 ft. 9 in. and eight thousand pounds, which fired a seventy-four pound shot. In the making of these pieces great activity and enormous heat had to be kept up:

> ... wealdon forests roared and flamed with scores of furnaces where iron founders smelted the ruddy ore which colours the wealdon rocks and stains the woodlands streams a ruddy brown. These were the days when the black country of the midlands and the north were unknown and the smelting furnaces were fed not with coal but with the southern forests ...

It was a time when water was operating so many forge hammers that the countryside never seemed to be without distant booming.

In spite of periods when the demand for shot and cannon rose and fell with the periods of war and peace, East Sussex retained a near monopoly in iron casting and John Fuller saw his Heathfield enterprise grow and be known not only for their wide variety of cannon, but also for their quality. He was in turn successfully followed by his son and grandson, each also named John. But signs of serious decline were eventually to emerge.

After using a casting technique that had remained supreme for many years, knowledge and events were overtaking. Wood fuel was being replaced by coal in the northern counties and other factors, including heavy transport costs on bad roads were now proving a serious burden.

It was in 1769 that a decision confirmed the changing times, when a naval contract for a powerful new gun, light in weight, was placed away from the Weald with a Scottish ironworks, which had made significant advances in both technique and economy.

In 1777, the fifth generation John Fuller took over what by now was a business that had declined to a trickle. The last guns had been cast in 1775 and the foundry limped on with lesser work until 1787, when it finally closed.

The famous neighbour of the Fuller ironworks was at Ashburnham and this formidable works closed at about 1810.

The vast and dramatic life of Sussex ironfounding, equally vital to the national and to the workers of the Weald, was not without its repercussions. For many generations roads in bad condition had been subject to the dragging and hauling, with tortuous progress, of the enormous weights of cannons and trees. Nothing could survive such treatment and the roads were often quite literally torn and churned into deep oozing clay that was without hope of repair. Only in dry summer or hard frozen winter was progress even reasonable. (*See* appendix 'F').

1697

At a time of increasing poverty made worse by recent years of bad harvests, many towns were alarmed to find they were now paying huge amounts in poor relief.

To meet the ever-growing demands of the poor, taxes were continually raised, to the resentment of those who had to pay. Stringent efforts were made to confine the poor lists to those in genuine need and part of the Settlement Act of this year was a determined effort to prevent unnecessary payments.

A decision instructed that pauper families listed for poor relief must now wear a badge with 'P' and the initial of the parish, for such identification would prevent abuse by the claiming of extra charity. This cruel measure provoked both bitterness and a disobedience that often led to harsh punishment.

1699

Of the burials recorded in the Hailsham church register between December and the following March in 1700, there were twelve from the,

> . . . terrible scourge of smallpox . . .

At this time there was much poverty and a low resistance to disease, in spite of the relief given by the parish in the form of food to those in dire need.

1700

1702

The Court of Pevensey Hundred expressed serious concern that the road south out of Hailsham towards Stone Cross had suffered neglect and '. . . the inhabitants of Hailsham are notified to repair . . . ' that part of it in their parish.

Some six years later similar forthright instructions were issued to save a dilapidated waggon bridge on the same bad road, destined in future years to be rebuilt as the turnpike to (east) Bourne.

1705

The Poll Book listed nearly fifty voters in Hailsham who were a privileged few of a larger population.

One of those names listed as being of a 'gent', was Anthony Trumble (*see* entry of 1722), a man of consequence in Sussex who was in 1707 appointed as deputy to Lord Pelham with duties at Sussex Courts.

c. 1708

The Vicarage was built next to Hailsham parish church during the early Georgian period and is architecturally, an excellent example of the Queen Anne style. Of dignified proportions and lacking ostentation, the house with its separate stable block is of grey and red bricks laid in the flemish bond, while a fine entrance doorway of fluted pilasters and Ionic caps support a neat and simple pediment.

Inside the house, a long hall extends back to where an elegant staircase rises to a tall circular headed window on a landing against the rear wall, a change of direction then takes the staircase to an upper landing.

Under a wide moulded handrail the bannisters are finely twisted, giving the staircase a prettiness that is enhanced by each tread having at its end the classical scroll and acanthus leaf ornament in wood, with all the subtle variations of hand carving.

The outstanding room of the house is the perfectly proportioned drawing-room with, at one end, the wall in a sweeping circular curve featuring a large central window flanked by panelling, and a cupboard meticulously concealed in the sweep of the wall. This room is also graced with a marble fireplace of the Adam period.

An exceptional house but today, no longer a vicarage; it was re-named Hailsham Grange at a time the kitchen garden, orchard and a barn were cut off to allow the building of the smaller vicarage in use today.

Hailsham Grange has now been listed on the authority of the Secretary of State for the Environment as a building of particular importance. This is the highest category of any building in Hailsham. *Note:* The Vicarage House, as it was first called, was probably built for the Rev. Thomas Hooper, vicar from 1701 to 1753. He was also Rector at Beckley, near Ninfield.

c. 1717

The growth of dissenting sects is indicated by the increased numbers now gathered at meetings. At this time one hundred and twenty Baptists came together at Warbleton, one hundred and ten Presbyterians at Glinley (Glynleigh near Hailsham), and thirty at Carter's Corner (Cowbeech).

It was but a year later that two anti-Dissenter Acts of 1711 and 1714 were repealed by the new Whig Government, determined to reverse certain restrictive legislation of the Church of England.

Nonconformists had for many years been denied certain civil rights including the freedom to educate their children in their own schools, it was a barrier created to limit Nonconformist entry into the professions and public life. The new Government cancelled such prejudiced measures.

There was however still a clear division separating these minorities from the Church of England which lost no chance of branding such people as dangerous. It was a false cry taken up all too often by the ignorant who frequently made trouble for people who, the new King George I, regarded with some sympathy and respect.

1722

Anthony Trumble of Hailsham became Under Sheriff of Sussex. He lived in the southern corner of the Market Square in a new house later to be named Sheriff Place.

A year later the first Duke of Dorset, Lord of the Manor of Michelham, leased to Anthony Trumble,

> ... the ponds of water on Hailsham Common within the precincts of the Lordships and Royalty of Michelham ...

The lease granted was for a period of twenty-one years at an annual rental of one shilling.

While living at his house in the Market Square Anthony Trumble sought permission to erect a family seat in Hailsham church:

> ... a seat in the Chancel of Haylesham Church so that he does not cause inconvenience or loss to any other person there being ...

The permission to build was granted by Sir Robert Fagg who was responsible for chancel repairs. It was near the chancel that Anthony Trumble was buried in 1733. (*See* entry of 1816).

1722

Parishes were encouraged to build or rent workhouses and to arrange for their maintenance and supervision by men chosen to be Masters. The choice by parishes of such men were not always happy and many workhouses were still not conducted as humanely and honestly as was hoped.

At this time it was possible for children of vagrants to be taken away and apprenticed against the wishes of their father or mother.

1722

Daniel Defoe, travelling in East Sussex, wrote about Dragoons riding to hunt down smugglers or 'owlers' as they were called. So powerful were the smuggling gangs that it was not unknown for the mounted Dragoons to be attacked and dispersed, when they would be powerless to prevent bales of wool being carried by pack horses down to the shore for loading on boats bound for France.

At this time smuggling was widespread, highly organised and very successful, bringing welcome rewards to the men of the coast and inland villages. Certainly Hailsham profited from the trade for many men were involved who would otherwise have earned little or nothing, or even been in the poorhouse and a burden on the local tax-payer.

To men intent on stealth, the rivers inland from the coast at Pevensey were ideal for the movement of smuggled goods in shallow boats. And it was the historian Sir William Burrell who wrote:

> ... the Pevensey river, though now so insignificant, was formerly ... of no mean consideration ... Herst Haven (this was a river reaching near to Herstmonceaux), about 3 miles inland shows there was a station for vessels at the wood. Herst Bridge ... now corruptly called Horse Bridge was formerly a pass of some consequence, as it combines the communication between the open country and the wild ... at the entrance of the great wood a neighbouring family seat now vilely corrupted into Horselunges but anciently denominated Herstlongue ...

1724

Richard Budgen the cartographer, '... skilled in mathematics and astronomy ...' published a new map of Sussex with the explanation that,

> ... all the Remarkable Places, are Determined from Observation, also An Accurate Delination By Admeafurement of the Sea Coast, Roads and the Rivers so far as navigable ...

The map was dedicated to Spencer Compton, then Speaker of the House of Commons and Treasurer to the Prince of Wales, later to become George II. In 1728 Spencer Compton became Earl of Wilmington, the owner of much land in the parish of Hailsham and the builder of Compton Place in Eastbourne where it still survives.

Budgen's map introduced a degree of originality with its grid lines and mile distances, quoted along roads and navigable rivers for use in the transport of oak timbers. There were also indications of large houses, windmills and churches by side-view drawings often suggesting simple characteristics, as with Hellingly church shown with a spire that was later demolished.

In particular, the map plots the little known old ruined chapel at Boreham (Street) and the Priory at Langney (*see* entry of 1624), but it fails to record even a track linking Hailsham with Priesthawes and on to Langney Bridge. But this unrecorded route was by 1754 to become a turnpike road.

An interesting feature of the map was an indication of the extent to which the land behind Pevensey was subject to tidal water. The former Hailsham miller Gilbert Catt, the final owner of Lower (later Hamblins) Mill in Mill Road, can recall that at a time of exceptional rainfall and high water in the rivers about 1930, flood water extended across Pevensey Marsh forming a complete waterway reaching to the end of Mill Road and within one thousand two hundred and fifty yards of Hailsham's Market Square.

1724

In a report on Hailsham parish church made to the Bishop at Chichester attention was drawn to the poor condition of the church seats and the need for new planking, for they stood on '... nothing but very damp earth ...'. The report stated the need to pave the church floor and repair the roof and much of the fence round the churchyard.

1724

Edmund Eeedes died. His wife died later in 1748 and their gravestone still stands at the southwest corner of Hailsham parish church tower.

Edmund Eeedes and his wife were Anabaptists, a sect originally from Germany and persecuted in the reign of Elizabeth for their rejection of child baptism as premature, favouring baptism in adult life.

At the top of a page in the church register is the note written in 1696:

> ... A register of the Children born to Anabaptists in this Parish And others Not Baptised ...

The record of such births ended in 1702.

Among the children listed below the note was Sarah the daughter of Edmund Eeedes. The simple entries in the register concerning this father, mother and daughter reveal the following different spellings: Eeds, Edes, Edman and Sara. Such variations in spelling however were not unusual in church registers but tend to reflect the low educational level of the writer. The essential was that the written word was understood.

1725

James Lambert the watercolour artist, was born in Jevington and became an illustrator of the important Sussex historic researches of Sir William Burrell.

Many of the paintings and drawings of Lambert are now in the British Museum, one of which is the drawing he made in 1780 of Hailsham Church, an interesting record of its appearance at that time for it illustrated the old entrance porch and south aisle demolished in 1870 '... a wretched erection of brick and stucco ... '. (*See* entry of 1733).

1730

While Dissenters were still not entirely free from malicious attacks, Roman Catholics continued to suffer from almost complete intolerance, being regarded as traitors. It was about this time that the 7th baronet Sir William Gage of Firle, renounced catholicism and

> ... conformed to the Established Church ...

an act that now denied to Catholics the use of his private chapel. (*See* entry of 1555–57).

1733

The birth of Sir William Burrell who was to spend many years of his life collecting historic Sussex documents and writing what was expected to be a definitive history of the county.

To illustrate this major work the artists Samuel Grimm and James Lambert, produced between them hundreds of drawings of places and buildings in Sussex.

Among their work was a study of Hailsham church in 1780 and an interesting landscape painted in 1784 called 'View of Hailsham from the Turnpike leading to East Bourne'. This particular picture was painted from a spot in open country where now would be the junction of Ersham Road with Windsor Road. The picture's foreground is of open fields before the houses of Windsor Road, Gordon Road, Garfield Road or Bellbanks were ever built, and beyond can be see the church tower and the cluster of houses that stood nearby.

Sir William Burrell who was in his lifetime to live at Knepp Castle, Shipley near Horsham, died in 1796 with his work of many years still incomplete but the hundreds of his manuscripts that were finished are now in the British Museum, together with the invaluable record of his artist's work.

It has been acknowledged that many of the pictures of Samuel Grimm and James Lambert now provide the only evidence available relating to some old Sussex buildings, long ago altered or even demolished.

1736

With the tremendous need for skilled and unskilled labour, the 17th and 18th cent. settlement of the American colonies owed much to the introduction of 'Indentured Servitude', the means by which at least half of the English emigrants were able to sail to America.

For a man or woman to sail without passage money, an indenture would be signed which sold him or her into American bondage for an agreed number of years. The arrangement was made through an agent in London, usually a tradesman, who acted for farmers or factory owners in many of the eastern states of America. Most emigrants sailed to Maryland, Pennsylvania, Virginia or New England and many as far south as Jamaica and the Leeward Islands. Not surprisingly there were many abuses of the system.

On the 5th July 1736 Benjamin Grove of Hailsham, a barber and periwig maker, signed an indenture with Joseph Taylor a barber of London in which he agreed to settle and work in North Carolina for a period of four years.

It is known that of the first English men and women to emigrate to North America about this time, most came from the larger villages in the counties of south-east England.

1740

In the records of the Hailsham parish for this year, the parish clerk has made thirty-two baptism entries of which were 'beas-born child' (base-born or illegitimate).

1741

George Gilbert was born at Rotherfield to live through a poor childhood and become first a farm labourer and then a carpenter. At the age of eighteen years he followed a father he never knew and joined the army with the light horse regiment of General Elliot, and during three years in Germany he saw hardship, action and victory against the French, at one time taking an enemy standard in battle.

Back again in England, George Gilbert grew to dislike the army and was attracted to the new Methodist thinking. His strong feelings led him to talking and delivering sermons to whoever would listen, and when his regiment moved to Kensington in London he asked to be stationed at Heathfield, where General Elliot, who was to become Lord Heathfield, had just purchased a house in Heathfield Park.

Gilbert continued with his sermons and made many enemies, for Heathfield at that time was

> . . . notorious for the immorality and ignorance of its people . . .

But slowly, the numbers who listened increased and he began to be sought at his small cottage for simple advice.

General Elliot knew of Gilbert's honest endeavours and released him from the army whereupon his sermons increased and he at last began to be taken seriously.

> . . . on many occasions tears flowed from every eye, and it has been the opinion of competent judges that no preacher since the days of Whitfield had a more powerful mastery over the feelings of his hearers . . .

When his own cottage became too small, meetings began to be held in barns or whatever shelter was at hand. Eventually in 1769 a simple wooden chapel was built by his followers in Heathfield.

Gilbert travelled and preached in many East Sussex villages including Battle, Rotherfield, Crowborough, Herstmonceux and on several occasions in Alfriston where in 1801, he preached the first sermon in a new brick and flint chapel, built by the people and still standing by the Tye.

When in Hailsham where he was very well known, it was in a barn but a few yards from what is now Vicarage Road that he preached.

> . . . his simple addresses produced a wonderful affect on his rustic audiences . . .

Such was his appeal that a Hailsham witness at the time recorded seeing from her window on Sabbath mornings:

> . . . a Godly woman . . . Mary Box starting, whatever the weather, to walk to Heathfield to hear George Gilbert preach . . . wearing high 'pattens' (wooden soles raised on iron rings to lift shoes above the road) on account of the bad roads, a long cloak reaching down to her heels and a 'calash' (a hood hooped with cane) to cover her bonnet . . . '

So widely known and trusted, Gilbert was able in areas lacking a medical practitioner, to make use of a box of instruments and his basic army knowledge of medicine and surgery. On occasions he was thus able to relieve the suffering of the poor.

With a new greatly increased congregation his small early chapel at Heathfield was demolished to make way on the same site for a chapel that was larger. Built in 1809 it is the same building that survives today as the Cade Street Chapel.

Standing prominently on rising ground the chapel design reflects Georgian simplicity in its clean cut lines, a plain but honest structure. The interior is simple, much of it in wood planking almost bare of decoration and its principle

1. The fine 14th-century south front of Wilmington Priory in flint, stone and brick. The upper floor was the Great Hall and each of the polygonal turrets has a spiral staircase. The early years of the priory were of extreme importance in the management of French land and possessions in England after William the Conqueror's victory in 1066 (see entry of *c.*1240).

2. The raised pew in Warbleton church dated 1722 was built for the squire and his family where they could be apart and above lesser mortals. It has a desk with bible box and a divided compartment for servants all above a flight of 12 stairs (see entry of 1559).

3. The impressive Gatehouse of Herstmonceux Castle showing in the carved panel the banner of Roger Fiennes who built the castle (see entry of 1441).

4.   Pevensey Castle, an aerial view showing the outer Roman wall with its west gate at the bottom of the picture. The ruin of the Norman Keep is at the top (see entries of *c.* 340, *c.*1175 and 1283).

5.   Herstmonceux Castle was one of the earliest and finest examples of a brick-built castle. But the superb warm red brickwork was not always appreciated for Horace Walpole, writing with clear disapproval complained that the bricks were '. . . without the luxury of whitewash . . .'. It was the depressing tendency to use this same substance that caused so many wall paintings in our parish churches to be covered (see entry of 1441).

6. The timbered 'Fleur de Lys' of the 16th century, originally an inn and during much of the last century, a Hailsham workhouse (see entry of *c.*1545).

7. Horselunges in Hellingly, built in the reign of Henry VIII, it is one of the finest timbered houses in Sussex (see entry of 1436).

8. The barn at Alciston, once the property of Battle Abbey (see entry of *c.*1320).

9. The Market Cross or *Smugglers* Inn at Alfriston (see entry of 1815).

10. These massive roof timbers are merely part of probably the longest aisled barn in Sussex. This formidable 500-year old structure is now part of Court House Farm (see entry of *c.*1320).

12. The stone jambs each side of the door to Hailsham's church tower show the worn areas caused long ago by the sharpening of knives, swords and arrow heads (see entry of *c.*1390).

11. The unusual pattern of chisel marks to be seen on all octagonal columns in the nave of Hailsham church (see entry of *c.*1390).

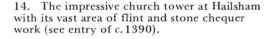

14. The impressive church tower at Hailsham with its vast area of flint and stone chequer work (see entry of *c.*1390).

13. An unusual group of flints in Hailsham's church tower of which three pairs each indicate they are halves of a flint boulder struck in two pieces by the mason and laid in the wall side by side (see entry of *c.*1390).

Items of jewellery found in the graves of the pagan Anglo-Saxon cemetery at Alfriston. The quality of the 'finds' indicated the burial of people of affluence.

15. A brooch of gilded bronze found on the breast of the skeleton of a young woman badly crippled in one leg whose grave was the most richly furnished in the cemetery.

16. A pair of saucer brooches of gilded bronze normally used to fasten a woman's tunic at the shoulders (see entry of 1912).

17. A belt fastener with two loose plates still with their rivets (once fixed to a leather belt), all tinned to resemble silver. From the grave of a wealthy male.

18. A grave in the Anglo-Saxon cemetery excavated on Ocklynge Hill. The skeleton is of a female, 5 ft. 5 ins. tall and thought to be between 18 and 20 years. A knife was found by the skeleton's left hip (see entry of 1909).

19. A typical Pevensey Marsh landscape with one of its many minor water courses (see entry of 1229).

20. An old 'Lookers' cottage on Pevensey Marsh. The 'looker' had his (sometimes a woman) own cattle, usually bullocks, or sheep, to look after but he would also do 'lookering' for neighbouring farmers (see entry of 1229).

21. The tower and stone spire of Chiddingly church seen from the village cricket green (see entry of 1621).

22. (*left*) Reminders of the Wealden iron industry. An iron 'gravestone' spiked at the bottom in Heathfield churchyard.

23. (*above*) A heavy iron vase in Herstmonceux churchyard (see entry of 1693).

24. The metalled surface of the old Roman road from Pevensey revealed beneath a field near the A22 road at Polegate (see entry of *c.* 340).

25. A charming Jonathan Harmer terracotta panel, set into a gravestone in East Hoathly churchyard. Of interest is that the baked clay panel has suffered less from age than the stone itself (see entry of 1806-25).

26. The old Chapel of Otham Priory in Polegate is now private property and after generations of neglect the east window is shown with its tracery restored in wood.

27. The south wall of the chapel over 750 years old with evidence of many repairs in stone and flint (see entry of *c.* 1175).

28. The Grange, formerly the elegant vicarage to Hailsham parish church (see entry of *c.* 1708).

. Carters Corner Place at Hailsham, an early centre of Nonconformist sympathy
d at one time, for many years, the home of the Hailsham family (see entry of
602).

30. Broad Farm in Hellingly, the house Joseph Calverly built in 1753 (see entry of 1626).

31. This calvary near Alfriston marks the place of burial of disturbed remains from a pagan Anglo-Saxon cemetery (see entry of 1912).

32. The wall paintings of Berwick church. In the nativity scene by Vanessa Bell the male figures are two local shepherds and a gardener with boys from local villages. The shepherds' crooks were from Pyecombe and the trug from Herstmonceux. The painting 'Christ in Glory' above the chancel arch is by Duncan Grant (see entry of 1943).

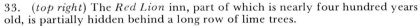

33. (*top right*) The *Red Lion* inn, part of which is nearly four hundred years old, is partially hidden behind a long row of lime trees.

34. (*below left*) Completely hidden in the attic, is a sawn-off tree trunk holding firm a locally-made iron contraption which, long ago, when the wheel was turned, worked for hours shredding tobacco leaves delivered by the smugglers (see entry of 1833).

35. (*below right*) A fireplace decorated by Duncan Grant in a room at Charleston Farmhouse (see entry of 1978).

36.   The simple chapel at Cade Street in Heathfield where George Gilbert preached. His wall memorial is next to the gallery (see entry of 1741).

37.   Cortlandt, the Hailsham home before its extensions were built, of Philip Cortlandt the American loyalist (see entry of 1775).

38.   Chiddingly Place, once a lavish Elizabethan mansion and former home of the Jefferay family. The centre is still lived in but on the left, a huge wing can be seen with its mullioned windows, now separate and used as a farm building (see entry of 1621).

39. The home at Halland of the Pelham family, demolished after the death of the Duke of Newcastle in 1768. This picture of the old house was painted by Frank Wootton from historical records (see entry of 1768).

40. Laughton Place, the moated home of the Pelhams was built on Laughton Levels in 1534 but only a tower now remains (see entry of 1356).

41. Exterior view of the chapel at Cade Street built in 1809 (see entry of 1741).

42. The 'Long Man', the giant figure of unknown age cut into the Downs at Wilmington (see entry of 1873).

43. The Court House at Pevensey where a death penalty could be inflicted. The spiked wall encloses the old prison exercise yard (see entry of 1370).

feature is a narrow balcony on three sides of the church, supported on cast iron columns. The entire balcony is full of enclosed box pews each with its door and again made entirely of thick planking left unpainted and unpolished, being today much as it was nearly two hundred years ago. This simple chapel may well be quite unique.

In his maturity, George Gilbert was a much respected man and an inspired speaker who worked ceaselessly for the 'Society for Spreading the Gospel in the Dark Towns and Villages of Sussex'. On occasions he was invited to speak in London, and has been acknowledged for having played an outstanding part during his lifetime, in the revival of religion in Sussex. He died in 1827 and was buried in the churchyard of his chapel.

c. 1745

The Manor House was built in Market Street, Hailsham.

An exceptional house built almost entirely of brick with the architectural ornament and classical design of the late Renaissance period.

The brickwork is of a high quality, the entrance doorway has heavily carved wooden brackets supporting a moulded porch and high in the roof are three unusual dormer windows, now little seen from the narrow Market Street. A fine house recently somewhat neglected but of a design little seen near Hailsham.

In the 19th cent, it was owned by a Josiah Pitcher of an old Hailsham and Hellingly family. (*See* entry of 1813). *Note:* The Manor House has now been listed as a building of special interest. It is an offence to demolish or alter such a building and in the event of undue neglect, consent may be granted for its compulsory purchase by a local authority.

1748

Th inland waterway or Pevensey Marsh as it is now known, was at this time an area full of streams and within limits, navigable rivers. Whenever the water was full from tributaries as far north as Dallington, Rushlake Green and Ashburnham a high level of water built up, which upon reaching the Old Haven river (now called 'Wallers Haven') a heavy flood would result if the outlet to the sea through the coastal shingle was restricted.

An attempt has been made to control such flooding even as far back as 1455 when appointed commissioners caused the waters to be diverted creating its faster flow to the sea. That the construction of a sluice followed as a further measure, is evident by a document of 1597 that refers to a 'Sluice House', while a map of 1610 quotes at the same coastal spot the words 'The Sluice'.

Repeatedly through the years, serious problems continued to effect both landowners and those who lived by the water until a final major work aimed at further controlling the inland waters of Pevensey was completed by 1748 when a 'New Cut' had been dug inland from the coast to ensure a permanent channel. A map of 1779 referred to the outlet as 'Sluice Haven' and the first edition in 1813 of the one-inch Ordnance Survey map for the Hastings area, named the outlet 'Pevensey Sluice'.

The eventual decline in the use of Pevensey Waters was when the infrequent passage of boats bringing iron down from the Weald finally ceased. It had previously been a vital export route for the iron products of the once great Wealden industry but now, the diminished need for a sluice house enabled a change of usage for today, on this same site, stands a vastly changed structure known as the *Star* Inn.

1749

The earliest newspaper with an interest, however slight in the area of Hailsham was *The Sussex Weekly Advertiser* and the first issue was that of Monday 19th June. This newspaper of four pages measuring 16 in. x 10 in. was of a strong but coarse paper with uneven edges and a dull grey/cream in colour. It was printed in Lewes by W. Lee who proclaimed on every issue that the,

> ...printing in general is performed in the neatest and most correct Manner, and Letter'd as well as in London...

The main news was set out under the headings of 'London Gazette from Whitehall' and 'Foreign Intelligence' which was almost entirely devoted to overseas wars, while general news was under the two headings 'London' and 'Country'. Finally the more local news was under either 'Brighton' or 'Lewes' and it was this latter heading that very occasionally mentioned places in East Sussex.

Much of the paper was made up of small advertisements, many dealing with patent medicines and assurances of cures, appeals for the return of cattle either strayed or stolen, property sales and offers of employment to those trustworthy enough to be servants or apprentices.

The issue of 20 May 1761 contained the following announcement:

> ...On Wednesday the 10th of this instant June will be fought, at the house of John Jones of East Hoathly.
>
> A MAIN of COCKS
>
> Between the Gentlemen of Hoathly, and the Gentlemen of Pevensey, showing nine Cocks of a Side for Two Guineas a Battle and Ten Guineas the odd Battle
>> Richard Summers, a Feeder...
>> John Head, a Feeder...

and some years later a report from Lewes said:

> ...Yesterday a boy only twelve years old, named Mitchell, was committed to prison in this town, charged with stealing two shirts, the property of an Artillery Driver...

1753

John Ellman while still young, moved with his family to Glynde where he grew up and became famous as a breeder of sheep.

During John Ellman's long farming lifetime he was to build a substantial reputation and was regarded by the Board of Agriculture as the county's leading farmer. On an occasion he was invited by the Board to advise on several questions. To one dealing with wages of farm employees, he commented:

... to fix the price of husbandry would be attended with many inconveniences to both master and servant ... by paying an idle, indolent fellow the same wages per day as you do a good working hand, I beg to know how long it would be before they all would come under the former description ... what is the language of the servant? ... 'why should I save any of my wages as the parish must keep me in case of illness, or a large family' ... This opinion being so prevalent in the minds of most common servants, is a big mischief ... it tends to encourage servants to frequent gin-shops and ale-houses, which rid them of what should be laid up ... and what is worse, corrupts their morals, and makes them discontented ...

Respected for both his character and his supreme knowledge of sheep, John Ellman was to greatly enhance the prestige of Sussex agriculture. Such was the success of his Southdown sheep in his later days that he frequently withdrew from shows rather than dominate the awards. He was unique in his lifetime and was consulted for his knowledge by landowners and breeders from all over England. His sheep were much in demand for breeding in New Zealand.

But John Ellman remained very much a Sussex man and was often to be seen in Hailsham market. He died in 1832.

1754

An Act was passed that allowed the establishment of the Horsebridge–Horam Trust which had as its object the building of a local Turnpike Road between Uckfield and Langney Bridge, later to be extended to Sea Houses in East Bourne. There was also to be an additional section between Horsebridge and Horam.

The road was one of the earliest in Sussex to be improved and was named the 'Horsebridge–Horam Turnpike', but generally it was referred to as 'the turnpike that runs through Hailsham' and meetings of the trustees were usually held

... at the house of Armgill Terry, known by the sign of the King's Head at Horsebridge ...

The positions of the toll houses were Union Point in Uckfield, Dicker Common, Horsebridge opposite the *King's Head*, Hailsham Common at the junction of South Road with Ersham Road, and Langney Bridge near Westham. The route through Hailsham was south from Horsebridge along London Road, through the town by what is now North Street and along Ersham Road past Priesthawes then to Stone Cross and Langney.

In a report on Sussex Turnpike Trusts drawn up in 1852 details were given on all the fifty-two turnpikes in the county and it was recorded that only three were free from debt and one of these was

... the turnpike that runs through Hailsham ...

The repair of loose road surfaces was a constant problem and the main material used was beach with broken stone and flint. In the year 1822–1823 over one thousand eight hundred tons of material was needed in repair work with beach coming from the nearby coast and most of the stone from the quarry near the sea front at East Bourne. (*See* appendix 'G').

Map of 1795 by
Gardner, Yeakell and Gream
showing turnpike roads and
proposed canal

Turnpike roads
Proposed canal   + + +

1755

At this time excited and packed gatherings were to be found at the *King's Head* in East Hoathly watching the fierce encounters of cock fighting when visitors, sometimes from distances, indulged in heavy betting. It was a sport that dated back several hundred years and at this time it was even more popular than horse racing, involving as it did all classes of people.

c. 1760

Just three miles from Hailsham, the house 'Montague' stands on rising ground at the edge of the marsh only a quarter of a mile from the river Pevensey Haven. The oldest part of the house is of 17th cent. brick and flint and for many years it was part of highly organised smuggling and a great deal of work had been carried out to ensure concealment.

In the house was a hidden entrance to a shaft down which men could lower themselves into a brick-built tunnel some nine feet below ground level. The tunnel was very cramped but enabled men to travel underground a considerable distance in a north-west direction. It broke ground in a narrow valley that gave ideal cover for moving towards a nearby road that could lead directly to Hailsham.

1762

The medieval building 'Fleur-de-Lys' in the Market Square was purchased by the Hailsham Vestry and prepared for its future use as a workhouse when it would give food and shelter to the poor. This new accommodation would be additional to other dwellings in the parish, some in appalling condition, that already housed paupers.

1762

In Hailsham a sum of £1 5s. 6d. was,

> . . . paid for peoples Learning to Sing in the Church . . .

It was about this time that music was provided in the parish church by a bassoon, a thick wooden double pipe about four feet long, a french horn and the more common and easily played pitch-pipe, a type of wooden slide-whistle.

At Hellingly church, music was provided on occasions by flute, bassoon, clarinet, cornet and more frequently by violin.

1768

Thomas Pelham-Holles, the Duke of Newcastle (the name Holles was added as a condition of inheriting land from a Will), died aged 75 and proved to be the last Pelham to live in Halland House, just half a mile east of East Hoathly village. Halland had been a Pelham home since the family moved from their low-lying and moated Laughton Place in 1595.

The duke had many properties and estates with several in Sussex, all having their own servants, but it was Halland House that in his lifetime he made famous for its excessive and lavish entertaining of London's leading figures and the famous families of Sussex.

He was a whig, and his political life in many high government offices also led to widespread spending, for as was the accepted custom and as his friends would say,

> ... Newcastle practically beggared himself through the expenditures in politics, in borough or county 'corruption', or 'in service to the public' ...

But Lord Chesterfield made it clear that,

> ... he took no specific personal financial advantages from his many offices ...

While through the whole of his life, the Duke of Newcastle allowed money to pour away in pursuit of living in the grand manner, so too did the financial pressures increase until at his death the incredible sum, for those times, of £300,000 was owed to people of every station including his bank.

Within a year of his death a vast collection of furniture, tapestries and pictures was sold and the old Halland House demolished, allowing the family to use their large house at Stanmer or the smaller house in Lewes (now called 'Pelham House', the property of the East Sussex County Council and containing the East Sussex Record Office).

In 1770 the farmhouse of the present Halland Park Farm was built on part of the site using much of the material from the ruins of the once great Elizabethan mansion. A reminder of the past is the huge brick structure of some dignity which once served the Duke of Newcastle as stables and a coach house. It is now used by the farm as a barn.

1769

A list of fairs and markets printed at this time did not list Hailsham as a market town.

1775

The American War of Independence began against England with the American family of Van Cortlandt deeply involved and one of its members, a Philip Van Cortlandt, was to reach the decision that he would remain loyal to the English Crown. It was a decision that proved both courageous and costly for at thirty-eight years it was to entirely change the course of his life.

Philip was educated at what is now Columbia University leaving with a Master of Arts degree. In 1762 he married Catharine Ogden of Jamaica in Long Island and they were to have a family of seventeen children of whom four died in infancy in addition to seven miscarriages.

In his early days Philip invested in a sailing ship for the West India trade but sold his share:

> ... having discovered that the owners had ordered her on a contraband trade contrary to our first arrangement ...

But his main interest, having considerable inherited land and wealth, was in a farm he bought in New Jersey which he described as,

> . . . being represented to us as the Eden of our northern world, the mountains filled with riches and the valley producing ev'ry luxury of life spontaneously . . .

He also had another estate with a mill, granary and a pearl-ash works and much of his own time he gave to honorary posts in civil affairs.

For many years, the relationship between the Crown and British Parliament and her colony of America had steadily deteriorated. As the 'new world' developed, so too did its confidence and intolerance of decisions made three thousand miles away in England and there were few Americans, either firm patriots for independence or loyalists, who were not for continuing with Britain albeit with a revised and more even partnership.

The strong inclination of Philip and others like him was to deal with an increasingly dangerous situation with a calm and open mind, that a solution might emerge best suited to the strengths of each country.

Patriots supporting the American cause were often prone to both violent language and hasty action and a man of Philip's wealth and prominence, together with his loyalist thinking, was soon to suffer indignities. When he made the serious decision to refuse a commission in the American army and had faced a court which with a serious warning had removed his guns and sentenced him to a fine, the court comment was of his unpatriotic behaviour but elsewhere the cry was of traitor.

Events eventually began to close in on Philip for there came strong pressure from patriots who asked for his pearl-ash works to be converted for making nitre, useful in the manufacture of explosives, but it was a request he refused. At a later date he was again charged with not taking up arms with the militia and again there was a fine with another warning about his neutrality.

There was no respite and Philip's failure yet again to join the militia brought a final court warning that he must either enlist or pay a man to take his place as was the custom. Still refusing to commit himself his reply was:

> . . . could a substitute be procured for the tenth part of a farthing, I would not send one, as I should look upon him as my representative, and therefore accountable for his conduct — at the same time that I looked upon this treatment as cruel, ungenerous, and incompatible with my notions of liberty . . .

With such an honest reply Philip had placed himself in an impossible position and in spite of the sympathy he felt for many of the American claims of injustice, his decision was inevitable and he declared himself a Loyalist. He was at once a target for armed patriots and his family reduced to the distress of suffering vile insults and a shortage of food until they could escape to a safe area.

In due course, after meeting Sir William Howe, the English Commander-in-Chief, Philip was appointed a Major in the New Jersey Volunteers. It was about this time that Philip's wife and children were turned out of their New Jersey house on an order from General Washington who converted it for the use of nearly six hundred sick and injured patriot soldiers.

Within a short time of joining his regiment Major Van Cortlandt was shocked to encounter an attitude of inexplicable prejudice displayed by British officers towards their comrades the American Loyalist officers. It was in many cases an arrogance directed at seemingly inferior people and the policy in the early phase of the war was to allocate the more subservient roles to Loyalist regiments. It was almost two years before this unpleasant attitude improved and the Loyalists saw hard action.

The war lasted with considerable losses until nearly the end of 1782. Copies of the Articles of Peace, signed on 30th November 1782, were sent out from Whitehall on 31st December and finally reached America on 18th March 1783. The treaty required that the defeated Loyalists be treated fairly, their property returned and persecution halted. In the event, these requirements were not honoured and in face of continued abuse the local committees,

> . . . assumed control and meted out punishments to loyalists in an inhuman manner . . .

To escape these intolerable conditions Philip decided to face the upheaval and a long sea voyage and sail with his family for England. Upon arrival in 1783 Philip was placed on half-pay of £120 per annum as a major while his two elder sons, now ensigns, were each allowed £30 per annum. With the need to support his large family without a private income Philip applied for a supplement and this was granted at another £120 per annum.

Philip at this time faced a near desperate situation. In a strange land he needed to provide a house with reasonable comfort for his wife and those of his grown children who had left America with him. What possessions may have escaped confiscation were thousands of miles away and money at this moment was vital.

With so many problems the future can only have been depressing and he was not encouraged when he encountered in London a somewhat shallow snobbish attitude of superiority towards the defeated Loyalists. It was indeed an unhappy time.

With the American attitude to Loyalists clearly vindictive in its quest for revenge, the British Government decided that its own duty was to ensure the defeated Loyalists were treated fairly. It was agreed to award part compensation to claims of confirmed losses especially where Loyalists were reduced to circumstances of genuine need.

The problem was to gather the proof of such losses from America where he now learned he had been declared guilty of high treason. Troubled with family sickness and the need to borrow money to meet expenses it was now that Philip, from an address in Chelsea, submitted a petition of some dignity to the Commissioners appointed by Parliament in which he outlined both his losses and his services to the Crown.

The petition was one of many and the delay considerable in spite of frequent appeals for money he desperately needed. Indeed it was some two years before Philip at last received a British compensation award of £1,500 against those losses the Commission could confirm. It was an amount of trifling size compared with what, in America, had been taken from him.

After a stay in Chester, Philip, in a quest for final security and happiness decided in 1786 to sail for Nova Scotia with his wife and nine of his children.

It was winter when their ship sailed from Liverpool and almost at once it was hit by a storm and forced to shelter in the Isle of Man. Once again the ship set sail but its passage was perilous for it met continual heavy weather and, at times, bad storms with the ship in dire trouble.

After three exhausting months and hundreds of miles south the ship limped into Madeira with much of Philip's property either damaged or completely lost. For Philip's wife the weeks on the storm battered boat were difficult for she was in advanced pregnancy and in Madeira gave birth to a son.

It was not until the end of 1787 that Philip with his family finally reached Nova Scotia and in the following year Philip was able to take advantage of a land grant scheme for Loyalists and was awarded three hundred acres with seeds, tools and medicines as well as other land elsewhere which he put to farming. With England now at war with France Philip was persuaded in 1793 to raise a regiment of militia and he served as Aide-de-Camp to the Governor, Sir John Wentworth. But the new life was not a success and in 1794 he again sailed with his family for England.

Enquiries and appeals concerning his former American properties were helped by his cousin and namesake now a Brigadier-General with the patriot army and later a political associate of Thomas Jefferson, a future President of America. With help, a sale of some property brought him £2,000, he also learned he still had property in Delaware and New York State.

With improved finance the family was to find London a friendlier place and after living for a period in Warwick it was from Binfield in Berkshire in 1803 that with immense relief he wrote to his American cousin:

> ... Since my arrival in this Country, I have been altogether in the Society of my children here and it affords me unspeakable pleasure with heartfelt gratitude to say so with as much earthly felicity as can fall to the lot of parents from their prospects in life ...

In 1804 at the age of sixty-five years Philip, due to his changing military circumstances, now a captain, obtained the post of Barrack Master in Hailsham controlling troops in readiness against a possible invasion by the French army of Napoleon. With his responsibility for several regiments in Hailsham at which time the troops far outnumbered the inhabitants, he was promoted to Major and finally to Colonel in the Royal Newfoundland Fencible Infantry.

To be near the barracks where there was constant activity, Philip lived at a recently built house in George Street known as 'Newhouse' (many years later to be given the name Cortlandt). The owner, John Bristow the elder, had recently died resulting in his two daughters, Marthaner a spinster, and Mary together with her husband the Rev. Matthias Slye from East Carleton in Northamptonshire, all inheriting an interest in the property as well as land at Coldthorn and Knock Hatch.

Van Cortlandt Manor, the old family home is forty miles north of New York City in Croton, Westchester County and stands on high ground overlooking the wide Hudson River. At one time the Manor House was surrounded by an estate of over two hundred square miles.

The Manor House was lived in by members of the Van Cortlandt family until 1940 and in 1953 it was purchased by John D. Rockefeller, Jnr., with the intention of preserving this historic place for the American nation. Work under the care of specialist architectural and historical researchers with experience of previous Rockefeller projects, has brought the house of wood and stone together with its subsidiary buildings to a state of excellent restoration.

Several family portraits originally from the house now hang in galleries throughout America including the Metropolitan Museum of Art in New York, but much of the original period furniture has been traced and returned to its place in the house. This property of a famous family is now open to the American public who are looked after by guides in costumes of the period when the Cortlandt family lived in the house. *Note:* The house 'Cortlandt' in George Street, Hailsham, once lived in by Philip Van Cortlandt, is now listed as a building of special interest. (*See* entry of 1814 and appendix 'H').

c. 1775

A modest house of brick opposite the market in Market Street called 'The Old Vicarage' has the appearance of being possibly two hundred years old, but inside the house, heavy timbers of great age can be seen. The presence of such a wooden structure suggests that at some time a brick rebuilding around the original frame has taken place.

Under the tiled roof are again timbers of immense weight with some still joined by wooden pegs, while among the minor rafters some have only been axed in a crude manner leaving much of the rounded tree trunk still visible. There appears no reason to doubt the thought that once this house was indeed an early vicarage.

1776

The Dicker area for many years yielded a clay suited to maintain several local potteries at different times. The products were mainly of a basic kind including land pipes and roofing tiles but some potteries produced among them such domestic items as jugs, spittoons, vases, simple crockery, flower pots and large unglazed earthenware for storage.

In this year, a time of keen competition among local potteries, Thomas Wood was declared bankrupt and his business assets auctioned at the *King's Head*, Horsebridge.

The last of the potteries at Dicker survived until *c.* 1964 and during its final phase, specialised in a range of small ornamental items finished with a distinctive black lustre iron glaze.

1776

The Rev. John Herring died aged sixty-seven and was buried in the porch of Chiddingly parish church. It was written of him by Mark Antony Lower:

...Mr. Herring is traditionally remembered as the first person who introduced potatoes into this district from Devonshire. That this esculent dates only from a very recent period here, is proved by the fact that the parish accounts of Mr. Herring's time contain an entry 'half-a-bushel of potatoes' bought for the work-house — probably as a delicacy for the sick ...

Later in 1813 the book 'General View of the Agriculture of the County of Sussex' quotes:

...the late and very alarming price of bread-corn ascertained the value of potatoes and directed the public attention to this root which in case of necessity might prove a substitute for wheat and the enquiry which the Board of Agriculture instituted with a view of determining the comparative merit and qualities of potatoes ...has naturally excited much attention. This root certainly possesses great merit as a food for man ...

This book, reporting on agriculture in the county, also recorded that:

...Mr. Calverley of Broad (Hellingly) on an old hop field, raised 700 potatoes per acre ...

In the same review on Sussex Agriculture, attention was directed to the worker and we read:

...Poor, by this term, is understood, in a general sense the labouring poor and those who at any time of the year, seek assistance from the parish ... the present state of this class of people is in many parts, inferior to what every humane person would wish ... too many of their houses are the residence of filth and vermin, for their clothes insufficient, their minds uneducated ... and their children from insufficiency of earnings, trained to vice. Give each man an interest, a stake in the welfare of his country and we shall no longer hear of so many crimes ...

Such a review is surely unworthy and biased against people so often disregarded and neglected. Of interest are the comments a year earlier in 1775 of Nathanial Kent in his book, 'Hints to Gentlemen of Landed Property', when he wrote:

...cottages as often in such disrepair that the wind and rain penetrated every part. They usually contained only one room, so that a man, his wife and family had to eat and sleep almost like animals ... the shattered hovels which half the poor of this kingdom are obliged to put up with, is truly effecting to a heart fraught with humanity. Those who condescend to visit these miserable tenements can testify that neither health nor decency can be preserved in them ...

and written twenty years later by another observer:

...humanity shudders at the idea of the industrious labourer, with a wife and 5 or 6 children, being obliged to live or rather exist, in a wretched damp gloomy room, of 10 or 12 feet square, and that room without a floor; but common decency must revolt ...

Conditions varied from county to county but the farm worker was all too often powerless against the whims and outlook of the landowner, just as he was against the harsh economic climate of his time.

1777

The home of Robert Hare was Herstmonceux Castle but influenced by his wife, and not without reason it is said, a decision was made to built a large house in the park north-west of the castle.

In so doing the castle interior was demolished leaving only the walls and towers intact, a scale of destruction that left a vast amount of material to be used in the building of the new house.

It was therefore from this unfortunate date that the exposed castle walls began a steady deterioration, ending in near ruin over one hundred and thirty years later. (*See* entry of 1911).

The new home of Robert Hare, to be named Herstmonceux Place, was in future years to have many distinguished guests among whom was William Wilberforce whose long and bitter campaign resulted in the end of England's participation in the slave trade. *Note:* The interior of Herstmonceux Place has been drastically remodelled and is now divided into family apartments overlooking the former castle park.

1782

The 'Gilberts' Act was passed. The introduction of this far-reaching Act was an attempt to humanise the administration of workhouses.

Independent inspectors were now to be appointed, orphan children were to be boarded out whenever possible and those under seven years not to be taken from their parents. Among the other humanities introduced were, ceasing to send paupers to a workhouse more than ten miles from their own parish and if a pauper was of good character, cancelling the need to make him wear a pauper's badge.

This Act also encouraged groups of nearby parishes to be linked together by the creation of a Union (or large workhouse) in which the paupers of the parishes would be housed.

The building of such Unions was calculated to increase the control of paupers and to lessen the harsh treatment so often suffered. There were many improvements including those of hygiene, sleeping quarters and medical attention.

Most of the inmates were female, many being widows and others, single mothers. There were children both with and without a parent but old men were fewer and able-bodied men were least of all. But wherever an inmate was able-bodied, an attempt was made to put them to work.

1783

At this time the demand for maps was increasing rapidly and in many early examples the date of the map did not always reflect the true state of road development in that precise year. With the time consuming problem of physically surveying the countryside it was not unusual for some parts of a map to have been repeated from an older edition. Indeed it was not unknown for a map-maker to copy the work of another, and unwittingly repeat his mistakes for such copying was not illegal.

When a map of 1783 was published two main tracks shown across Hailsham Common had already become roads in spite of still being indicated by dotted lines. Furthermore the track leaving Hailsham due south had by now been made into a turnpike road that carried on past the house 'Priesthawes' and on to Stone Cross, Langney and Sea Houses in East Bourne. *(See* entry of 1795 and appendix 'J').

1784

It was estimated in this year that the unloading of smuggled tea along the coast, much of it in East Sussex, had reached such an enormous volume that of the total weight of thirteen million pounds of tea consumed in the country, duty had only been paid on a mere five and a half million.

On 2nd March of this year there was written in East Bourne:

> ... Yesterday evening two cutters from the continent landed their cargoes a short distance from this place, a great part of which was conveyed away by men with horses, but leaving some bags of tea behind, the officers carried them away, to the amount of 200 L being all hyson ... (hyson was green tea from China).

This was an occasion when, pitted against overwhelming odds, the Revenue Officers were prepared to be bribed and avoid physical violence.

1784

For attending sick paupers in Hailsham parish:

> ... Mr. Kerby Salvey for Docttering the poore £12. 12. 0. for the half year ...

and much of the sickness was from smallpox which so often proved fatal.

Such payment could be made from local taxes in return for the simple medical services from men calling themselves surgeons, bone-setters, doctors, apothecaries and physicians, while the inevitable midwives, with their varying attitudes and talents, were largely expected to help pauper women and unmarried mothers.

Those with the means to pay could freely indulge in the services of a 'doctor', but for others, their medical attention could only come from a 'doctor' paid by the parish. The payment was an agreed sum for medical attention given over a period during which time 'doctors' could ignore attending smallpox and broken bones; and should the agreed sum be low, then there was a tendency for the poor to be deprived.

Where a parish preferred not to agree a contract sum in return for 'doctor' services, then payment was made strictly against whatever medical attention had been given.

Of burials at this time, most of the bodies would have been carried from the church to the graveside in a coffin, then removed and buried in a shroud, often wrapped around with strips of canvas. In the years following the turn of the century, 'uncoffined' burials slowly decreased but the use of a coffin depended on a family's ability to pay: it was therefore likely that poorer agricultural areas were slower to indulge in this display of respect.

1785

In a handbook of roads with details of routes and coach destinations, Hailsham was still listed as a Post Town and the route from London was quoted as being to

Tunbridge Wells, from where the horses would have to pull the coach along poorer roads so often impassable in bad winter weather. Hailsham was still an important centre for the distribution of mail to villages in the area and letters and parcels addressed to East Bourne or Meads were still quoted as 'near Haylsham'.

1785

Thomas Burfield was born. He was to become a ropemaker and to found the Hailsham firm of Burfield and Son.

1786

On 15th December, Hailsham market was revived after a long period of stagnation.

With a steady rise in the population, the improvement in roads and the introduction of turnpikes, there had been a steady expansion in farming. The land was improved by the ploughing of rough pastures and in some areas, new crops were introduced.

The return of the market now offered a steady and useful service to agriculture until by *c.* 1850 it had become of very considerable importance, being the largest cattle and corn market in the county. On market days, the volume of cattle being driven into Hailsham transformed the town, now dominated by the noise of animals and people, with carts, wagons, movement, obstruction and even occasional danger.

1787

At this time a printing office was operating in Hailsham High Street where it met the needs of people for many miles around. It was a time when there was no printer in East Bourne.

1788

An advertisement of 21st July on the front page of the *Sussex Advertiser* read:

... CRICKET

On thursday next, the 24th this instant July, will be played at Broad Oak on the Dicker, in Chiddingly, a match between the Gentlemen of Alfriston Club, with Baytop of Wadhurst, against the parish of Chiddingly, with five men, one of which can be selected from any Part of the County ... From the situation of the Spot, and the numerous Avenues thereto, a great Number of Spectators are expected; and a good Dinner will be provided at the 'Bat and Ball'.

The Wickets to be pitched at Ten in the Morning ...

The name 'Bat and Ball' referred to an inn on Dicker Common, long since converted into a house of the same name situated just west of Golden Cross and a few yards from the junction of the B 2124 road with the A 22 road to Lewes.

1788

The Hon. John Byng, later to become Viscount Torrington, was a Lieutenant-Colonel in the Guards and a lover of the countryside. During his rides through the counties he kept a travel journal and while passing through east Sussex he wrote:

> ... I walked my horse to Boreham; here was a most tempting public house, and it was now the right hour of appetite; so I ordered cold beef to be laid forth in a clean bow-windowed room ... Three miles hence, leaving the high road to the right, we enter'd Herstmoncoeux Park (a name pronounced with such variety by the natives, as scarcely, to be found out) a place once glorious ... Mr. Hare-Naylor, the owner, having built a paltry citizen-looking house at the edge of the park ... has within these last years, stript, destroy'd, and pulled down all the interior parts of this grand old mansion of Herstmonceux ...'. (*See* entry of 1777).

Later in his ride after passing through Magham Down, John Byng wrote,

> ... at Horsebridge, where seem'd to be a very good public house, the *King's Head*; my horse being put up, and a double bedded room put into preparation (our baggage was arrived), ... the evening now closed, we were soon at supper, ... mutton chops, and boil'd ham; in a sitting room of most spacious extent, being 36 feet, by 21. Our bed room, too was of noble dimensions ...

1789

Thomas Turner died. In his early life he was a schoolmaster, but later, in 1750, he became a grocer and general dealer in East Hoathly, near the parish church. As village grocer Thomas Turner assisted in supplying food for many of the lavish dinners hosted by the extravagant Duke of Newcastle at his nearby home in Halland.

During the years 1754-1765 Thomas Turner kept a diary written in a meticulous and attractive copperplate style, recounting the happenings of his everyday life which in the course of years, was to prove a remarkable record. Commenting on Thomas Turner, J. B. Priestley has written:

> ... he knew none of the great, he never travelled far from his home but what he wrote provides a picture of village life in the 18th Century. It shows us what people during the last days of King George II thought, read, ate and drank ...
> ... as an historical account of village life at the time it is probably without parallel ...

Thomas Turner Wrote 20 June 1755:

> ... this day being my birthday, I treated my scholars with about 5 quarts of strong beer ...

He wrote of 11 January 1757:

> ... this day I gave a man 6d, who came about a-begging for the prisoners at Horsham Gaol, three of which are clergymen, two of them for acting contrary to the laws of men ... that is, for marrying contrary to the Marriage Act. The other is for stealing some linen; but, I hope he is innocent ...

He wrote on 22 May 1757:

> ... about 4 oclock, my wife and I set out for Lewes, on our roan horse, where we arrived about 20 minutes past 7 ...

A comment made on conditions at this time was:

> ... almost the only mode of getting about in Sussex was on horseback, the husband riding with his wife on a pillion behind him. There was generally a narrow strip of road made hard by the refuse slag of the extinct iron works along which they jogged in winter, the rest of the road being available only in summer ...

He wrote of 3 August 1758:

> ... what seem very surprising to me in the Duke of Newcastle, is, that he countenances so many Frenchmen, there being ten of his servants, cooks etc., which was down here ...

He wrote of 25 December 1758:

> ... this being Christmas-day myself and wife at church in the morning. We stayed at the Communion; my wife gave 6d., but they not asking me I gave nothing ...

He wrote on 9 July 1759:

> ... in the afternoon my wife and I walked to Whitesmith to see a mountybank perform wonders, who has a stage built there, and comes once a week to cuzen a parcel of poor deluded creatures out of their money, by selling his packets, which are to cure people of more distempers than they ever had in their lives, for 1s/– each ...

He wrote of 15 November 1759:

> ... after dinner set out for Allfriston, in company with James Marchant, Durrant and Tho. Davy they on foot, myself on horse-back ... to see Mr. Elliss ... plaid at bragg in the even; and, though we plaid as low a game as possible, it was my unhappy lot to loose 3s. I think almost to give over ever playing at cards again ...

He wrote of 7 April 1760:

> ... after dinner I went down to Jones, to the vestry. We had several warm arguments at our vestry to-day, and several vollies of execrable oaths oftentime redouned, from allmost all parts of the room. A most rude and shocking thing at publick meetings ...

He wrote of 10 June 1761:

> ... was fought this day, at Jones's, a main of cocks, between the gentlemen of Hothly and Pevensey. Quere. Is there a gentleman in either of these places that was concerned ...

He wrote of 1 August 1761:

> ... there being only prayers in our church, Sam Weller and I took a ride to Seaford, where we took a walk by the seaside, and took a view of the two forts newly erected there, one of which has five 24 pounders ...

He wrote of 12 March 1762:

> ... myself and both the servants were at church in the morn; we had a very crowded audience ...

He wrote of 29 January 1763:

> ... The frost began to thaw today, after having continued very severe for five weeks; the ice was seven inches thick ...

He wrote of 24 March 1763:

> ... I went to Jone's (this would have been the Inn for it was to Jone's where Thomas Turner went to witness cock fighting) there being a vestry (meeting) there to make a poor rate. We staid till near one oclock, quarrelling and bickering ... the design of our meeting was to have made a poor rate, every one to be assessed to the racked rent. But I do blush to say, what artifice and deceit, cunning and knavery was used by some to conceal their rents ... to be robbing every other member of the community that contributes his quota ...

He wrote on 24 November 1763:

> ... Mr. Banister having lately taken from the smugglers a freight of brandy, entertained Mr. Carmen, Mr. Fuller, and myself, in the even, with a bowl of punch ...

He wrote on 7 December 1763:

> ... I think since of having lived at Hothly I never knew trade so dull or money so scarce, the whole neighbourhood being almost reduced to poverty ...

The diaries in which Thomas Turner wrote over a period of eleven years filled a total of one hundred and thirteen booklets each of one hundred pages. The simple booklets with paper covers, made by Thomas Turner or possibly for him were as small as four inches by six inches tall of unlined rag paper sewn together with fine string. The daily entries are written in straight lines and almost entirely in a very clear and legible hand.

The collection of diaries with the exception of two missing volumes is now in the Manuscript department of Yale University, U.S.A., and is still in excellent condition.

1790

The desperate flight from the French Revolution with its pitiless massacre and the guillotine still continued, and for those who could escape,

> ... the savage and unrelenting fury of their persecutors ... a stream of assorted boats carried distressed families to the Sussex coast at Brighton and Seaford ...

In particular, it was reported on 10th September that in the last few days boats had landed nearly one thousand three hundred people on the shore at East Bourne. From the beach they were taken in coaches and waggons to inns and country houses, some near Hailsham, for food and rest.

A meeting at the *Star* Inn in East Bourne of men from the country discussed how help could be given to the sad refugees. The chairman, Lord Sheffield of Sheffield Park, said

> ... the arrival of these unfortunate persons was not a matter of choice ... if we rejected or refused relief to men in their distressed situation, it would be an everlasting reproach on the national character ...

1791

Influenced to a degree it is thought, by the recent escape to England of clergy victims of the Revolution in France, a sympathy towards Catholicism helped the Act of this year for the Relief of Roman Catholics.

From now, it was lawful for Catholics to say Mass and to enter the legal and medical professions. There was also to be a toleration of Catholic schools and places of worship.

1791

William Child, a farmer, took over a lease at Michelham Priory where his family were to live and farm until 1861. William and later his son Thomas were to build up a remarkable reputation for breeding Sussex cattle and establishing, for the first time, accepted standards by which cattle should be judged. The farm at Michelham had by 1825 become a centre for farmers who sought to breed from cattle of pure Sussex stock.

c. 1792

Hailsham had for many years been,

> . . . a stronghold of Dissenters who objected to Romish practices carried on inside the parish church . . .

Many were those whose religious belief was simple but strong, and about this time regular meetings began to be held in what had become known as Chapel Barn. The barn was a sturdy structure in brick and boulder walling less than two hundred yards from Hailsham parish church. It was here where the gospel as preached by George Gilbert of Heathfield was followed (still standing today close to the market, Chapel Barn is now an abattoir).

From the meetings of those early believers in a simple doctrine in 1795, the Hailsham Baptist chapel was destined to emerge.

With the need for a more suitable place of worship, the old Chapel Barn was, about 1798, replaced by a small weather-boarded structure erected in a field adjoining what is now Market Street. Religious animosity of the time however caused the Meeting House to be burned down:

> . . . the work of an enemy opposed to the truths preached in the place . . .

but it was soon to be rebuilt.

Increasing support enabled the wooden Baptist chapel in c. 1830 to yet again be rebuilt and enlarged, making it possible for the pastor in 1839 to create a large classroom for boys at a time of almost total neglect in teaching for the poor. Finally in 1909, with the use of brick and stone, the structure was substantially enlarged and improved to become the chapel with its churchyard we know today. The porch of the chapel now stands exactly over the grave of the first pastor, a Francis Brown from Diss in Norfolk who long ago, had preached in the old Chapel Barn and married, soon after coming to Hailsham, the devout Mary Box. (*See* entry of 1741).

1792

The Gibraltar Tower was built in Heathfield Park as a monument to Lord Heathfield who had died two years earlier. It was as General George Elliot that this man, at the end of a long military career, defended and resisted a seige of Gibraltar from 1779 to 1783 by numerically, a vastly superior force of French and Spanish troops. It was a brilliant defensive campaign of four years and the reward was when General Elliot, whose home was Heathfield Park (bought from the Dacre family of Herstmonceux in 1766), was created Lord Heathfield of Gibraltar.

Many of the cannons defending Gibraltar were made by Fuller of Heathfield.

1792

Following many meetings involving, among others, the landowners and farmers between Hailsham and Lewes, there emerged a proposal that a canal be built from a tributary of the River Ouse in the Beddingham area, to Hellingly. Such a scheme would create, from the busy waters of the Ouse even as far away as Newhaven, a continuous waterway enabling shallow draught boats to make a journey inland as far as Hellingly.

There could be many advantages to those within reach of the waterway but in particular, it would be farmers needing to reach the mills at Horsebridge and Hellingly who would clearly benefit. There was the possibility of reliable transport with the avoidance of adverse road conditions, and on turnpike stretches, there was the saving of high toll charges incurred by teams of horses pulling heavily laden wagons.

A statement prepared on 3 September 1792 advised of a petition to be presented to the next session of Parliament. It spoke of a Bill to,

> ... improve the navigation of the Glynd River (now Glynde Reach) from the River Ouse to Hollebone's Bridge (now probably Beddingham Bridge at the foot of Mount. Caburn) ...

and the statement next explained the hope,

> ... to extend the said navigation through the several Parishes of Laughton, Ripe, Chalvington, Chiddingly, Arlington and Hellingly ...

The extended navigation referred to was by canal which in its final stages would cross Dicker Common and reach the River Cuckmere just north of Michelham Priory. The canal would then follow the level ground near the river to Horsebridge Mill then past Horselunges Manor and possibly on to the medieval mill at Hellingly.

From a survey to establish the land contours along the entire length of the proposed canal, a drawing was prepared entitled:

> ... Profile of the Landfall between Hellingly Mill and the South end of Ranscomb Brooks at the Verge of the River Ouse near Lewes ...

The highest land along the canal route was on Dicker Common where now stands 'The Mount', over one hundred feet above sea level. Also plotted was a draft map on which the course of the canal was drawn. Along the route on both banks the names of landowners and tenant farmers were written-in, no doubt with the question of compensation in mind against the disturbance of their farm land. A total of thirty-nine landowners were listed together with twenty-one tenant farmers.

Also on the draft map was shown a much smaller 'collateral cut' named the 'Selmeston Canal' starting at 'Edlee' (now renamed Headlee Bridge) on the 'Glynd' River. This short canal ended at the road from Selmeston to Lewes just north of Tilton and some six hundred yards west of the *Barley Mow* inn.

There can be little doubt that the research and planning for the building of both canals involved a great deal of expense and the time of many people among whom were major landowners: Lord Gage, Lord Pelham, Ellison of Glynde, Fuller of Boship and Calverley of Hellingly. The final decision however was that that project be abandoned.

It was in this year that the House of Commons required any planned public project such as a canal, to be surveyed and drawn on a plan for depositing with the clerk of the peace. (*See* entry of 1795).

c. 1793

A house in the simple style of the Georgian period was built with care for the Bristow family on a Hailsham corner site of ground rising away from two roads. To the front was George Street and to the side was a road that had become a turnpike in 1754. The house faced south and looked over isolated cottages and fields, gently losing height towards Pevensey Marsh beyond which, from the upper windows, could be seen the sea at Langney and Pevensey.

Standing away from the house at the rear were stables and a coach house with a yard allowing entry from the turnpike road (now North Street). This house of some prominence was for many years to be knows as 'Newhouse'. (*See* entry of 1881).

1794

Among the entries in the Hailsham parish Vestry Minute Book dealing with the poor were:

> ... Peter Bradford requested a load of wood but was refused on account of Selling
> Gin. Offer to lighten the Family by taking one Child into Workhouse ...
> ... to allow Widow Rich a little wood ...
> ... to allow Mrs. Brown one Handkerchief ...
> ... to allow Walter Carey one Quarter of Oats to fatten his Hog ...

In this year the harvest was exceptionally bad causing corn to double in price. With wide unemployment and low wages there was,

> ... extensive distress among the labouring class ...

Such was the poverty in some areas that there was a real threat of starvation and the demand on parishes to provide relief with food and clothing was very heavy.

1795

The map section of 1795 is from the one inch scale 'Topographical Map of Sussex' by W. G. Gardner, and T. Yeakel and completed by Thomas Gream. The map was plotted and drawn from triangulation surveys carried out by engineer officers of the government Board of Ordnance who normally worked with draughtsmen in the Drawing Room at the Tower of London.

This new map was sold as a large canvas-backed folding map fitting into a leather case and was considered at the time to be of an extremely high standard. Features of particular interest that have been indicated on the map by the writer are the turnpike road to (east) Bourne and the proposed canal that was intended to link Glynde Reach with the mills at Horsebridge and Hellingly.

In the area south and east of Hailsham, well-drawn contour shading served to emphasise the higher ground on which villages and houses of importance were built. Similarly, the indication of the low-lying ground north of Pevensey, in a darker tone, reveals how near to Hailsham was the water-fed marsh even after the action taken in 1748 to control flooding. (*See* appendix 'J'.)

1799

On a map of this time, there was in Lullington still an indication of dwellings south of what little remained of the church, for it had by now fallen into a ruined state.

Built *c.* 1180 one hundred and fifty feet above sea level, the church was enlarged *c.* 1350.

Lullington was one of the villages that suffered a severe loss of life during the Black Death plague and its slow decline from that time led to it eventually becoming a deserted village.

In such a village, nothing could save its church and so today only the chancel survives.

With the collapse of the old church a vast source of stone was created for as many who might feel the need to take it. Through the years, stone from the church ruin would be used for farm walls, barns, cottages and houses of the area, or wherever a horse could transport it.

c. 1800

1800

What appears to have been the first Post Office in Hailsham was in a shop in George Street where a glass pane of the shop window was removed to allow letters to be posted through the gap. The site of this shop is now occupied by the offices of the Sussex County Building Society. (The first Post Office in Eastbourne was in 1806).

c. 1800

The stone Market Cross, probably similar to that at Alfriston, which had stood in the Hailsham Market Square and been the centre of the town's life for many generations, was now considered cumbrous and an obstacle to the increasing movement of carts, coaches and waggons. For this reason the Cross was demolished and the Square made into a clear space.

Sussex
Pevensey Rape } towit

An Abstract of the several Persons Matters and
Parishes hereunder mentioned within the said Rap...

Parishes	No. of Persons bet. the Ages of 15 & 60 willing to serve in what Capacity		How they can Arm themselves				No. of Persons between the Ages of 15 & 60 willing to Act
			Cavalry		Infantry		
	On Horseback	On Foot	Swords	Pistols	Fire locks	Pikes	
Hailsham	3	10.	1	1	8	2	9
Hellingly	5	5	5	.	5	.	25
Chalvington	.	.	.	.	.	.	13
Ripe	.	2	.	.	2	.	23
Laughton	4	5	4	.	2	.	4
Eastgrinsted	64	133	20	28	70	2	60
Hartfield	1	.	.	.	.	.	77
Wythyham	7	16	.	.	3	.	52
Lindfield	16	22	8	9	21	6	60
Buxted	16	22	.	.	.	.	44
Framfield	20	57	10	16	43	14	10
Isfield	.	1	.	.	.	.	21
Uckfield	.	.	.	.	.	.	3
Mayfield	12	10	12	3	6	.	27
Wadhurst · No return							
Frant	2	.	1	1	.	.	4
Rotherfield	24	10	10	8	4	2	11
Fletching	25	20	4	5	9	.	77
Horstedkeynes	.	10	.	.	10	.	36
Littlehorsted	4	3	.	.	.	.	14
Maresfield	10	9	.	4	3	.	14
Chiddingly	4	4	2	4	2	1	4
Easthoathly	7	23	4	4	9	.	13
Waldron	13	40	2	2	34	11	35

*As a result of widespread enquiries this schedule provided information showing the various
weapons and implements held in villages and likely to be of use in the event of an invasion
by the French. Other schedules listed statistics equally useful in the event of an emergency.*

	Pick Axes	Spades	Shovels	Bill Hooks	Saws	Hedges	For any other Instrum the Pioneers may engage to bring		No of Persons between the Age of 15 & 60 willing to act as Drivers of Cattle	No of Persons between the ages of 15 & 60 willing to act as Drivers of Pack	No of Persons between the ages of 15 & 60 willing to act as drivers of ...of Feb not	No of D.º as Workmen or Bargemen
6	.	5	3	2	2	2	.	.	20	24	24	.
5	4	6	2	3	3	.	.	.	22	13	16	
4	5	3	.	.	3	.	.	.	6	9	11	.
10	1	.	2	.	3	.	.	.	0	7	16	..
3	1	.	.	.	.	.	.	.	35	40	10	
30	17	34	16	16	36	.	.	.	90	49	50	
48	14	18	12	1	2	.	.	.	49	25	30	
16	2	14	11	.	9	.	.	.	20	19	40	
24	0	17	6	4	8	.	.	.	38	21	31	
0	5	7	11	10	6	.	.	.	27	16	10	
17	11	12	11	6	13	.	.	.	23	10	19	
9	3	2	1	3	4	.	.	.	15	15	20	
	.	.	.	.	.	.	.	.	13	10	7	
0	14	1	.	.	2	.	.	.	67	45	37	
4	2	2	3	4	4	.	.	.	6	6	3	.
	.	4	.	4	.	.	.	.	17	23	20	.
1	14	16	15	3	10	.	.	.	37	25	24	.
4	.	12	2	7	7	.	.	.	43	33	.	2
	.	.	.	.	.	.	.	.	13	6	16	
7	6	1	.	.	11	.	.	.	17	19	14	
3	1	2	.	.	.	.	.	.	6	12	19	
3	5	3	.	.	3	.	.	.	0	0	11	.
3	29	37	20	9	29	.	.	.	24	19	16	.

1801

The first official census revealed:

Population of Hailsham   897
Population of Hellingly   936

The result of the census divided the population into male and female and attempted to place people into categories of agriculture, trade or manufacture and those without the previous occupations.

In addition to people, this census also included figures for houses, both inhabited and uninhabited. The resultant figures however produced widespread complications and proved in many cases to be unreliable.

1803

The prolonged state of war with France had now developed into a serious threat of invasion and determined steps were being taken to defend the south coast of England.

On the 7th and 8th days of July at the *Castle* inn in Brighthelmstone (Brighton), a meeting was held,

> ... of the lieutenancy of the County of Sussex ... headed by the Duke of Richmond with Lords, Baronets, Knights and 28 Esquires ... to enable His Majesty more effectively to provide for the Defence and Security of the Realm during his present War ...

In a long and detailed report from the gathering it was said:

> ... we trust that no circumstance can arise which would induce His Majesty to carry into execution so devastating a measure as to burn and destroy some of the Richest Provinces in England ... it is not by ourselves making a Desert of our own Country that an Enemy will be stopped, but by our Army backed with the Energy and Spirit with which every individual will to a man arise in Arms on Actual Invasion ...

A decision of this crucial meeting was an immediate and detailed survey of the County to produce statistics vital in the emerging defence plans. From the Rape of Pevensey the following three schedules were among several drawn up to provide the military with every aspect of local information that could assist them.

Schedule No. 1, dealt with animals and indicated in complete detail against every parish, the types and numbers that needed to be driven away from an invading enemy. The many entries against Hailsham included one hundred and fifty oxen, two thousand one hundred and fourteen sheep, one hundred and thirty-six cows, ninety-one horses and eighty waggons and carts.

In Schedule No. 2, six columns listed countrymen between the ages of fifteen and sixty who were separated into groups best suited for the removal of different types of cattle.

The 3rd Schedule was a detailed report showing the numbers of local men available to assist the army in defence. It also listed every possible weapon in the parishes including Hailsham, that could be put to use against the enemy.

1803

Hailsham Barracks were built to house some of the troops that were quartered in strategic areas along the south coast, as a defence against the threatened invasion. It was in 1804 that Captain Philip Van Cortlandt was posted to Hailsham to be barrack master.

The barracks were built on that part of the old Hailsham Common bounded on the north and west by what are now London Road and Summerheath Road, and the large triangular shaped barrack area was lined along each side by long wooden huts leaving a central parade ground.

To meet the needs of the soldiers an agreement was made between William Stevens of Berwick, John Worger of Alfriston and Isaac Clapson a gentleman:

> ... to erect a temporary building for the sale of beer for the use of the barracks on Hailsham common ...

With the barracks likely to be active for many years the perhaps inevitable step meant the building of the aptly named *Grenadier* inn (now hotel) on the edge of the barrack area.

The constant troop movements along the south coast meant that Hailsham saw many different red coated regiments march in and out of the town and for some years the soldiers considerably outnumbered people in Hailsham as indeed they did in Alfriston. In 1815 with the Duke of Wellington victorious against the French the soldiers finally left and the barracks closed. Hailsham sorely missed the transient if hectic prosperity the army had brought to the town.

1803

With local unemployment high and parish relief scarcely able to help, many of the poor were in a desperate condition. It was a time of hardship and great discontent among the poor.

With the need to act, the vestry approved a plan to repair the workhouse in Market Square (part of it is now the timbered shop opposite the entrance to Vicarage Lane) and agreed on changes to improve the working conditions of the inmates. Increased attempts were being made to provide work and the success in the past of flax spinning, prompted the actual purchase of land by the parish especially to grow flax.

One of the occupations for able bodied male inmates was helping in the building of cobble or boulder walls and this would mean several men pulling a hand cart to the coast at Langney, loading it with large stones from the beach and returning to Hailsham. It was a heavy and unpopular task that on occasions led to trouble and even violence, but it did enable boulder walls to be built in the town as for instance, the nine feet high and forty yards long wall in Stoney Lane leading from the Market Square. This wall was part of the original workhouse property and it is still in very good condition.

The collecting and carting back to Hailsham of 'beach' was hard, and carried out regardless of weather with very little reward as the Labour Book of the time revealed. As with other books for record keeping, the Labour Book was hand-made of uneven pages with its paper covers cut from old printed notices.

1804

In the early weeks of this year the first regiments of soldiers marched into the barely completed Hailsham barracks and during the first twelve months the following deaths were recorded in the register of the Parish Church:

27 Feb. burial of Pte. James Wiltshire, R.A.
28 Mar. burial of Pte. William Morgan, Glamorgan Militia
 8 April burial of Sgt. Lancelot Lancelot, Glamorgan Militia
 8 June burial of Pte. William Hunt, 8th Regiment of Foot
25 July burial of Sgt. John Beaver, 8th Regiment of Foot
 2 Aug. burial of Elizabeth, daughter of John Webb, soldier
 2 Sept. burial of Pte. John Salsbury, 23rd Regiment of Foot
23 Nov. burial of Ann, daughter of John Golden, 29th Regiment of Foot
27 Nov. burial of Ellen, daughter of James Locklin, 29th Regiment of Foot
23 Dec. burial of John, son of Thomas Marchant, 29th Regiment of Foot
28 Dec. burial of William Wiseman, 48th Regiment of Foot

1804

On the morning of Saturday 26th August the Commander in Chief, H.R.H. the Duke of York, attended at Hailsham Barracks where he inspected the Royal South Gloucester Militia under the command of the Earl of Berkeley. A few days later this regiment marched away to new quarters at Brighton.

At this time there was a constant movement of troops between the barracks of Hailsham, Eastbourne, Pevensey, Bexhill, Hastings, Battle, Steyning, Brighton, Ringmer, Seaford and those overlooking the sea each side of the river Cuckmere, mainly with the object of keeping the soldiers fit, alert and fully occupied.

1804

In the *Sussex Weekly Advertiser*, an advertisement read:

. . .   William Wildish
                           of the *White Hart* Inn, Lewes
Takes the liberty of informing the Nobility and Gentry that he has for the better accommodation of the Public sent two Post Chaises with able horses and careful drivers to the *Crown* Inn, Hailsham and all those who will favour him with their commands may depend on having the same Chaise from Hailsham through Lewes, with fresh horses at the *White Hart* to Cuckfield or Brighton without changing luggage and the same from the *White Hart*, Lewes to Hailsham and forward to East-Bourne, Battle or Hastings . . .

1804

On 31st December, Mr. Rickman was returning from the market at Lewes to his home at Hellingly Park when he was dragged down from his single horse chaise, severely beaten and his pockets rifled.

1804

At a meeting of the Hailsham Vestry on 7th May it was after discussion agreed that,

... it appears necessary at this meeting to erect a Gallery at the West end of the Church; the materials of the Singing Seats to be made use of which is agreed ...

To defray the expense involved in other church repairs and the erection of the new gallery it was agreed, '... to have a church rate of 12/- in the pound ...'. It is of interest to reflect upon the mental discipline towards economy and conserving public money practised by the vestry. Such bodies, invariably all male, were incidentally of people from a social strata that formed the backbone of ratepayers.

The Vestry Minute Book from which this entry was taken was hand-made and very crude with covers of thick coarse paper and pages unlined and having irregular edges sewn together somewhat loosely. No particular talent appears evident in this thin, limp hand-made book but it was certainly put to official use and proved adequate. The book was used for many years and the records can be seen today in the faded brown ink, but it has nevertheless survived one hundred and eighty years in good condition.

1805

The immensely popular sport of bare knuckle fighting, notorious for its boisterous followers and their heavy betting, was against the law and contests arranged by affluent supporters were always in safe country areas away from disapproving eyes:

... upon such illegal riotous assembly which be a breach of the peace ... seek the detection and punishment of all persons ...

An important contest between John Gulley and Henry Pearce was arranged to take place,

... in the village of Hailsham near Lewes ... on a green adjoining the village at one oclock on 8th October ...

John Gulley at twenty-two years had been in Bristol prison for debts before they were paid off to allow his release and journey to Hailsham. It was an occasion that drew many people from Brighton and London both on horseback and in carriages of every description and among the spectators were the Duke of Clarence, later to be William IV, and Beau Brummell.

The fight lasted sixty-four rounds when Gully was defeated but the exciting contest had enhanced his reputation. With a Captain Robert Barclay as his patron (friend of former Prime Minister William Pitt the younger), Gulley went on to become champion of England.

Other prize fights took place in Hailsham, one of which was between the famous Tom Cribb and

... Bill Richmond, a man of colour from America ...

in whom the Duke of Cumberland was interested.

1805

Martello Towers were being built along the south coast as a defence against the threatened attack by the French. The towers were at their most effective at

Pevensey Bay where an enemy ship could it is said, be within the range of guns from fifteen towers at one time.

The circular towers were considered impregnable, being up to thirteen feet thick towards the sea and five feet facing inland with fifty-thousand bricks being used on a single course. After tests with cannon balls carried out by the Royal Engineers at Woolwich it was decided to set the brickwork in what became known as hot lime mortar, a mixture of lime, ash and hot tallow which it was said, set as hard as iron.

So great became the number of soldiers in barracks, billets and encampments behind the Sussex coast that even large barns were converted for the use of troops and cavalry. The expectancy of an attempted invasion by the French was great and a constant state of alert was maintained with incessant training, artillery practice, and '. . . sham fights . . .' between regiments.

To strengthen the defences at Pevensey, the sluice outlet was repaired and improved to ensure that if the enemy landed,

> . . . the level will be immediately inundated and they will have to content with fire and water . . .

Some sixty years on, when the martello towers had long outlived their useful life, the four towers east of Eastbourne Redoubt were used for artillery target practice by guns of a new design. It is recorded that the towers withstood considerable firepower.

1806

A deed of 30th August was concerned with the sale of No. 4 George Street in Hailsham. Previously occupied by C. Elphick, saddler and collar maker, and John Curl, plumber and glazier, it now passed into the hands of Isaac Clapson, Gentleman.

This small property together with the adjoining No. 6 was once in the past named the 'Crown Inn' with heavy oak beams and areas of stonework. But its postal and legal address of George Street was somewhat misleading, for the site was in fact mere yards from both the old market cross and the town's ancient parish church; even more important, it was at the precise intersection of four roads into the town, two of which were once old tracks down to the inland waters behind Pevensey. This significant place was, and is still called Hailsham's Market Square and the property being sold was long ago part of the 'Crown Inn', an inn which quite simply was at the very centre of Hailsham life.

The closure of the inn, possibly about 1770, was probably when it underwent structural alterations resulting in it becoming two separate shops. One of the shops, for many years the grocery business of the Ellis family, was demolished in 1974 to provide an extension to the National Westminster Bank.

It was the act of demolition that confirmed the old 'Crown Inn' as a past hostelry of great age, for surviving from centuries ago was a fireplace with an oak bressummer beam across its opening into which had been burnt a design in the shape of a crown. Even more impressive were the areas with beams and stonework that clearly dated from the distant past for the type of stone used was identical to the stone of the nearby parish church and for both buildings it had come from the old quarry at (east) Bourne.

There was also a substantial stone opening with a low pointed arch long ago bricked up; but more important was the crucial part of the old inn, a second vast open fireplace where a huge fire would have cooked the meals for countless market days.

The age of such stonework cannot accurately be traced but bearing in mind it was from a quarry of great age and when transported to Hailsham, possibly by water, it was built into low pointed arches of the 16th century, there is little doubt there was a 'Crown Inn' facing the market square in the reign of Queen Elizabeth I.

Due to the initiative of Maurice Thornton, a Hailsham man with knowledge of this old fireplace, its heavy stones were rescued at the demolition and are now stored at Michelham Priory awaiting reconstruction by the Sussex Archaeological Society.

1806-1825

This was the main period in the output of terracotta plaques cast from local clay by Jonathan Harmer. He lived and worked in Clappers Wood by the river Cuckmere near Vines Cross.

Harmer's work, much of it charming, was based on classical architectural designs but quite often arrangements of flowers were also featured in a manner which suited the Georgian and Regency periods. The terracotta was made by pressing the fine clay found in the Horam-Heathfield area into a mould then baking the cast plaque in an oven.

Jonathan Harmer died in 1849 at the age of eighty-six and examples of his work, in the distinctive reddish brown colour of the clay he used, can be seen in the churchyards of Chiddingly, East Hoathly, Glynde, Hailsham, Heathfield, Hellingly, Herstmonceux, Mayfield, Warbleton and Wartling.

In the course of time Harmer's work has earned great respect and his designs have been made available in a published form. A collection of his terracotta plaques together with moulds can be seen in the Museum of Local History at Anne of Cleves House in Lewes.

1806

There can surely be little doubt that an entry of baptism in the Hailsham parish church register on 25th May was not unconnected with a flight from France of a Baron and Baroness.

... Philip Cato Henry Charles Leander, son of John Charles, Baron de Glen and Ann Christiana Juliane Antonie, Baroness de Schmit.

Unlike other entries at this time the date of birth was not written in the register.

1807

The rope making activity to become Burfield and Son of Hailsham was founded by Thomas Burfield at the age of twenty-two years. One of his rope-walks was situated behind a medieval timbered cottage in the High Street and next to the busy *Crown* inn (known in previous years as the *Crowne* Alehouse). Opposite was a narrow pathway between two shops leading into Hailsham's parish church-yard. With the burning down of a gun shop next to this path (*see* entry of 1894) a space became available which in time was used for the erection of the wrought iron gates in memory of Queen Victoria.

It is probable that the timbered cottage with a wide brick paved side entrance was owned by Burfield for by 1900 it had been used as a saddler's shop for many years. In 1956 the very old saddler's business still existed but was known by the name 'Larkin'. It was in this year that the shop was demolished and together with the land at the rear, where once was a rope-walk, it provided the site for the store 'Woolworth'.

Rope-making about 1800 was largely confined to long narrow rope-walks sited about the town, each usually with a small hut for the storage of materials and winding gear.

The rope-walks were an essential in enabling the rope maker to walk while feeding in fibre to spin yarns, these were then twisted into strands before laying the strands into a long rope. A vital part of this work was usually a young lad known as a 'spinnerboy' who turned a wheel at the end of the rope-walk to 'take up' the yarn as it came from the spinner.

Probably the oldest rope-walk in the town was by the road (now South Road) leading south-west out of Hailsham. On the site of this old rope-walk now stands the factory of Burfield and Son.

1808

A new Act gave power to Justices in Quarter Sessions to order that county asylums be built in which lunatics could be lodged. A further Act of but seven years later made parish overseers responsible for advising the Quarter Sessions of these pauper lunatics in their parish, for there was now concern about their care.

1808

Two soldiers of the Berkshire Militia stationed at Hailsham Barracks were charged before a magistrate with having attacked a young man by the name of Sands. The attack was denied.

The incident was alleged to have occurred near Herstmonceux when Sands was walking home from Broomham Wood where he had been working when two soldiers stopped him:

> ...strongly importuned him to enlist, which he peremptorily refused to do, and persisted in his resolution, until they at length forced him down and for his refusal, punished him with castration...

Every effort was made in the magistrate's Court to seek the true facts but the guilt of the soldiers could not be proved.

c. 1812

An improvement in postal communication was apparent due to private coaching beginning to operate along shorter journeys.

The route from London by mail coach was through East Grinstead and on to Uckfield where a daily ride was made to Hailsham by horse post, unless part of the road was impassable. At this time there were one hundred and thirty-five houses in Hailsham.

In 1816 a petition from Pevensey for a mail delivery was rejected for it was said that less than thirty letters and packets were sent there each week. Thus the Pevensey mail continued to be collected from Hailsham.

There was also a horse post from Lewes but winter conditions could still prevent the horses getting through. Even the road between Horsebridge and Hailsham caused serious trouble in bad weather and 'Hailshamers' were warned that unless the road was made good, their mail would stop at Horsebridge.

1813

Josiah Pitcher was born to grow up and farm with his father at Priesthawes Farm and on the death of his father he took over the farm's management. Josiah's interest and knowledge increased and led to him taking up the breeding of Sussex cattle at which he was very successful.

A first prize with a Sussex Bull at the Royal Agricultural Society Show at Lewes in 1852 was the beginning of a career which saw him consistently win at County, then National shows, and finally in Paris. Josiah went on to become a famous judge of any cattle in almost any breed, officiating at Smithfield and all over England for the Royal Agricultural Society.

In 1883 he died while living at South Lawns almost opposite the cattle market in Market Street, Hailsham. This old house is now called The Manor House and over the side entrance door is a stone panel Josiah had erected many years ago on which was carved a jar or pitcher with a capital 'P'.

1813

Mark Antony Lower recalled:

> ... I was born in the obscure agricultural village of Chiddingly in the Weald of Sussex on 14th July 1813 ... I learnt music and drawing so early, that I cannot remember my first lessons in either science. I have not the slightest recollection of the hours when I learnt my gamut (*see* note below), and a certain facility in sketching from nature. This I recollect, that I was a tolerable proficient on the flute, and a sketcher, before I was seven years old ... *Note:* The gamut is the 'great scale' of seven hexachords consisting of all the recognized notes used in medieval music.

Lower was the youngest of six sons, four of whom died in infancy and at the age of seventeen years he became an assistant to his sister who opened a school in East Hoathly. Later he established his own school at Cade Street, Heathfield. After a period of living and teaching in Alfriston he finally moved to Lewes where he once again had a small but successful school of undoubted quality.

It was appropriate for him to live in this historic town for he became an important figure in the Sussex Archaeological Society and, in later years, was famous in Sussex for his research and writing on county history to which he sometimes added his own illustrations. Lower also became known for his work in the fields of dialect and poetry. He died in 1876.

1814

The Emperor of Russia and the King of Prussia with their Empresses accompanied by an armed escort halted and rested at Amberstone Grange, Magham Down where the Quakers, Nathaniel and Mary Rickman, lived. The royal party was on its way from Portsmouth to Dover.

1814

In May, the American loyalist Colonel Philip Van Cortlandt died at 'Newhouse' in George Street, Hailsham in his seventy-fourth year. This fifth generation American-born officer of Dutch descent had displayed both strength and integrity in his decision to fight his fellow countrymen as a loyalist in the American War of Independence. The decision was to cause him great hardship and personal loss.

Philip was buried in his martial robe inside Hailsham parish church, where a memorial tablet of stone and marble on the north wall near his place of burial, reflects the degree of respect in which he was held. The last line on the tablet being:

> The memory of the just is blessed.

The last Will and Testament of Philip Van Cortlandt was dated 30th April, mere days before his death. In it he revealed a great concern for his . . . beloved wife Catharine . . . and seemingly was without regret at the decision that changed his life.

> . . . my body to be interred at the directions of my surviving friends without any unnecessary show or expense, the small portion of property remaining from the wreck occasioned by the American Revolution (at which period I took an active and zealous part in favour of my King and the British Constitution) I dispose of as follows . . .

A few months after her father's death his youngest daughter Sophia married Captain W. H. Mulcaster, R.N., who in later life was to become Sir William, Sword Aide-de-Camp to King George III. Philip's wife Catharine was aged eighty-two when she died in Torquay, Devon. (*See* entry of 1775).

1814

Francis Howlett was a churchwarden and among other of his duties in Hailsham was that of vestry clerk, tax collector, postmaster and an overseer of the poor. In later years he was also to become the town's first schoolmaster when the schoolroom was the church vestry and the churchyard was the playground. It was all inadequate but it was a beginning that at least faced up to the problem of children in need of education.

... the old vestry ... a poor, miserable, cold, dingy place was the schoolroom for
the parish and for children of both sexes ... and at the northern base of the tower
stood the office for all, the drainage running off into a ditch almost close to the
church wall and passing the doorway until the moisture became absorbed by the
earth in the journey onward ...

The schoolroom was closed in 1827 when the 'Free School', paid for by voluntary contributions was built south of the town near the edge of Hailsham Common. Francis Howlett died aged eighty in 1831 and a white painted wooden
grave-board can still be seen in the churchyard over his grave.

1815

An official complaint was made out by Francis Howlett, an overseer of the poor,
who recorded that,

... Francis Foster of the parish of Hailsham, a labourer, being a poor person and
able to work spends his money in Alehouses and does not apply a proper proportion of the money earned by him towards the maintenance of his wife by which
wilful neglect and default he hath permitted her to become chargeable to the
parish ... whereupon this informant prays that the said Francis Foster may be
punished as an idle and disorderly person ...

1815

The Battle of Waterloo was won.

At this time, agriculture in East Sussex was in a distressed state. Many years of
war had seriously affected the economy and with victory, came men back from
the war to rural areas where affairs of the nation had slowly created appalling
conditions.

Born at Firle into a farming family Edward Boys Ellman, a son of the illus-
trious John Ellman (*see* entry of 1753), grew up knowing the suffering of men,
women and children in the surrounding areas of which Hailsham parish was one.
Edward was destined to be vicar of Berwick for sixty-six years and his latter day
book *Recollections of a Sussex Parson*, recorded in its final chapter a comment
by his daughter:

... during the long war prices of everything had gone up terribly. The country was
impoverished. Corn was at almost famine prices. Labour was so cheap and plentiful
that even men in full and regular work could hardly support their wives and families
upon the poorest of food, and often and often they starved to death ... starving
caused much extra crime which was harshly and cruelly dealt with ... to save their
children from starvation men stole sheep, field turnips or anything eatable, and
when caught were condemned to death or transportation for life ...

The Reverend Edward Boys Ellman died in 1906.

1815

The *Market Cross* Inn of Alfriston was sold to James Collins a butcher of
Chiddingly who eight years later, passed it on to his son. In due course, the son,
Stanton Collins, became deeply involved in smuggling and proved to be leader of
the Alfriston Gang with its headquarters at his inn, the *Market Cross*. After

operating for some years, often using the nearby river and Cuckmere Haven, the gang lost Collins when he was arrested, it is said, for sheep stealing and sentenced to seven years transportation.

1816

Thomas White was the grocer in Market Square who lived with his family next to the shop in the house called 'Sheriff Place'.

The shop supplied many things and traded with people from villages around Hailsham. It distributed stamps and issued licences for much of East Sussex covering guns, horses, dogs, servants, hawkers and pedlars.

The business had a considerable local fame and used on its premises a malt mill, salt mill and pepper mill. Through the years the shop passed from Thomas White to Daniel, then to Reginald and finally Harry who sold the house and business and retired in 1946.

The original part of Thomas White's property was Tudor, but rebuilt *c.* 1710 it can be seen today with the shop now a chemist's business. Little has changed and the house still has its modest but charming entrance doorway with wood panelling to the sides and curved arch above. This doorway facing the Market Square is now the entrance to 'Sheriff Dry Cleaners'. (*See* entry of 1956).

1817

Willingdon Windmill was built on a site a few yards from the parish boundary. In 1939, a change in the boundary line found the mill in the next parish; thus it is now known as Polegate Tower Windmill. (*See* appendix 'K').

1818

The Vestry was in early times always a church body, but gradually over the years it assumed a wider responsibility towards the people and became the preserve in many ways of the wealthy and influential. Landowners, a group always heavily taxed to pay for poor relief, usually had a strong voice and in the 1818 Sturges Bourne Act, parliament recognised this burden and on a scale in proportion to their tax assessment, they were given corresponding extra votes.

Formerly, members of a vestry were ratepayers at a substantial level and there were occasions in Hailsham, when a member's personal circumstances fell below a certain minimum level, he was required to relinquish his position as a member of the vestry and be replaced.

It was of little surprise that vestries could in small communities exercise almost a complete control, leading on occasions to abuse. Certainly vestry efficiency varied from place to place. The Vestries Act of 1831, although primarily intended for towns, did slowly introduce a more balanced selection of members and towards the end of the 19th cent. a certain amount of democracy was beginning to appear in public affairs.

Over many years vestry meetings were held in several different premises throughout the town including: the south chapel of Hailsham church, the *King's Head* inn at Cacklebury, *George* inn, *Crown* inn, Terminus Hotel and the Infants'

School, until finally a special Vestry Room was built above the first fire station in Market Street. (*See* entry of 1889).

1821

The famous artist, Samuel Palmer, painted a landscape called 'Storm over Hailsham'. The picture is a watercolour painted from the outskirts of the town, and to capture the mood of the heavily overcast scene the fields and storm clouds are all vigorously painted in tones of dark grey. A small area of blue suggests water on a foreground field but the picture comes remarkably to life when small touches of bright green on the otherwise dark fields indicate where light has penetrated the storm clouds. The buildings of Hailsham in the distance are shown in tones of brown.

It is a vigorous picture of some value and on the back are several pencil-written notes concerning the scene. It is now part of a collection given by Paul Mellon to his 'Yale Centre for British Art' at Yale University in Connecticut, U.S.A.

1823

A letter of 17th December addressed to,

> . . . the Churchwardens and overseers of the Poor of the Parish of Hailsham . . .

from Samuel Flint, a landowner of the parish, laid down his strong objections to the billeting by the overseers of,

> . . . labourers being Paupers of the said Parish upon certain Occupiers of land therein without their consent to be employed by them and in some instances where such Occupiers have no employment for such labourers . . .

In this case, and in a winter month, the landowner had been sent men from the workhouse for whom he had no use. They were sent with the expectation that he would find them a day's work, but in fact, it was not unusual for a farmer to dismiss many if not all his labourers in October should he no longer need them through the winter.

The pauper sent from the workhouse, took with him a printed ticket upon which was quoted, the number of days work to be provided. Work would be from 7 a.m. to 6 p.m. and the rate often 8d. per day, at the end of which the farmer would collect the work tickets and deduct their value when he paid his poor rate.

At this time, there was discussion concerning food served in the workhouse, and within the limits that could be afforded a '. . . weekly bill of fare . . .' intended to be regarded as typical was drawn up to allow for three meals each day. It was likely that the food given in seven days would be the same in the next seven days, but even for a man or woman to eat regularly was a godsend.

Breakfast was always either gruel or porridge with milk; the midday dinners on each of seven days were: Sunday, boiled beef or pork; Monday, pease soup (made of the preceding day's liquor and one pound of fresh beef to four quarts of liquor); Tuesday, beef pudding; Wednesday, boiled beef; Thursday, as Monday; Friday, meat pudding and on Saturday there was Irish stew. With these main meals there was an insistence that bread and 'proper' vegetables should be available.

Supper alternated from day to day with either milk porridge or bread and cheese and measures of beer were given to both adults and children. The food was plain, wholesome and monotonous but without question, it saved life.

1825

On a list of men in the parish of Hailsham called for a period of duty with the Militia were the names:

> No. 15 — Thomas Burfield Snr.
> Aged 40, a harness maker. He appealed against the duty but was not exempted.
>
> No. 65 — George Green.
> Aged 27, a rope maker. He found a substitute willing to be paid to do the duty and was exempted. At this time George Green was employed by Thomas Burfield.

The National Militia was created by Charles II and in each year up to four periods of training and one general muster were held.

Each man on the militia return was accorded a number and in the event of men being required, small numbered slips of paper were used from which were drawn the numbers of however many men were needed.

The Hailsham parish militia list of this time revealed the names of one hundred and ninety-two men between the ages of eighteen and forty-five of whom ninety-five were ruled exempt. The main occupation was that of labourer but also listed were: wheelwright, cooper, miller, shoemaker, sweep, glover, ostler, surgeon, tailor, blacksmith and pedlar.

c. 1825

The Hailsham Petty Sessions at which sat two magistrates, were still mainly held in the confined space of two upper rooms at the George Hotel.

1826

Late on a February night a single horse chaise was after a day at Hailsham market, taking Mr. James Pagen a farmer, home to Willingdon when it was attacked by three footpads on the narrow and lonely Hailsham to Polegate road.

A fight ensued with the armed farmer and his driver, and the three men were driven off and afterwards traced, imprisoned, and sentenced at Horsham Assizes to transportation to Botany Bay. The footpads all the knew the road well having once lived in Hailsham.

1827

Thomas Gooche, a man from Norfolk, settled in Hailsham and at the old Brewery in Brewery Road (the premises are now part of Apaseal Ltd. in the re-named Battle Road), he brewed 'Gooche's Strong Beer'. This Hailsham beer was widely known and John Hollamby wrote of it:

> The foreigners they praise their wines
> (tis only to deceive us)
> Would they come here and taste this beer
> I'm sure they never leave us.
> (*See* appendix 'M').

1828

A simple paper book of blank pages, some of which had been hand ruled, was used to record details of 'Christmas Beef' issued to the '. . . poor and needy . . .' persons of Hailsham parish.

In a column following the name of the person in need and the number in family, was the place of abode, and among the areas written-in without further detail were: Summer Heath, Cold Thorn, Carters Corner, Highlands, Otham Quarter, Marshfoot, Stone Lane, Barrack Ground, Cacklebury, Town, Sandbanks, Harebeating, Starve Crow, Common and 'near the Chaple'.

Seldom was there an entry of a single person or of a childless couple but most were of families with children. With a beef allowance of 2 lbs. for each person, a total of 968 lbs. of meat was distributed to one hundred and seventy-one families.

By this time, with many farms in poor condition, the agricultural labourer of East Sussex, in contrast to the west, had suffered many years of acute poverty bordering on starvation.

Of the casual employment now being found for able-bodied men from work-houses, was work on road repairs. It is known that in places, poor roads were much improved by this hard relief work.

1829

After centuries of religious danger, prejudice, hostility and fear, there was still a reluctance felt by the Establishment to,

> . . . give privileges to people owing allegiance to a foreign power and frankly hostile to the Anglican Church . . . but in spite of the dangers, public opinion became increasingly in favour of emancipation . . .

In this year, with public support, the Catholic Emancipation Act was passed allowing Catholics to become Members of Parliament.

1830

George Green, a rope maker, left the employment of Thomas Burfield following a disagreement.

At this time Thomas Burfield had been established for many years as a maker of rope and controlled many rope-walks in and south of the town on Hailsham Common. Apart from rope, his products also involved canvas and leather for they were used in farming and in particular with horses.

George Green began to work for himself and was later to have a rope-walk of over one hundred and fifty yards, sited along the hedge line of a long narrow field, previously the boundary of the old barrack area. George Green's business grew and from the simple wooden shelters and buildings of the early years, it slowly developed into the complex factory known today as Green Brothers Ltd. in Summerheath Road.

The site of today's factory is precisely on the ground of the original rope-walk.

1830

FIRES AT BERWICK

... great excitement in consequence of the fire last night ... these horrible affairs of nightly occurence, no one can detect the perpetrators ... most likely to be the peasantry who for years have been ground down. Patrols established and special constables appointed ... another five at Berwick and public fearful at alarming state of things and yet the landlords will not call the farmers together to make arrangements to pay peasantry in adequate manner ...

This extract from the journal of Gideon Mantell the surgeon and humanist describes the feeling behind acts of arson at Berwick. These incidents however were typical of what during the period of August 1830 and September 1832 was repeatedly happening in the parish of Hailsham and all over East Sussex, due to the intense anger and desperation of farm workers who for far too long had been underpaid in a time of terrible unemployment.

The troubles in agriculture were felt in nearly every county for when the Battle of Waterloo ended the Napoleonic Wars, vast numbers of soldiers were released to find work. This was at a time when simple farm machinery was beginning to be used thus reducing the need for man-power still further.

Steadily, unrest built up and local riots were sparked off with acts of machine smashing, particularly where there was a thresher.

In East Sussex scarcely a village failed to witness the bold gangs of workers who concentrated at night on burning ricks and even barns. Sometimes a crude and threatening letter would be sent to a farmer signed by a Captain Swing, probably a mythical figure which nevertheless gave the letter a substance that was nearly always followed by destruction. This troubled period came to be known as a time of the 'Swing Riots'.

On all sides of Hailsham there was arson and riotous meetings in protest against low wages and even gatherings at the houses of landowners and rectors demanding money or food. One such gathering reported in the *Morning Chronicle* of 23rd November 1830 at 'The Broad' (now Broad Farm) at Hellingly involved Lord Chichester. Dealing with a noisy mixed gathering protesting for more money,

... he separated the Hellingly men from the assembled mob and invited them into the farmyard ...

A discussion followed and the result was a rise in wages.

... the unruly gathering still outside the farm refused to leave and only when Lord Chichester sent for troops from Battle did the mob disperse ...

The prolonged intensity of feeling and the violence that it produced brought a fear to farmers, landowners and townspeople who were shocked and for the first time became aware of the strength of frustrated workers intent on forcing justice.

There was on occasions a sympathy from farmers for they too were known to join protest meetings when a general outcry against crippling tithes was made. Even now the payment of tithes to the church still amount to 10 per cent. of produce and stock or its equivalent in money, and this was in addition to heavy taxation.

After two years of unrest and suffering when the courts did not hesitate to inflict the most savage punishments, over four hundred and eighty men, women and even children were transported, and a total of nineteen men and boys were hanged of whom sixteen died for rick burning.

Although improvements in living conditions were sadly small, a great awareness was now felt and even parliament was moved to take notice. There can be little doubt that the Acts that followed in 1834 and 1836 were influenced by more realistic thinking.

c. 1830

A man of these hard times who knew Selmeston and understood how men could sometimes earn a reward, has written:

> ... when smuggling was carried on in these parts the 'free-traders' had a rendez-vous in the churchyard. An old altar-tomb served as their temporary storehouse. By lifting the encumbent stone they could safely deposit their goods and it is said they never failed to leave a 'tub' or two for the parson! I have this anedcote on good clerical authority ... (Mark Antony Lower M.A. 1870).

1831

In June, with great expectation, the installation took place of John Sterling as a curate at Herstmonceux parish church. The son of a Scottish farmer, he was acknowledged as a brilliant intellectual.

A writer and traveller of outstanding character, he chose to enter the church but was curate for only eight months before deciding that his entry into the church had been a mistake.

> ... cheerful and rapid in thought, word and action ... his visit had been like a shower of rain bringing down freshness and brightness on a dusty roadside hedge ...

Thomas Carlisle in his biography of John Sterling also wrote:

> ... there are many poor people at Herstmonceux who affectionately remember him ... a poor cobbler now advanced to a much better position, who gratefully ascribes this outward and other improvements in his life to Sterling's generous encouragement and charitable care for him ...

Never a robust man, John Sterling died aged 38 years just twelve years after leaving Herstmonceux and the church.

1831

The census of this year, following others in 1801, 1811 and 1821, emphasised a need to record the numbers of men in different occupations. Those listed were:

> ... agriculture, manufacture, retail trade and handicrafts, capitalists, bankers and professional men, industrial labourers of all types, servants and 'all others' ...

In this census it was recorded that 1,445 people lived in the Hailsham area contrasting with 1,504 listed against Hellingly. The higher population figures in the areas north of Hailsham are probably due to the effects of the former prosperity enjoyed by the iron industry.

Whereas, It is in contemplation to raise a sum of Money not exceeding £500 for the purpose of sending Labourers to America belonging to the Parish of Hailsham, & as it propos'd to raise the sum requir'd either on the Parish rates, should a Law be so enacted otherwise by the aid of the Principal Landed Proprietors either by their advancing the money or being security for it — We the undersigned Occupiers of Land & Houses pledge Ourselves so long as we remain rateable to the Parish to liquidate yearly from the Poor rate 'till the whole is paid off, so much of the debt as the Paupers would have stood the Parish in annually had they remain'd at Home, taking the expenditure of each for the year previous to their departure as the Sum to be paid off ———

An agreement in which certain men of Hailsham pledge themselves to lend sums of money for pauper families to emigrate to America (see entry of 1832)

Not until 1851 did the population of Hailsham (1,825) exceed that of Hellingly (1,761). (*See* appendix 'L'.)

1832

To relieve the increasing burden of the Poor Rate caused by widespread unemployment, a vestry decision was reflected by a document in which the 'Principal Landed Proprietors' of the parish would raise or be security for a sum not exceeding £500 to pay for thirty-two families of the parish to be sent to America.

> . . . We the undersigned Occupiers of Land and Houses pledge Ourselves so long as we remain rateable to the Parish to liquidate yearly from the Poor Rate 'till the whole is paid off, so much of the debt as the Paupers would have stood the Parish in annually had they remained at Home, taking the expenditure of each for year previous to their departure as the sum to be paid off . . .

It was calculated that if the thirty-two families would agree to emigrate, then the ratepayer signatories to the agreement would in time each recover their outlay by being paid yearly, an amount from the poor rate that would otherwise have been paid out to the pauper families until the total of £500 was repaid. From then on the burden of these families would no longer exist in Hailsham.

Just eleven years later in 1843 the sum of one hundred pounds was borrowed by the churchwardens and overseers of Arlington to pay the expenses '. . . of poor persons being willing to emigrate . . . '. (*See* entry of 1834).

1832

In this year a fundamental change was introduced into the manner vestry meetings were conducted. From now, all ratepayers in a village were not only able to attend, but more important they were able to vote on the affairs of their community. Hitherto, members of a vestry had almost exclusively been confined to those with influence through the possession of wealth; exceptions to this tendency were inclined to be rare.

1832

Julius Charles Hare became rector of Herstmonceux and later, the Archdeacon of Lewes. He was to be acknowledged as a writer and man of letters.

> . . . I once heard him preach in (Hailsham) our own parish church what I considered to be a very dull sermon — prosy, long winded. Little did I ween I was listening to a man who would one day become famous in the world of letters . . .
>
> Thomas Geering

Among the poets and writers who stayed with Julius Hare at Herstmonceux were: William Wordsworth, Walter Landor, Thomas Carlisle and Mathew Arnold.

1833

John 'Jolly Jack' Fuller died at Brightling. He was the last of the iron master Fullers but lived on after the days of the furnaces.

A popular man, he was also wealthy and spent a good deal of time in London as an M.P. and enjoying the company of intellectuals for he was a patron of science, music and painting. The great artist J. M. W. Turner, while staying at Brightling visited Heathfield Park and painted his famous 'Vale of Heathfield' now in the Tate Gallery.

'Jolly Jack' was generous and he was greatly concerned when Bodiam Castle was to be sold merely for the value of its stone and he ensured its survival by buying the castle himself. He was also responsible for building Brightling Needle and a fine observatory on his land.

1833

The Battle of Pevensey Sluice took place at the outlet from the marsh of the Wallers Haven river, and this place where it enters the sea is now known as Normans Bay.

It was here that the last bloody encounter between smugglers and the new Coast Guard Service took place and only after a long running fight covering many miles of the marsh were the smugglers finally beaten.

Much contraband was captured and during the fighting three smugglers were killed, many others wounded and five were captured to eventually suffer transportation. The smuggling by ruthless men using open brutality and murder was now becoming a far greater risk.

The following is an extract from an account of the 'battle' printed in *The Sussex Weekly Advertiser* of November 1833:

> . . . On Monday morning about four o'clock, a boat laden with contraband goods, came on shore, near No. 28 Tower, Pevensey, which was perceived by one of the Coast Guard, who discharged his piece as a signal for assistance, when a great number of smugglers rushed down to the boat, and commenced unshipping her cargo, consisting of contraband spirits and tea; the boat was surrounded and protected by armed smugglers, who kept up a constant fire during the period of unloading the boat. Having cleared the cargo, the smugglers, proceeded with it towards the marsh, flanked and covered in the rear by their armed companions; they had gone about a mile and a half from the boat across the marsh, when the Coast Guard had concentrated their force and came up with them, upon perceiving which the smugglers drew up in line, and upon the word 'fire' being given, some guns were discharged at the Coast Guard, who instantly returned the fire, and the smugglers again commenced a retreat . . . a sort of running fight was kept up for nearly two hours, covering a distance of six or seven miles . . .

Against growing armed resistance smuggling had begun to decline, but in spite of work at night in hard weather on windswept beaches and mud-torn tracks, the increasing risks, when capture could mean death, were still taken for the welcome reward that kept many families better fed than did parish relief or ill-paid work on the land.

Depending on the task, pay for unloading a vessel to the beach at Pevensey meant from two to six shillings each night, while the 'common' man was paid a guinea a week. As a farm labourer his pay would have been from sixteen to eighteen pence per week. An earlier official report to the Board of Agriculture had quoted:

> . . . in the neighbourhood of the sea are seen many old labourers, as the young and active find smuggling a more lucrative employ . . .

1833

A petition in Atherstone, Warwickshire, drawn up as a protest against high taxes, claimed that too much was allocated to the relief of the poor and it was accompanied by a table setting out the rate for each county.

It was shown that Warwickshire paid 3s. 4½d. in the pound, Middlesex, Durham and Worcestershire each paid 3s. 0d. and most other counties paid under 3s. 0d. Kent paid 5s. 8¾d. while Sussex had the greatest burden with 6s. 9½d. in the pound.

1833

In the book *Coast of Sussex* by J. D. Parry:

> . . . executed in the most unshrinking style of expence . . .

considerable space was given to descriptions of places and buildings as they were seen at the time.

> . . . . from Ashburnham to Lewes . . . is a lonely road . . . with the sole grand feature of the distant range of heights near Eastbourne . . . we pass through Gardner's Street, a dull village, and soon after leave to the left the tower of Hailsham with its lofty and elegant pinnacles . . . Horsebridge the next point, is a hamlet to the parish of Hellingly, whose mean church, with a pointed Steeple, is seen on the right . . .

1834

The Poor Law Amendment Act substantially changed a system originally established in the reign of Elizabeth when each parish was responsible for its own poor. It had been a reluctant duty with the almost inevitable sad results.

The hardship of life in many rural areas with their widespread unemployment aggravated an already inadequate system and caused a Commission of Enquiry to reveal parishes that had tolerated appalling conditions in which the poor and destitute had to live.

The new Act resulted in the parishes of Sussex being divided into convenient groups to enable each group to be served by a new central workhouse now to be called a Union. It was from this year the Board of Guardians of the Poor were introduced to administer the Poor Law, but members of such boards needed to be owners of property before their election was possible.

The group of eleven parishes of which Hailsham was one was to be served by Hailsham Union, a new building which reflected a serious effort to solve a piteous problem.

In 1836 the Union was built at the junction of Union Road (now Hawks Road) and the Horsebridge Road (A 271) to serve the poor of the following parishes:

> Arlington, Chiddingly, Hailsham, Heathfield, Hellingly, Herstmonceux, Hooe, Laughton, Ninfield, Warbleton and Wartling, with Chalvington and Ripe added in 1898.

With the creation and use of the new Hailsham Union, the age old practice of providing individual relief was largely discontinued. For those paupers in dire need and incapable of helping themselves, it was now the intention to take them into the new workhouse or Union as it was called, where there was both discipline and help. The workhouse, built to house up to three hundred inmates was large and grim and surrounded by a high wall. It was self sufficient with a kitchen garden, kitchens, laundry, a delousing oven, an infirmary and a mortuary.

A system of separation was operated in the workhouse when men, women and children were housed in separate quarters, and not even married couples with children were treated otherwise. The 'casuals' or tramps had to stay two nights, sleeping on boards, after which they often moved on to another union. While they were in the union however, they were expected to work and if they were tough and difficult they were enclosed in what was referred to as 'the cage', where they had to break flints.

One of the improvements of this drastic re-organisation was that able men could with a measure of dignity, be allowed out to work when employers were forced to pay them a fair working wage. With the thinking of the times it was inevitable that union life would be hard, for the intention was that inmates would seek outside work rather than prolong a stay. A rough justice was the object.

1834

A Vestry meeting of 5th April agreed to 'hire' a sum of money repayable with interest to pay for a pauper John Smith, his wife (unnamed) with eight children to be sent to America. The ages of the children were: Harriett, 18 years; George 17 years; Francis 16 years, James 11 years; Joseph 10 years; Charles 6 years; Eliza 2½ years; John 5 months.

The main expenses involved in this emigration were: clothing for the family, 10s. 0d. each; conveyance to London 4s. 0d each and 2s. 0d. for the four youngest. Passage money £6 5s. 0d., half price for the four youngest. Dock fees for parcels 2s. 0d. each. Landing money £2 0s. 0d. for parents, half price for children.

From correspondence beginning on 11th April it appears that John Smith and his large family were conducted on an early morning coach from Hailsham on Monday 21st April to arrive at the *Spur* inn in Borough High Street at 8 o'clock in the morning the next day. At a meeting with the shipping agent the money for the passage was handed over, some simple refreshment given to the family after which they were taken aboard the *Catherine* in the London docks.

Other similar passages were arranged and recorded up to 1849.

1835

The market in Hailsham was now beginning to enjoy a prosperity and it was written at the time that,

> . . . to the great rejoicing of the inhabitants, be it said, that it can boast of having one of the greatest markets for cattle and corn in Sussex . . .

A huge volume of cattle was sold in the market, purchased for consumption in many large southern towns.

c. 1835

At a time when smuggling was often proving no longer worth the serious risk it had become, the brewing of an illicit beer was to be a profitable activity.

A strong beer called Dicker Flint, brewed locally proved popular and was distributed in the parishes around Dicker.

1836

The requirement, in force for many hundreds of years, of tithe payments to the church in the form of,

> ... a tenth of the annual produce of agriculture etc. conceived as due to God and hence payable for the support of priesthood and religious establishments ...

was now discontinued.

From this year payment to the church by produce to be stored in tithe barns was replaced by an agreed monetary payment, such amounts to be reviewed every seven years and adjusted to match the market price of corn.

1836

On 19th November, a rain storm with winds of frightening intensity was experienced over Sussex when widespread damage was done. In particular Hailsham parish church was '... unroofed ...' leaving just the bare rafters:

> ... a mighty storm swept over southern England. Buildings were unroofed, trees torn up by their roots, barns, churches and many other structures blown down ...

In due course the roof was repaired and a large area had to be patched with slates, instead of the usual tiles which were in great demand everywhere for house repairs.

1836

The first book for recording births in the new Hailsham Union began with the entry of 13th April when Mary Wright gave birth to an illegitimate baby girl to be named Harriott.

In the first three years a total of twenty-three children were born in the Union of which fourteen were legitimate.

1837

In this year the book *The Unlettered Muse* was published. It was a book of poems written by John Hollamby who was born in Frant, but spent nearly all his life in Hailsham.

Hollamby lived in an old cottage on St Wilfrid's Green at the north end of Hailsham's High Street where he was the miller in the Post Mill.

> ... the cottage just by the mill held his all, a good wife and a large family of boys and girls ... he was happy in his home ... reading and observation were his teachers ...

The local fame of John Hollamby was sealed by the success of his book, printed by the 'Hailsham Press' (now Jenners the bookseller and printer), for the poems survived to become both widely read and respected. (*See* appendices 'K' and 'M'.)

1842

The Tithe Award Map of Hailsham parish was completed by Thomas Hughes to a scale of 26.6 inches to one mile. The map was of vast size and weight, for backed with heavy canvas it covered nearly one hundred square feet.

Shown on the map were roads, paths, fields, woods, ponds and boundaries, but most important of all were properties, accurately plotted and each one numbered. On an accompanying schedule were the property numbers against which were recorded details of size, value, use, owner and occupier. Where the property was land, the field names were listed.

The survey and creation of the map was a requirement of the Tithe Commutation Act of 1836. The object of the map was that it should be used for assessing properties in the process of converting the old complicated, and sometimes unfair tithe payment to churches, into an acceptable monetary payment by the State.

1844

Up to this date, children in workhouses were without education except on occasions for instruction of a rather primitive kind. There now came into force a Poor Law permitting the appointment of a teacher in Unions, when basic schooling could be attempted.

1845

The Duke of Wellington, former Prime Minister and Foreign Secretary, visited Pevensey to inspect the Martello Towers which had recently been re-armed.

The distrust and violent turmoil in France had led to prolonged unrest in Europe, and the possibility of war against France with the threat of the invasion of our shores was again causing real concern.

1846

The Rev. John Hobart Caunter left Hailsham, having planted during his three-year stay as vicar, the superb chestnut trees now growing along the boundary of the parish churchyard.

1846

A school for boys and girls to be known as the Hailsham National School was built and paid for by voluntary contributions aided by a small grant from Parliament. Many National Schools were built at this time and were free, having been founded by the 'National Society for the Education of the Poor according to the principles of the Church of England'. They were schools with a strong church influence that did not always please families of dissenting religions.

The site of the new school was on land facing the end of a lane, now Garfield Road, while the playground at the rear adjoined the turnpike, later to become South Road.

1846

The first meeting of the Sussex Archaeological Society, one of the earliest to be founded in England, was held on 9th July in Pevensey Castle, when Chiddingly born Mark Antony Lower read his paper dealing with the history of the castle.

This work proved to be in advance of anything hitherto written, and was used later as the nucleus for Lower's book *Chronicles of Pevensey* which he lived to see regarded as the definitive book on the subject.

1846

In an essentially agricultural area Hailsham was beginning to emerge from a period of low wages and poor living. Heartening signs for the future were the preparations for building the railway into the town, and the steadily increasing number of men and women needed by the two small factories mainly specializing in ropework.

With the fortnightly market continuing to be one of the busiest in the county, there was indeed more money to be earned, but with this modest prosperity came an unwelcome complication.

Strangers were attracted to the town and with two new beer houses there was hard drinking, noise and argument causing a concern that prompted a special vestry meeting. From the meeting a letter was sent to Captain Mackay, head of the Sussex constabulary with an appeal that Inspector Dawes of Horsebridge be sent to Hailsham to control and quieten,

> ...the congregating of many disorderly persons which is frequently a great annoyance to the inhabitants...

A vestry meeting nominated Thomas White the grocer and Thomas Burfield the rope factory owner to,

> ...wait on Captain Mackay should he feel disposed to communicate...

1847

During the removal of soil and the preparation of the ground before laying track for the railway extension between Polegate and Eastbourne, a cast lead coffer was uncovered in the area of Lower Willindgon.

A square-shaped container of considerable weight, now misshapen from the pressure of earth after centuries of burial, it had simple and somewhat crude patterns of the Anglo-Saxon period, where raised ridges took the form of ropes.

Measuring twelve inches by eleven inches with a depth of six inches, this lead casting, almost certainly over a thousand years old, is now in the possession of the Sussex Archaeological Society at Barbican House in Lewes.

1849

Hailsham station was opened for the railway to Polegate and on the first journey John Hield, a passenger standing on a carriage step, was killed when he was struck by the crossing gate at Mulbrook. The coaches were of three different classes, the first two being covered but the third class was of open trucks.

To celebrate the opening a commemorative dinner was held in the market room of the *Crown* Hotel in the High Street. Attending, according to a contemporary report of some charm, were gentlemen, railway officials and strangers in a room with a very low ceiling, poor gaslight and no ventilation.

At a later date a short branch line was laid from Hailsham station to a then nearby brickfield adjoining a lane that is now Gordon Road.

c. 1850

At this time a total of thirty-six windmills could be seen from the top of Hailsham church tower, for now was the time that the windmills of East Sussex were enjoying their greatest prosperity. Almost every village had a windmill or watermill within reach and certainly it was difficult to travel across country and not to have a windmill in sight.

Within Hailsham there were two mills. A smock type called Lower Mill in Mill Road, later to be called Hamlins Mill, was built in 1834. David Catt moved from Cowbeech windmill to work at Lower Mill and eventually became part owner with two others in 1879, but within seven years the mill was entirely with the Catt family who continued to control it until its final destruction. (*See* entry of 1923).

A steam engine used by David Catt was sold in *c.* 1912 to the Berwick Bone Mills for grinding bones in the making of fertiliser, and part of the original mill is still on the Drusilla site at Alfriston.

The other mill in Hailsham was a post type on St Wilfrid's Green dominating the nearby site in the High Street soon to hold an infants school (still existing today). It was called Upper Mill and it was here in 1869 that the miller John Kennard was tragically killed when his loose fitting Sussex smock became caught in the mill mechanism causing him to be crushed. (*See* appendix 'K').

In spite of an age approaching one hundred years, the task of moving this old mill was undertaken in *c.* 1892 with the aid of bullock wagons and it was eventually working again on a new site at Harebeating. Now of extreme age and after some years of neglect, it was in *c.* 1932 that the mill sweeps finally collapsed. The lower part of the structure in brick still stands today in Harebeating and but a few yards from Battle Road. (*See* appendix 'K').

1850

At a meeting of the Ratepayers of the parish of Arlington, consent was given for the Board of Guardians to assist George Lambert, his wife and two children, to emigrate to Australia by providing the sum of four pounds.

1851

At the Great Exhibition in Hyde Park, Thomas Smith of Herstmonceux exhibited his trugs with painted decoration and was awarded a medal and diploma of merit. A special trug with silver nails was presented to Queen Victoria.

> ... at the exhibition the trugs were much admired by Queen Victoria and Her Majesty gave instructions for a number to be specially made. These trugs

were personally delivered by the maker Thomas Smith who made the journey from Herstmonceux to Buckingham Palace on foot . . .

With further awards from Paris, the fame of Herstmonceux trugs resulted in the word trug being accepted in *c.* 1860 for inclusion in the Oxford Dictionary. Trugs have been made in East Sussex since 1600, the word being derived from the old English word 'trog' meaning 'boat-like'. They are still hand made, usually in willow for the boards and ash or chestnut for the frames.

1851

Called to consider,

> . . . the propriety of removing the old three decker pulpit . . .

a meeting of the Vestry was held in Hailsham parish church.

It was resolved that the very old panelled pulpit should be removed and paid for by voluntary subscription and not from the church rate. The total expense was £2 4s. 0d.

1852

A meeting of the Vestry decided, that a letter be sent to 'Lord Delewar' (Lord De la Warr) with the request that he consider giving the Hailsham Common Pond for the use of the people in the parish. The letter was duly sent but the request met with a refusal.

1853

Following a discussion at a Hailsham parish vestry meeting it was agreed that letters be sent to 'the prominent people' of the town. The letters were to advise of a proposal that the protective posts and rails along the main street of the town be removed.

In reply, the following extract is from a letter of 26th April sent to the overseer, Stephen Breads by the ropemakers Burfield and Son:

> . . . We beg to acknowledge receipt of a requisition signed by several of the respectable inhabitants of the town of Hailsham . . . in relation to the removal of the posts and rails standing in front of our property in the town; we beg to say that our agreeing to such requisition would be attended with much greater loss and inconvenience to ourselves we think, than would be felt by all the rest put together, but we would not wish to be guided altogether by private interest, when the public good is thereby effected. We will therefore agree . . . but with this understanding that the whole town shall be cleared of posts and rails on the outside of the pavements and that the Parish shall agree from and after that time to pave all the public footpaths in the town on both sides of the road which is now done at the expense of private individuals in some few excepted cases. *N.B.* Allow us to say we do not consider the posts and rails that have been here almost from time immemorial to be near so dangerous to the public safety as goods carts so being allowed to remain in the town after dark . . .

The date the vestry issued the instruction to have all the posts and rails in the town sawn down was not recorded in the vestry minutes.

1854

Henry Isted, the secretary of the Hailsham Horticultural Society, distributed printed folders to selected people inviting donations towards prizes. These awards were to be given for the best cultivated cottage gardens.

1854

A Vestry meeting of 3rd June discussed the disposal of the 'Old Workhouse' in Market Street, and it was decided to apply to the Poor Law Board for their sanction to allow a lease to be granted:

> . . . a freehold messuage or tenament with yard and garden and appurtenances formerly an Inn known as 'Flower-de-Luce: . . . we are of the opinion that the letting will be advantageous to the said parish. The premises are estimated to be of the value £500 and yield an annual rent of £25 . . .

In reply, permission was granted and the lease advertised, but the decision to close this old workhouse was controversial in spite of the large Hailsham Union having been in use for eighteen years. The reason the old workhouse was kept open so many years after the Union was built is not clear, certainly it was known to have been well run, humane and economical. The sad decision so shocked Mr. E. E. Vidall of Ersham Lodge that he resigned his position as Chairman of the Guardians.

> . . . in consequence of the decision to remove the old and infirm from the Hailsham Poor House (now named Fleur-de-Lys) to Hellingly (Hailsham Union) . . .

'Ersham Lodge' was an impressive Victorian house of some grace, with ornamental gardens, woodland and tall pine trees lining the drive to the former turnpike, now Ersham Road. Demolished *c.* 1930 the land from the estate allowed the building of houses over the area now known as Ersham Park, comprising The Avenue, Park Close and Ersham Way.

1854

At a public meeting of the Ratepayers of the parish of Arlington held at the workhouse at Caneheath, it was agreed to employ William Gosden '. . . on the roads at nine shillings per week provided he earns it . . . '.

Five months later Gosden was elected Surveyor at fifteen shillings, five pence per week so long as he entered into an agreement to resign should he fall sick or be unable to work.

1855

A considerable area of open ground both south and west of Hailsham had for centuries been common land for the pasturing of cattle and other uses of the people.

The wide common stretched from Ersham Farm by the turnpike road (now Ersham Road) in the south, then westward round the town to reach the road (now London Road), north out of Hailsham, towards Horsebridge. The only features were a few isolated cottages especially in the Cacklebury area (the

King's Head in South Road) and a broad straight track north-west across the common from the south (the *Bricklayers Arms*, now at the junction of Ersham Road and South Road).

When at this time five acres of common land was enclosed as a town recreation ground the old track, used for centuries by travellers, could no longer be used as a route avoiding the centre of Hailsham.

1855

Making the purchases for a large Union with on occasions, nearly three hundred inmates, was a demanding responsibility, ranging as it did from food to commodities for every eventuality. The invitation:

> ... the Guardians of Hailsham Union will take tenders for the supply of coffins ...

was indeed a sad reminder that many inmates after years of hardship and neglect had deteriorated into a wretched condition.

1859

An additional Order made to an Act of 1835 was addressed to the 'Guardians of the Poor'. The intention of this instruction was to ensure that the religious principles of any workhouse inmate would be respected and that he or she could be protected from having,

> ... to attend any religious service celebrated in a mode contrary to the religious principles of such inmate nor should authorize the education of any Child in a Workhouse in any religious creed other than that professed by the parents or surviving parent ... or in the case of an orphan, to which the godfather or godmother of such orphan should object ...

The schedule of workhouses to which this Order applied listed the Union at Hailsham, where the master was required to record the religion of every orphan child under fourteen years of age and to ensure such a child attends religious instruction.

c. 1859

On those occasions when information needed to be conveyed to people of the parish, the method was by use of handwritten notices pinned up at strategic places including the parish church door. Such notices would advise of petty sessions courts, public meetings and town events as well as to warn churchwardens, vestry members and overseers of the poor, when their presence was required at vestry meetings. *(See* following page).

1862

Richard Lower, an eighty year old schoolmaster of Chiddingly and uncle of Mark Antony Lower, wrote the book *Stray Leaves from an Old Tree*. Having in mind the fame of Sussex for sheep breeding, he referred to the unique shepherd:

> ... decidedly the chief servant and generally, from generation to generation, a kind of heirloom to a farm. For, whatever changes occurred, the shepherd was still a

Parish of Hailsham

Notice is hereby given that a Vestry will be held at the Crown Inn in this Parish on Thursday the 5 day of January at 8 o'clock in the evening 1860, to appoint an Assistant Overseer for the said Parish (to collect all Parochial Rates) and consult on other Business All persons wishing to fill the said office are requested to attend

        Edward Browne   *Churchwarden*

        William Burny   *Overseer*

Hailsham
    Dec 31 - 1859

A typical notice announcing to the public that a meeting of the Vestry will be held. Such hand-written notices were pinned up at prominent places in the town. (See entry of c. 1859) fixture there. As for parting with a shepherd, Master Giles would almost as soon have thought of separating from his good old spouse . . .

1862

The first Hailsham school for infants was built in the High Street. This was a time of considerably increased awareness of the need to extend and improve educational standards. It was but eighteen years later in 1880, when attendance at school for children up to the age of ten years was made compulsory, that the infants school was enlarged.

1866

Thomas Burfield, the founder of Burfield and Son died leaving his son, also Thomas, to carry on the family rope making business. Established over fifty years ago, the firm made many types of rope and line and by now had extended its activity into the manufacture of sacks, matting, harness and tarpaulins.

Through long periods of widespread unemployment, the work this man was able to provide proved of immense value. Certainly he made life more secure for many men and women in and around Hailsham and on the day of his funeral, an impressive and spontaneous gesture was to be seen when huge numbers of men and women rope workers formed ranks in long columns, and followed his coffin through the town where many of the shops had closed to show their respect.

1867

With the passing of the Second Reform Bill, the Test Act of 1673 was finally repealed.

For one hundred and ninety-four years this malicious Act against Dissenters had proved an unjust handicap, but now, Nonconformists were at last allowed their complete political freedom and it became possible for them to hold both State and Municipal Offices.

1867

The Hailsham Postmaster, a Mr. Harvey was suspended from duty for being £35 19s. 9d. 'in debt to the Post Office'. The debt was paid later and he was reinstated.

At this time the Post Office operated from a small shop in George Street, a few yards from the Market Square.

1868

The Methodist Chapel was built in High Street, Hailsham.

1868

The use of the High Street and other roads on market days for the buying and selling of cattle and dealing in other commodities, was no longer permitted. After this date the new walled-in market in Market Street was used.

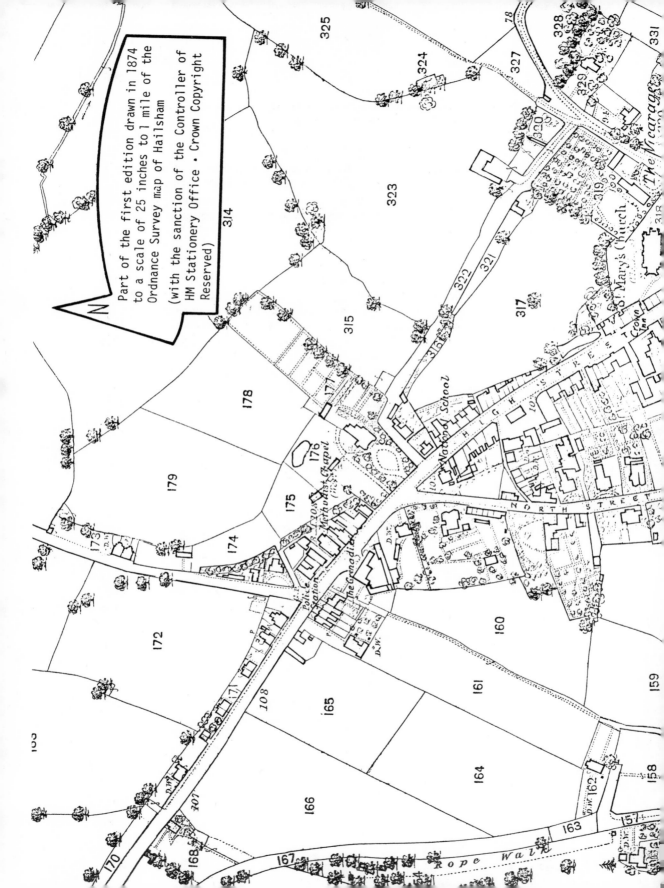

Part of the first edition drawn in 1874 to a scale of 25 inches to 1 mile of the Ordnance Survey map of Hailsham

(with the sanction of the Controller of HM Stationery Office • Crown Copyright Reserved)

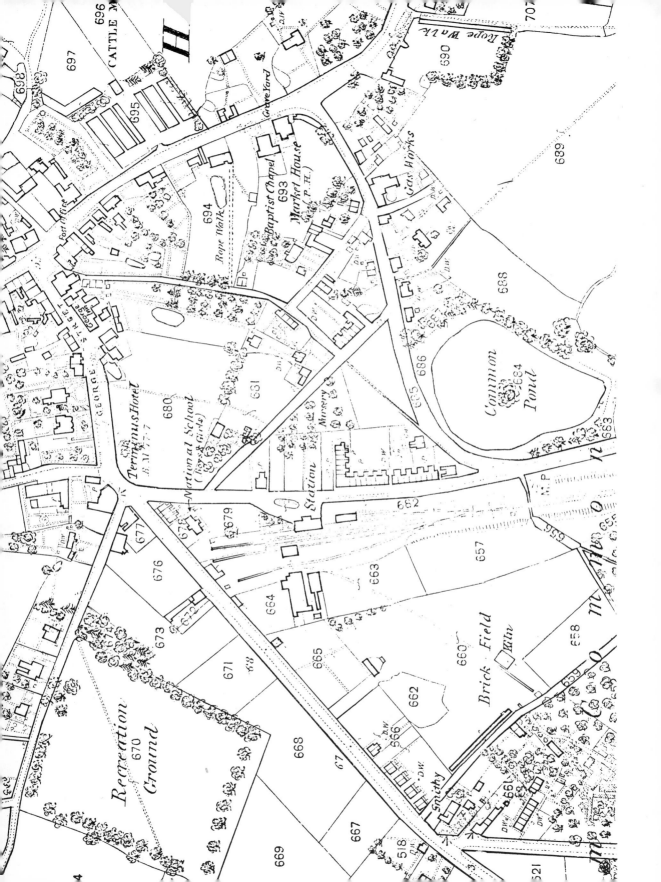

1873

The 'Long Man of Wilmington', the figure of a man believed one of the largest in the world, was first cut into the chalk of the steep side of the Downs facing the Priory, at least nine hundred years ago and maybe even earlier. Being of great age and overgrown for many years, it could only be discerned by at times the growth around its outline, or if seen when the light was in a certain direction.

It was decided at this time to establish the Man as a permanent feature and the figure was outlined in yellow bricks. (*See* entries of 1925, and 1969 and appendix 'Q').

1874

The first edition of an Ordnance Survey map of Hailsham to a scale of 25 inches to a mile was published. Several old rope walks in different parts of the town were indicated as were field numbers taken from the Tithe Award map of the parish.

1874

Thomas Burfield, son of the founder of the Hailsham firm of Burfield and Son, died on the 9th September aged sixty-three years.

1876

Stone Cross Tower Windmill was built by F. Neve & Sons the millwrights of Heathfield. (*See* appendix 'K').

1877

A public meeting on the 6th March was held in the Hailsham National School (soon to be demolished) having as its object,

> ... to consider the best means of equiping a Fire Brigade and maintaining same in a state of efficiency ...

The meeting, with the Rev. F. Clyde Harvey, vicar of Hailsham parish church as chairman, agreed that the town needed such a brigade and that it should be supported by voluntary contributions. The loan offer of a manual fire engine by William Strickland was accepted and it was housed at the *Terminus* Hotel where two horses also on loan, would be taken when needed.

The first fire the brigade attended was a burning oat stack at Buckwell Farm, Herstmonceux, and the second was the lamp room at Hailsham railway station.

For thirty-six years William Strickland, J.P. showed exceptional generosity to the Hailsham Volunteer Fire Brigade and in 1913, as chairman and honorary captain, he transferred to the brigade thirty ten pound shares in the Hailsham Water Company to ensure the brigade had a sound future.

1878

The Prime Minister William Gladstone's recent far-reaching Education Bill of 1870, introduced a system of primary education in what were to be known as Board Schools. The new schools were to be controlled by local authorities and, no doubt to avoid favouring any particular denomination, religious instruction was not to be given. In the course of time however the rule was relaxed and such instruction was left to the discretion of individual school boards.

The board school for Hailsham opened in 1878 on a site in Brewery (now Battle) Road some three years after the School Board held its first meeting in the *Terminus* Hotel, when the Rev. F. Clyde Harvey was elected Chairman and Thomas Geering, Vice-Chairman. During these three years the ambitious project of the new school was constantly discussed and at almost every stage, the Education Department in Whitehall needed to be informed and their approval sought.

Such planning of a new school at this time was crucial to the town and it solved a problem created by the impending extension of the railway to Heathfield, for the old National School site was now needed to provide land for a new siding and a house for the station master.

The Rev. George Luxford had much land north of the town with its income in lieu of the old tithes, and it was part of his land along what was to become Battle Road, that became the site of the new school.

With the prevailing opinion that boys and girls older than ten years should be separated, the school plan was of two buildings each to hold one hundred and fifty pupils thus allowing for the increasing population of Hailsham. The land was purchased for £350 and after enforced economies, the cost of building including drains, water supply, playgrounds and earth closets was finally reduced to £2,350 making a total of £2,700.

When the posts of certificated schoolmaster and schoolmistress were advertised there were one hundred and twenty-three applications. The master was to receive £125 per annum and the mistress £105 and both teachers were forbidden to take private pupils.

Until 1891 when elementary education was made free, the charges made by the Hailsham School Board were 3d. per week each for the first two children of agricultural labourers with the rest free, while the children of mechanics and others were to be charged 3d. each for their first three children. It was recorded that Thomas Burfield, grandson of the founder of Burfield and Son (*see* entry of 1807), was the only member of the Board to vote against the school charges.

In March of 1878 a census of school age children was taken by Samuel Wenham, the attendance officer. The number recorded in Hailsham and with visits to Hellingly, Herstmonceux, Polegate and Willingdon reached a total of five hundred and twenty. These children were attending nineteen schools of which thirteen were private and there were sixty-six children not attending any school.

Not all the pupils at the new school were full time and among the part-time pupils were boys from the now closed Burfield factory school in Carriers Path (later to be the Hailsham Gospel Hall).

Such boys were often very young, some a mere nine years old, but known as spinner boys they were employed on the rope walks about the town. Their work was hard from 6 o'clock in the morning until 1 p.m., sometimes involving running up and down the 'walks'. The boys were tough and smoked tobacco like the men with whom they worked; old beyond their years they could be aggressive and difficult to subdue for teaching.

1879

The Hailsham branch of the London, Brighton and South Coast Railway was now being extended northwards from Hailsham. While workmen were removing soil and forming the railway cutting some four hundred yards from Hailsham station, many pieces of Roman pottery were discovered.

1880

The railway from Hailsham to Heathfield was opened in spite of the station buildings at Heathfield not being completed. The extension of the line at once created the need for a major bridge allowing the road south out of Hailsham to be re-routed across the new railway lines.

Just a few months later in September, the line from Heathfield was extended to Mayfield and Tunbridge Wells, allowing with a change of trains, the complete journey to London.

For Heathfield, this rail connection with London was of tremendous help to the local enterprise of specialist chicken farming, for with its rate of growth a success was achieved that was of great benefit to many people in the area. By 1894 the value of dead poultry sent off from Heathfield had reached, for those times, the startling figure of £140,000.

1881

The Georgian style property in George Street known as 'Newhouse' was purchased for £1,250 by William Strickland, a prominent and successful corn merchant. With the knowledge that the former American officer Col. Philip Van Cortlandt had once lived there, the house was renamed 'Cortlandt'.

Upon taking possession the new owner embarked upon plans to extend the house at each end, taking meticulous care in matching the new brickwork and windows to the period and quality of the old structure.

Much of the original interior of simple Georgian design tended to be overshadowed in the enlarged house by features of the somewhat heavy and ostentatious Victorian era. Of interest in the new work was some oak panelling from the old three decker pulpit, discarded many years ago from the parish church, and the door of the pulpit complete with its iron hinges, built into a clothes cupboard.

William Strickland later purchased among much other land in the town, the field that faced his house across George Street. With some flair and amid local enthusiasm, the field was converted into a large paddock enclosed by ornamental iron railings. In the centre an impressive brick shelter was built surmounted by a tower with a clock that automatically illuminated during the house of darkness.

A herd of deer together with peacocks were to live in the paddock and be a feature of the town for many years, indeed such was its status that the Southdown Foxhounds occasionally held their Meet in this place.

The creation of a paddock with such a display, was for those times in a small town, quite unique. No doubt the spectacle prompted the somewhat extravagant phrases in the *Eastbourne Chronicle* of 17th December 1887 when the view from Cortlandt was described:

> ...to look out of one of the broad windows, he would see, instead of the bare unenclosed common, with hissing geese and braying donkeys, 'a park in miniature' covered with emerald green, stocked with deer, 'poor dappled fools', poking their cold noses between the bars of the ornamental iron fence that bounds the public roadway and fearlessly caressing the hand of the loitering passer-by, as he stops to look into their full and liquid eyes ... for this boon we all owe a meed of thanks to the present owner of Cortlandt House ...

1884

Thomas Geering, who lived all his life in Hailsham, died in 1889 aged seventy-six years just five years after his book *Our Parish, A Medley* was published. It was a remarkable collection of essays dealing with Hailsham characters and parish institutions and Arthur Beckett, a Fellow of the Royal Society of Literature has said

> ...Geering's work is unique in the literature of the county; there is no other Sussex book of the same kind, in fact I cannot call to mind any other book of such descriptive flair of any rural parish in England ...

An edition of five hundred copies was printed to sell at 1s. 6d. while a smaller number were priced at 2s. 6d. For his friends however, twelve special copies were prepared bound in leather with gold decoration, each having seventy-two illustrations. A much abridged version was published in 1925.

Thomas Geering inherited his father's shoemaking business in Hailsham's High Street and was also deeply involved with parish duties in which he served the town well. He was a member of the vestry and elected at the age of thirty-three to serve as a constable. In this position he was concerned with the welfare of the poor, inspecting alehouses, apprenticing pauper children, supervising militia training and,

> ...ensuring the upkeep of local means of punishment and imprisonment such as stocks and cage ...

Following Geering's death his only daughter lived on in her father's High Street property, next to the gun shop which was later to burn down. Today, Geering's old shop is still a business retailing footwear.

1889

In Horseye Road, later to be called Market Street, a serious fire broke out on 25th September in the long 15th cent. building once the 'Fleur-de-Lys' Inn but later to become parish property and a workhouse.

Built of heavy timbers with a tall wooden gable at each end, this impressive tudor structure housed a butcher's shop at the Market Square end, then a post office, a confectioner, and at the other end, a carriage works, all with homes above the business.

The fire started in the carriage works store and spread along the building until it was quelled after two hours with the post office badly damaged but its mail safely evacuated. Just three days after the fire, an inconclusive vestry meeting expressed its deepest gratitude to captain Towner and members of the Eastbourne Fire Brigade for their early and willing response to an appeal for assistance. It was also agreed,

> ... that the Sanitary Authority be called on to fix a sufficient number of hydrants for the effectual protection of the town ...

With the realisation that much more time was needed to solve the problems caused by the fire, a new vestry meetings was called for 3rd October to

> ... consider the best thing to be done with the parish property (the old workhouse) lately damaged by fire, and to discuss anything arising out of the above mentioned fire ...

At a vestry meeting on 24th October at the *Crown* Hotel it was proposed that the part of the parish property (Mr. Verrall's carriage works and home above) lately destroyed by fire, be utilised as a station for the fire engine and appliances. Next was a proposal for part demolition and a sale of what remained but this too was rejected until at a meeting in the *Crown* Hotel on 5th December it was finally agreed that

> ... a committee of eleven be formed to thoroughly enter into the disposal of the old workhouse and that they report at a future vestry meeting ...

The eventual findings of the committee of eleven was to

> ... repair the old workhouse and to build a Fire Engine House and Vestry Room ...

and at a meeting of ratepayers on 20th December at the Infants School it was decided a vote should be taken. There was an adjournment and at the resumed meeting of 2nd January 1890 the result of the poll was announced:

For the report	204
Against	81
Majority for	123

In accordance with the wishes of the ratepayers the damaged parish property was rebuilt to become Hailsham's first fire station, while the floor above was converted into a large room for vestry meetings. For the first time, the Hailsham Vestry was able to meet in their new chamber instead of using the school or one of the local inns. This original vestry room later served the parish council and is still in use for town council meetings.

Also as a result of the fire and the destruction of Hailsham's post office, it was decided that a new post office should be opened on the opposite side of the road. It was this building that many years later was to be converted into the present Midland Bank in Market Street.

While vestry opinion on the fire damage conflicted over many meetings before a final solution was found, the vestry had only a single dissenting voice in urging the replacement of the old manual engine by a more efficient model. As the cost was to be met from the poor rate a poll of ratepayers was held on a market day, but the confident vestry proposal for a new engine was rejected by one hundred and nine votes to thirty-eight. *Note:* That part of the old 'Fleur-de-Lys' structure that remained with its medieval timbers, unaffected by the fire, is now listed as a building of special interest. (*See* appendix 'N').

1892

At a vestry meeting of 7th January,

> . . . it was resolved that the overseers and churchwardens be allowed to provide the following furniture for the new Vestry Hall . . .
> Sixty light coloured cane seated chairs . . . . each not to exceed 2s. 6d.
> Two deal tables on twined legs with deal tops coloured to correspond with chairs
> . . . . not to exceed £1 15s. 0d.
> Hat pegs, blinds, mat and scraper . . . . not to exceed £2 0s. 0d.
> A stove to be fitted . . . . not to exceed £2 10s. 0d.

and at a vestry meeting on 25th March a vote of thanks,

> . . . was accorded Mr. William Strickland for his present of two chairs suitable for the chairman and the vice-chairman of the vestry . . .

1893

A public meeting was held at the *Woolpack* Hotel on 22nd July to consider the formation of a fire brigade for Herstmonceux. Mr. C. S. Arkoll informed the meeting he would be willing to buy the Hailsham horse drawn manual engine if the Hailsham Brigade would bring the engine to Lime Park and give a demonstration to prove its good condition. The engine with its equipment was purchased for £30 and used by the newly formed Herstmonceux and Wartling Volunteer Fire Brigade.

1894

In this year the Local Government Act marked the end of the old vestries and enabled the planning of parish councils. It was at this time that Rural and District councils were also created.

1894

The railway extension to Heathfield of 1880 began through a deep cutting and during its excavation some four hundred and fifty yards north of Hailsham station, it cut through an old footpath used by children to and from school. Since the new extension, children now needed to cross the railway lines and use steps up and down the steep embankment each side.

With the railway busier and more children crossing the lines, a meeting of ratepayers in this year voted strongly that the attention of the London, Brighton and South Coast Railway be drawn to the need for a bridge to be erected for the safety of the children.

In spite of increasing danger it was to be twenty years later in 1914 before a steel bridge was built to form part of what is now Eastwell Place, still a busy walking route to Hailsham School.

1894

In the early hours of 27th June, the gun shop of Austin and Son in High Street, Hailsham, where it adjoined the churchyard, caught fire and burnt to the ground.

The *Eastbourne Chronicle* reported the fire and said:

> . . . the occurrence provoked great excitement in Hailsham and crowds assembled at the scene of the fire. The furniture was removed from the neighbouring dwelling house and piled in the churchyard. The premises and the stock were insured . . .

A decision was made by the owner not to rebuild the property and four years later the ruin and the land on which it stood was purchased jointly by the corn merchant William Strickland, the Hailsham vicar the Rev. F. Clyde Harvey and Holland Southerdon. It was these new owners who arranged for the site to be cleared and grassed, before it was given to the church as a small but significant extension to the churchyard.

There had always been a narrow path through which the church could be reached from the High Street but this new area of grass between the shops, now opened up an impressive view of the entire church tower.

Following the death of Queen Victoria in 1901, tall wrought iron gates between ornate stone pillars were erected across the grassed gap in her memory.

At the opening ceremony conducted by the vicar with music from the Hailsham brass band, it was Mrs. Strickland who cut the red, white and blue ribbon and declared the Victoria Gates open.

1895

The first meeting of the newly-elected Hailsham parish council was on 3rd January, and among the council members were all three clergymen in the town.

The Rev. F. Clyde Harvey was elected chairman and Major Harold Parminter Molineux was appointed treasurer. To ensure the safety of public money, the council minuted:

> . . . providing he enters into a bond to the satisfaction of the council . . .

1896

With the need to seek water for steam engines at Heathfield station, the London, Brighton and South Coast Railway sunk a borehole near the mouth of the nearby tunnel. As the boring went deeper the presence of gas became apparent until at a depth of three hundred and seventy feet, while no adequate supply of water had been reached, the increased gas pressure when piped, supported a sixteen feet jet of flame.

The new gas supply provided the lighting for Heathfield Station and in 1902 a new company, 'The Natural Gas Fields of England Ltd.' began a serious programme of boring and extended the exploration into surrounding areas.

An increased supply of gas was found, enabling the streets of Heathfield and some of its houses to be lit but more serious production was uneconomic and ceased in 1904. The railway station continued to be lit by local natural gas until the supply was sealed off in 1963.

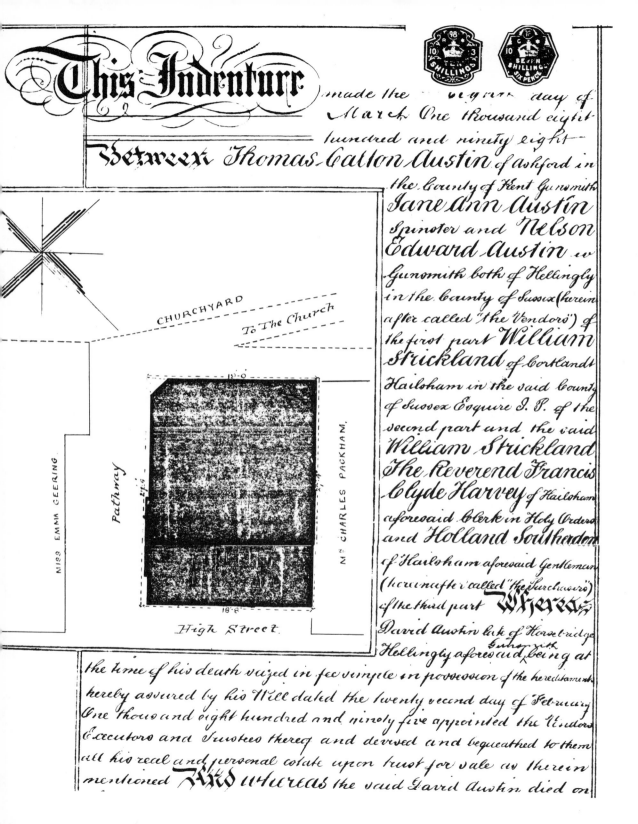

This Indenture

made the *[eighth]* day of March One thousand eight hundred and ninety eight

Between Thomas Catton Austin of Ashford in the County of Kent Gunsmith Jane Ann Austin Spinster and Nelson Edward Austin Gunsmith both of Hellingly in the County of Sussex (hereinafter called "the Vendors") of the first part William Strickland of Cortlandt Hailsham in the said County of Sussex Esquire J.P. of the second part and the said William Strickland The Reverend Francis Clyde Harvey of Hailsham aforesaid Clerk in Holy Orders and Holland Southerden of Hailsham aforesaid Gentleman (hereinafter called "the Purchasers") of the third part Whereas David Austin late of Horsebridge Hellingly aforesaid Gunsmith being at the time of his death seized in fee simple in possession of the hereditaments hereby assured by his Will dated the twenty second day of February One thousand eight hundred and ninety five appointed the Vendors Executors and Trustees thereof and devised and bequeathed to them all his real and personal estate upon trust for sale as therein mentioned And whereas the said David Austin died on

Map labels: CHURCHYARD — To The Church — MISS EMMA GEERING — Pathway — Mr CHARLES PACKHAM — High Street.

The indenture or contract of sale concerning the purchase in 1898 of the site where formerly stood the gun shop in High Street, Hailsham. (See entry of c. 1898)

1896

Augustus J. C. Hare was a member of the Herstmonceux family, one of whom lived at the castle, while three others were consecutive rectors of the parish church.

A friend of European Royalty and a prolific writer of biography and travel books, many of which he illustrated himself, he wrote in his book *Sussex*:

> . . . peasants still walk with 'backsters', flat pieces of wood fastened to the soles of their boots to enable them to get across pebbles at Pevensey . . .

In the same book, Hare wrote of Hailsham as a '. . . dreary little market town . . .' and excelled himself with recording that the famous T. W. Horsfield's *History of Sussex* was . . . 'both dull and inaccurate . . . '.

Described by a friend as 'dapper, old-maidish and undoubtedly a snob', his critics preferred the words 'garrulous, indelicate and trivial'.

1896

The 'Clergy House' at Alfriston, built close to the parish church in the 14th cent. as a priest's house, was purchased by the National Trust for £10. The house at that time, in a ruinous state, was the first property purchased by the then new organisation, founded in the previous year.

This now impressive restored structure is a fine and typical example of a Wealden House of massive timbers with the usual large central hall reaching the full height of the building.

1897

To celebrate the sixtieth year of Queen Victoria's reign, a public appeal was launched for donations towards providing the church tower with a striking clock. It was to be a replacement for the very old clock that still indicated the time with a long single hand.

The appeal raised £157 4s. 9d., and the clock was installed to be,

> . . . set going at 7.57 a.m. on Friday 19th November at a special service of dedication . . .

1898

The Sussex County Council authorised negotiations for the acquisition of land at Park Farm, Hellingly, to build what in later years would be known as Hellingly Hospital. A comment at this time written by the vicar of Hellingly, the Rev. Alfred Metcalfe, in his church magazine read:

> . . . Whether we like it or not, it seems that the new County Lunatic Asylum is to be built in Hellingly . . .

The site, nearly four hundred acres of farmland, was surveyed and pegged out in 1900 but it was not until 1903 that the East Sussex Asylum was opened. In its first year an average of six hundred and eighteen patients were cared for at a weekly cost for each of thirteen shillings and four pence, almost everyone of whom was a pauper.

1901

A Memorandum of Agreement was drawn up on 7th February between the Managers of the infants school at Polegate and Lucy Alice Beard:

> ...the teacher shall teach...under the direction of the Managers in accordance with the requirements of the Board of Education...the Managers shall pay the sum of £28 0. 0. per annum in monthly payments...

1902

On Tuesday 18th March the Hailsham Brewery was sold by auction. The business was fully operational and was advertised as,

> ...a modern concern with electric light...

With the brewery were sold its two tied houses: the *Yew Tree* at Arlington and the *Welcome Stranger* at Herstmonceux. *Note:* The old brewery building still exists just a quarter of a mile from Hailsham School.

1902

Almost facing the parish church in Willingdon's Church Street, an intriguing residence of unusual character was created by restructuring and adding to an old house to effect a remarkable transformation.

Extensive new work was of stone, flint and superb brickwork with an entrance through an archway into a small walled courtyard. The impressive rear of the house with three new gables and oriel windows, overlooks a stone terrace with steps descending in circular groups down to a garden flanked by high walls and two small pavilions.

This dramatic re-built property, named 'The Hoo', was designed by Sir Edwin Landseer Lutyens, architect of The Cenotaph, The Somme Memorial at Thiepval, and the unique government buildings of New Delhi, said to be,

> ...one of the finest palaces in architectural history...

The building is acknowledged as of considerable architectural importance and has a statutory listing in the category as being of outstanding interest.

1908

The first Hailsham Telephone Exchange was installed by the National Telegraph Co. in the front room of a private house at 29 High Street (later to be converted into W. T. Mitchell, tobacconist).

The caretaker/operator who lived on the premises controlled a small exchange panel with a capacity of fifty lines, many of which remained unused for a considerable period.

1909

In March of this year, while workmen were engaged on moving soil to level an area of land on Ocklynge Hill, a trench in the chalk, long since filled in, was uncovered. The trench, some two feet below the surface, extended for well over a hundred yards and was found to contain skeletons buried shoulder to shoulder without space between them.

Further excavation revealed the presence of a parallel trench but in this trench there were skeletons spaced as much as ten feet apart. The bodies in both trenches were of Anglo-Saxons who had been buried with feet roughly towards the east and considered opinion was that where the bodies had been spaced apart, it probably indicated they were once men of significance. (*See* entry of 1970 and appendix 'U').

1909

Upon the retirement of Mr. Snashell, the Postmaster of the Hailsham Post Office in Market Street, his family who were owners of the property, refused to allow the postal authority to continue its tenancy thus at once creating the urgent need to secure new premises.

The dilemma was resolved when an offer of land together with an opportunity for a specialist building was made by David Guy. The Post Office thus became a tenant of a new building in North Street with complete postal facilities for the first time.

It was in 1928 that the premises were purchased by the government.

1911

The partial restoration of Herstmonceux Castle was begun by Col. Claude Lowther but he died before the enormous task could be completed.

1912

While digging the foundations of a new house barely seven hundred yards north of Alfriston, an Anglo-Saxon cemetery was uncovered resulting in finds of considerable importance.

The site was a hundred and twenty-five feet above sea level where the road through the hamlet of Winton goes west, and crosses the road north-west out of Alfriston, itself becoming a track across fields to Berwick church. The new house of 1912, once severely interrupted during its building, stands today on the site of the cemetery and is called 'Sanctuary'.

During the course of the archaeological excavations some hundred and twenty graves were uncovered, most of which lay in an east–west direction. There was no trace of cremation but many skeletons were in a poor state of preservation.

The remarkable range of finds recovered, some rich in design, included: small swords, knives, bronze buckles, an ivory ring and others in silver. There were many brooches, two in the shape of a swastika and an interesting range of beads; some simple but others were of amber, rock crystal and glass with several threaded on silver wire.

An exhibit showing a scale model grave and a range of objects and jewellery is at the museum of the Sussex Archaeological Society in Barbican House, Lewes.

Today, against a roadside hedge of the garden of 'Sanctuary' stands a crucifix marking the southern end of the Anglo-Saxon cemetery.

High on the bank the tall cross with its narrow tiled roof reaches fifteen feet above the road and supports the figure of Christ carved in wood. It is behind this crucifix that were re-buried the disturbed human remains from the cemetery.

1913

In the dry summer of this year certain indications on the grass of farmland at Exceat suggested there once having been a building sited just three hundred yards south of the Exceat to Friston Road.

On a prominent spur of land overlooking the Cuckmere river and visible from the sea, an excavation controlled by the Rector of Westdean and the Sussex Archaeological Society discovered between nine and twelve inches below the turf, the stonework of the lower walling of what proved to be the parish church of old Exceat.

The uncovered remains revealed the lower course of stonework to a very small church comprising a nave, a narrow south door and a semi-circular chancel built soon after the Norman Conquest about 1080. The thick walls were of a mixture of chalk, greensand stone from (east) Bourne, flint and Caen stone, while in the dug soil were pieces of moulded stone as if from a font. Still further investigation revealed occasional fragments of coloured glass dating from *c.* 1290 and of a beauty closely resembling that in the windows of North Stoke church near Arundel. Those discoveries dating from more recent times were fragments of stoneware and bottle glass.

Of particular interest was the discovery nearly two feet below the turf and in the centre of the nave, of a stone grave slab covering a grave situated some two feet deeper and holding a complete human skeleton with its feet towards the east. With the skeleton was another human skull and some large human bones. The grave itself was very well made of chalk sides smoothed with a plaster finish and this grave, together with its human remains still intact below a stone slab, is again deep under the turf of Exceat.

Records of 1342 indicate that Exceat suffered, as did many other villages, from the ruthless coastal raids of the French; such raids when much was destroyed and so many slain, were the reason, it is thought, the village was eventually deserted.

Of the vicars known to have been at the church of Exceat village, the earliest was '. . . Richard, parson of Excete . . .' in 1255, a date that confirms a Norman origin.

1914

On Tuesday 4th August, Britain entered the Great War, mere days after the German invasion of Belgium.

A few days later, in response to a government introduction, horses from the surrounding farms were brought to the Pleasure Ground (by the Common Pond) about which the Hailsham vicar the Rev. F. Clyde-Harvey wrote:

> . . . they were inspected and those selected commandeered for the war. Though some faces looked strained as they parted from their favourite horse, and were left without any for agricultural purposes, yet there was no murmuring . . .

At this time a territorial detachment of the Royal Artillery was based in Hailsham with their horses in Parsonage (later Vicarage) Field, the Deer Paddock in George Street and the Market.

1914

It was reported at a meeting of the Hailsham parish council on 16th October that the mantles of the gas lamps in Station Road opposite the Railway Cattle Dock were often broken. The damage was caused by boys climbing the post and swinging on the bar.

> ... it was resolved that some barbed wire be placed on the upper part of the post ...

The cattle dock was a long row of strong cattle pens extending along the platform of a railway siding. This allowed animals to be driven from the pens into the cattle trucks of a goods train.

1915

In July, the Royal Naval Air Service under Dover Command established a Royal Naval Air Station at Lower Willingdon. The airfield and hangars were on land, bordered by what are now Coppice Avenue, Broad Street and Wannock Lane with entrances near to the *British Queen* inn and another from the Polegate to Jevington Road.

Known as the Polegate Station its duty was to patrol shipping in the Channel and to seek the menacing German submarines. Both the station and the increasingly efficient range of its airship patrols quickly established an excellent reputation in the Naval Air Service.

On 22nd December 1917 in conditions of thick fog, patrolling airships were instructed to return to base. Arriving back in darkness and appalling conditions of fog and rain, an airship mistook other lights for field landing lights, and crashed on top of another airship. Both airships were burnt out with loss of life.

The station closed in 1919.

1916

On 30th June, the day before the terrible killing battle of the Somme opened in the Great War, Company Sergeant-Major Nelson Victor Carter of the 12th Battalion Royal Sussex Regiment (Lowther's Lambs), won a posthumous Victoria Cross for his bravery during action at Boar's Head, Richebourg L'Avoue near Lille in France. The citation for his award read:

> ... For most conspicuous bravery. During an attack he was in command of the 4th wave of the assault. Under intense shell and machine-gun fire he penetrated, with a few men into the enemy's second line and inflicted heavy casualties with bombs.
> When forced to retire to the enemy's first line he captured a machine-gun and shot the gunner with his revolver. Finally after carrying several wounded men into safety he was himself mortally wounded and died in a few minutes.
> His conduct throughout the day was magnificent ...

Several comrades of Nelson Carter wrote to his widow telling of their sorrow at his death, but ironically their letters were followed by an official notification

It is a matter of sincere regret to
me that the death of Serjeant-Major Nelson
Victor Carter, 12th Battalion Royal Sussex
Regiment, deprived me of the pride of personally conferring upon him the Victoria Cross,
the greatest of all rewards for valour and
devotion to duty.

George R.I.

Mrs. Catherine Carter,
    33, Grey's Road,
        EASTBOURNE.

Letter from King George V

reporting Carter as only 'Missing'. Many weeks later, on 17th November, Mrs. Carter wrote to the War Office seeking a correction to their unfortunate error and on 14th December came two replies: the first was notification of Nelson Carter being 'Killed in Action' and the second, an apology for their previous incorrect letter quoting him as missing and explaining that it was '. . . owing to conditions prevailing at the Front . . .'. The 'conditions prevailing' were that nineteen thousand men had been killed and fifty-seven thousand were casualties on the first day of the Somme battle, mere hours after the attack in which Nelson Carter died.

The award (confirmed in *The London Gazette* 9th September 1916) of the supreme medal for gallantry to this Hailsham man provoked tremendous local sympathy for his widow with her six month old child named Jessie. A fund was set up for their welfare with one of the contributions being the income from an evening show at the 'Hailsham Electric Cinema'. The wholehearted response to the appeal involving both Hailsham and Eastbourne, paid for the education of Nelson Carter's daughter in addition to an annuity on her twenty-first birthday.

The last letter written by Nelson Carter to his wife was but a few hours before his regiment moved into action and just two days before he was killed. In it he reveals concern for his men.

> . . . it seems a long time since I had a letter from you, how are you and young Jessie getting along? . . . one day its pouring and the next day its boiling hot, just the right sort of weather to lay the lads up, but I suppose we shall get a rest shortly and some of the poor devils need it too . . . have a devil of a lot to do before we move off tonight so I suppose that I must draw to a close . . .

Nelson Carter was born 9th April 1887 and lived all his boyhood at Harebeating in a Brewery Road (later re-named Battle Road) cottage. He was educated half a mile away at the Board School, which much later, when greatly enlarged for comprehensive teaching, became Hailsham School.

In 1911 Nelson married Kathleen Camfield of Rotherfield at St Mary's parish church in Old Town, Eastbourne. (*See* adjacent illustration and appendix 'O').

1918

William Strickland, Justice of the Peace, died on 25th May aged eighty-two years. He had lived in the old house 'Cortlandt' for thirty-seven years and proved to be an outstanding man. (*See* appendix 'P').

1918

On 28th November the Hailsham parish council resolved to,

> . . . take the initiative for providing by public subscription a permanent memorial for the men of Hailsham who made the supreme sacrifice in the great world war whilst serving in His Majesty's Forces upholding the cause of Freedom and Justice . . .

A public meeting of the 4th March, 1919 discussed how best the town could express their respect and gratitude for those who had died in the Great War. The decision of the meeting was that a monument, together with a memorial hall, be erected in the High Street and that the house 'South View Villa' in Western Road opposite the Recreation Ground, should be purchased for conversion into an institute.

While efforts were being made to raise the money, a letter was sent by two brothers: J. Robert Green and Arthur Green, offering to purchase the house and present it to the council in memory of their brother Ewart V. Green, who was killed in action at Poelcapelle in Belgium, north of Lille on 30th October 1917. The acceptance of the gift was confirmed by the council on 14th November 1919 when it was agreed the house would be converted into a library with reading room and an 'institute' for recreation.

In April 1920 the library was opened together with a Memorial Institute that had a games room with a billiards table.

The library was under the supervision of two honorary librarians and with a total of seven hundred and fifty books, one hundred and ninety-six people were enrolled. The cost of furnishing both the library and the reading room was a little over £100.

A council meeting of the 28th November 1918 had also favoured the erection of a monument to the fallen together with a war memorial hall somewhere in the High Street. Once again a fine gesture solved this second public approved plan, for a Mr. J. S. O. Robertson-Luxford offered a suitable plot of land to the council. The land, next to the old chestnut tree in the High Street, was accepted and a grey Cornish granite War Memorial was erected in 1921.

Later in this same year the rest of the land behind the war memorial was let by the council to the 'Comrades of the Great War' at a rent of 5s. 0d per year, and on the site was built a wooden memorial hut named the 'Old Comrades Club'.

Over many years the club was to prove of considerable benefit to the town and its demolition when a shopping precinct was constructed enabled it to be rebuilt but a few yards from its original site in a more permanent form, to become in 1968 the successful and prosperous 'Hailsham Club'.

1920

A plot of land in South Road, Hailsham, was after several years of legal enquiry and investigation, transferred for the use of the Southwark Catholic diocese of which Hailsham was a part.

For centuries the land had lain waste as common land until in 1845 the Enclosure Act resulted in the common land of the manor of Michelham being divided up among tenants. It was part of this land, once owned by John Thatcher of Priesthawes who died in 1649, that was assigned to the trustees of a charity devoted to Catholic purposes. (*See* entry for 1546).

This land was destined to become the site upon which the future Catholic parish church was to be built.

1921

On 21st October the Hailsham parish council sent a letter to Lord Sackville asking him,

... if he was prepared to hand the Common Pond over to the council on easy terms ...

There was at this time a serious unemployment problem and the aim of the council was to provide employment by improving the pond and making the area into a 'pleasure ground'.

Also with the hope of providing employment, letters were sent out to business-men in the parish and to the East Sussex County Council from whom it was hoped, work on building and the making of footpaths could be agreed.

In January 1922 a reply from Lord Sackville's agent offered to sell the Common Pond to the council for £300. It was at a public meeting that, with the help to the council of private subscribers, the purchase was agreed.

1922

Mass was said in St Wilfrid's, Hailsham's first Catholic parish church, a simple wooden structure built in spite of initial public protest.

In previous years, use had been made of a loft over stables, all part of the old brewery and approached by an outside wooden staircase. This property is now part of the Apaseal factory in Battle Road.

1923

A meeting of Hailsham parish council on 19th October decided that if there should be enough ice on the Common Pond in the coming winter to allow skating, a charge of 6d. per day would be made.

1923

Hamblins Mill (formerly Lower Mill) in Mill Road, Hailsham, was destroyed by fire. The structure was rebuilt in 1924 when instead of the normal wind driven sweeps, an engine was installed to drive the machinery.

1925

The Duke of Devonshire conveyed to the Sussex Archaeological Trust his property, Wilmington Priory, and in pursuing their policy of care and preservation, much work was undertaken in the interest of restoration. In due course the society introduced to the priory a small museum devoted to the display of agri-cultural exhibits.

Also at this time, the Duke conveyed to the society the land upon which the 'Long Man of Wilmington' had been cut and outlined in bricks. With the need to improve its condition the society in 1969 replaced the ageing bricks with more permanent white concrete blocks. (*See* appendix 'Q').

c. 1925

Horselunges Manor built at Hellingly in *c.* 1487 was restored with meticulous care by Walter Godfrey, C.B.E., F.S.A. of the Sussex Archaeological Society. It is now recognised as one of the finest moated timbered houses in the south of England.

c. 1932

The large brick building of the old Hailsham Union was demolished after being derelict for many years.

The site, on the western corner of Hawks Road and the A 271 (Lower Horsebridge Road) lay waste until 1938 when a few bungalows were built. In c. 1948 the rest of the site including the corner portion was taken up by new council houses and a few years later, it was on the surrounding fields of Lansdowne Farm that the many houses of the Lansdowne Estate were built.

1932

On a beam in the attic of 'Cortlandt', the old house in George Street, an interesting leather and brass diary was found. Dated 1808 and well written in sepia ink it was a record for that year of the activities of Matthias Slye, a Hailsham farmer.

The diary clearly reflected the farming year and also revealed a close social life with many friends in outlying places, and frequent visiting with much tea drinking. Seldom did the weather discourage these many journeys along the lanes, sometimes by horse and often on foot. There is also mention of tythe feasts, oyster feasts, the Horsebridge fair, days at the market and a Ball at the *Crown* inn.

Matthias Slye also enjoyed an excellent relationship with officers at Hailsham barracks:

> . . . six lambs sold to Col. Van Cortlandt at 14s/- each . . .

and those soldiers who could play musical instruments were themselves it appears, sought for social events in the town.

1932

The house 'Cortlandt' was, within months of the death of William Strickland's widow, purchased by the Rural District Council for conversion into offices. The price paid was £2,500.

Still remaining of the house, built before the Napoleonic wars was much of the plaster work, wide plank flooring and the by now frail windows. Also intact was the very narrow twisting staircase that led out of the old kitchen and up to the low ceilinged servants' attic.

To the rear, the old coach house with stables and the small building for implements, straw and horse feed, are even now much as they always were, for they still have their uneven rafters of split silver birch trunks complete with bark as the carpenters left them nearly two hundred years ago. Also to be seen today are the clay roof tiles, fastened with simple wooden pegs just as they were left by the same carpenters of long ago.

Reflecting the care with which the original builders worked, the brickwork of the outhouses exactly matches that of the house with the subtle decorative feature of nails sunk into the wet cement joints.

The house 'Cortlandt' is now protected by being listed as a house of special interest but in 1982, its use as council offices finally ended when a large block of new office accommodation was built in Vicarage Lane behind the Hailsham shopping precinct.

1933

An archaeological excavation near the parish church at Selmeston exposed some six thousand four hundred worked flint implements dating back to prehistoric man, of a period between one thousand five hundred to six thousand years B.C. The flints were found in and around the dwelling pits lived in by men and women of the Mesolithic time, and of such interest were the finds that the discovery was considered the most important made in Sussex, and one of the first of its kind in Britain.

Of the flints recovered many were burnt, having been repeatedly made red-hot for use as cooking stones when they would be dropped into water to heat it; such stones were also used for heating food. The traces of ashes that were found as the remains of fires, revealed evidence that oak, hazelwood and hawthorn had been burnt.

1933

Horatio Bottomley the journalist and financier died. Born at Bethnal Green in 1860 and reared in an orphanage, Bottomley during his life handled immense sums of money, sometimes with brilliance but often with dishonesty until in 1922, he was convicted of fraud and sentenced to seven years penal servitude.

An obituary of this colourful personality quoted:

> ... opportunities sadly wasted ... personal magnetism, eloquence, enthusiasm and power to convince ... he might have been a leader at the Bar ...

Elected an M.P. in 1906, he entertained liberally at his country house at Upper Dicker where he spent vast sums of money living in luxury within reach of his racehorses in training at Alfriston.

Apart from building cottages for the workpeople, Bottomley created considerable local employment over the years which, with his generosity, made him a popular figure in the village.

Returning from prison to his home 'Crossways House' with enormous debts, he was made bankrupt for the fourth time and died in a state of poverty. The house complete with its man-made lake and private racecourse is now a day and boarding school called St Bede's.

1933

The restoration of Herstmonceux Castle was completed by Sir Paul Latham, M.P.

1935

Queen Mary and the Princess Royal, who were staying with the Duke of Devonshire at Compton Place in Eastbourne, came to Hailsham on 10th March. The journey enabled a visit to the High Street shop of Kerridges where antiques were purchased for delivery to Buckingham Palace.

It was close to this time that Queen Mary was a visitor to Herstmonceux Castle.

1937

In March, at a meeting of the Air Raid Precautions Committee of the Hailsham Rural District Council at 'Cortlandt', Colonel Agg presented a progress report dealing with the results of alerting the rural district parishes to the need for the creation of a civil defence organisation. Contrary to the response in other parishes, it was recorded that in Hailsham:

> . . . there is no training; general apathy in the village, no volunteers coming forward.
> Col. Agg has got the matter in hand and will try new methods to get volunteers . . .

A year later the situation had improved and there were then sixty wardens in the parish.

1939-45

The Second World War

Sections of Pevensey Castle were fortified and occupied at different times by British, Canadian and United States troops. In 1940 an Observation and Command Post was set up to be followed by 'pill-boxes' for machine gun defence and a 'block-house' with anti-tank guns. Later the U.S. troops built a Radio Direction Centre for the detection of enemy aircraft. Some of this special defence structure has been retained to record a phase in English history.

In 1941 Canadian troops moved into Michelham Priory and remained in training until they embarked on the tragic commando raid on Dieppe in 1942 when of five thousand Canadians who took part, three thousand three hundred and sixty were casualties, many of whom knew Hailsham well.

A map of the English Channel drawn on the wall of an upper room of the priory gatehouse and used in connection with the Dieppe assault can still be seen preserved behind glass.

In 1942 the Downs between Jevington and Willingdon were used for testing the Churchill tank during its final development stages and it was on Combe Hill that the Prime Minister, Winston Churchill, witnessed a demonstration of the tank.

During the war years enemy aircraft dropped over the parish of Hailsham a total of one hundred and ten bombs and one thousand two hundred and twenty-five incendiaries. (*See* appendix 'S').

1940

The defence plan for the South East of England against which the German Army was expected to launch its main invasion attack, designated certain towns within reach of the channel coast as Nodal Points. These strategic towns were regarded as being within the area expected to be in the path of enemy bridgehead troops and their initial objectives.

Hailsham was listed as one such Nodal Point to be manned by both army and home guard troops with the task of controlling movement of the civilian population and defending the locality with its strategically important road junctions.

In direct contrast to the army and its defence role of resisting the enemy attack, there had been much planning and undercover work involving the formation of Resistance units located behind vulnerable coast lines. And with great urgency such secret units were organised behind the threatened coast of Kent and Sussex.

Each unit of selected men had a well-equipped underground hide-out from which to emerge for sabotage or attacks on enemy troops. This organisation was created in 1940 and was in a state of readiness in the Hailsham area as well as other places in the south of England. (*See* appendix 'R').

1943

The mural paintings to the interior of Berwick church were dedicated by Bishop Bell of Chichester. They had been designed and painted by the artist Duncan Grant, who lived close to Firle Beacon, and Vanessa and Quentin Bell.

Berwick church had been chosen as suitable for the experimental renewal of the ancient tradition of wall painting in Sussex churches, for having suffered the destruction of its stained glass by bombing, the new clear glass windows now flooded the church with light to create the perfect setting.

Dominating the interior is the vast 'Christ in Glory' by Duncan Grant that fills the space above the chancel arch, while the large wall areas of the nave have fine murals with many details significant to Sussex, some portraying local men of the wartime period.

The pulpit has painted floral panels and the chancel is enlivened with many paintings reflecting the Downs, seasons of the year and the religious ceremonies encountered in the span of life.

Sir Kenneth Clark, the art historian, has said,

> ... these decorations will remain a fine monument to English painting of this period ...

1946

A tentative venture into wine making produced some four hundred and fifty gallons of red currant wine and vintage cider in the garage of a house called 'Merrydown', and this simple initiative was in time to prove the humble beginning of the now famous Merrydown Wine Company.

Following the purchase of the burnt-out ruin of Horam Manor and much re-building, steps were taken by Ian Howie and Jack Ward towards serious production. The encouraging result was a new concept of vintage cider that at once proved commercially acceptable.

Many years of steady expansion has seen improving techniques and specialist equipment, some for the first time in England, achieve a turnover of over five million pounds and a world-wide reputation. Of this now vast output of both cider and vinegar, much is exported to Europe, in addition to Africa, U.S.A., West Indies, Australia and even to mid-Pacific. This company has contributed much to the prosperity of Horam and the prestige of Sussex.

1948

The Royal Greenwich Observatory was moved from Greenwich to Herstmonceux Castle where clearer observing conditions were to be found.

Among the functions of the establishment were: telescope and instrument design, providing navigational tables, measuring the positions of the Sun, Moon and Planets and a worldwide responsibility for time keeping.

In 1958 the observatory was visited by H.R.H. The Duke of Edinburgh and in 1967 H.M. Queen Elizabeth II also came to Herstmonceux to open the new Sir Isaac Newton telescope.

1953

During the digging for foundations of the equatorial group of telescopes at the Royal Greenwich Observatory, Herstmonceux, six pottery vessels were uncovered from a circular area of ground ten feet across.

The pottery, made over one thousand nine hundred years ago, was the work of a tribe thought to have come from Brittany who were prominent in East Sussex until the Romans landed in A.D. 43. Five of the vessels were found to contain the burnt remains of human bone.

1953

The amalgamation took place of Burfield and Son with Green Bros., two very old Hailsham companies with established national reputations, who by now had both extended their manufacturing activities far beyond that of ropemaking. It is however with rope that such incredible technical progress has been made.

In a world away from the physical tasks early in the century when men and boys toiled daily for simple results on their individual rope-walks, there is in Hailsham today a machine of advanced design producing the largest synthetic rope in the world. This eight-strand plaited rope of twenty-four inches circumference is used in the major ports of the world as well as nearer home with giant tankers in the oil fields of the North Sea.

1954

The ringing each evening of the curfew on the tenor bell in the tower of Hailsham parish church was discontinued.

1955

The new permanent Catholic parish church of St Wilfrid's in South Road, Hailsham, was blessed and the first Mass offered by the Bishop of Southwark on Ascension Day 19th May. This momentous day for Catholics came over three hundred years after John Thatcher had dedicated his land and the site to God. (*See* entries of 1920 and 1922).

1956

The last owner of the old family grocery business in Hailsham's Market Square, Harry White, gave the North Street house called 'Hardwycke' with its large garden, to the East Sussex County Council to allow the building of an infants school. The school opened in 1964 and was called White House School.

The house 'Hardwycke' was last lived in by the late Lady Winifred Corkran before she moved to 'The Old Thatch' in Hellingly. Her husband was Major-

General Sir Charles Corkran, whose brother was for many years Comptroller of the Household to Princess Beatrice, the youngest child of Queen Victoria.

1958

The first specialist-built and fully-equipped Fire Station for Hailsham was opened in Victoria Road. This major improvement allowed the vacated fire station in Market Street to be converted into an extension of the parish council offices.

A heavy bell of great age, with signs of having had much use was presented in 1972 to the Hailsham Fire Brigade by Mrs. Monica Bowen, the daughter of William Strickland. It now hangs in the new Fire Station but once it hung on the rear wall of the house 'Cortlandt' where it served as a fire warning bell.

Previous to the presentation, Monica Bowen commissioned a report on the bell from a campanology specialist.

The evidence that emerged indicated the bell having been cast in either Russia or more probably Poland in *c.* 1580, with signs of it having survived great use. Of unusual shape, the bell is without inscription but is profuse in religious decoration including a crucifix and priestly figure.

It is probable, bearing in mind their early history, that the bell was linked with the Van Cortlandt family.

1959

Michelham Priory was purchased by Mrs. Stella Hotblack who, after embarking on a programme of repairs and improvements, presented the historic property to the safe keeping of the Sussex Archaeological Society.

1960

The Reverend John D. Bickersteth, Vicar of Ashburnham, gave the mansion of Ashburnham Place together with 220 acres of gardens, woods and lakes originally set out in 1767 by Capability Brown, to the trustees of the newly-formed Ashburnham Christian Trust for use in '. . . extending the kingdom of our Lord Jesus Christ throughout the world . . .'.

During the twenty-two years since this date, Ashburnham Place has become famous as a residential centre for Christian conferences, lectures and spiritual renewal, until it now receives some seven thousand people in a year from churches of all denominations. Much of the work of maintaining the centre is undertaken by young volunteers especially from other European countries. (*See* appendix 'T').

1961

The hoard of Roman coins dating from the 3rd cent. nearly one thousand seven hundred years ago and found in a garden at Polegate were sold to the City Museum in Birmingham.

1961

New offices for the East Sussex River Board were built on the waste ground in George Street, once the site of the paddock for William Strickland's herd of deer.

Later, in 1967, these offices were converted to become the sub-divisional head-quarters of the Sussex Police.

1965-68

The Vicarage Field shopping precinct was built in these years incorporating the first Health Centre in Sussex.

The precinct was built on what was once church property called Parsonage or Vicarage Field and the site, during the second world war, held an underground air raid shelter.

In the process of clearing the field for building work, a number of old but very small shops were demolished. At the same time, several fine old oak trees along the edges of the field were also lost to the town.

1967

Hamblins Mill in Mill Road, Hailsham, owned at this time by Gilbert Catt, finally ceased to work. Up to now it had operated as a provender mill, grinding oats, barley and other cereals for animal feed.

1968

Following the closure of the railway line for passenger trains from Hailsham to Heathfield in 1965, it was just three years later that the line from Polegate to Hailsham also ceased to be used. This resulted in the closure of Hailsham railway station on the 9th September 1968.

Serious consideration was given to the possible conversion of the former railway route from Polegate to Heathfield into a public nature walk, but in 1980 the site of Hailsham station and goods-yard was cleared to become a housing estate.

1969

Major restoration work was undertaken on the outline of the 'Long Man of Wilmington'. The work involved replacing the once yellow, but now very old bricks with white concrete blocks. In so doing, there arose an opportunity to carry out exploratory digging at selected places on the Long Man figure, when it was hoped such digging might produce evidence of age.

Apart from the pursuit of age there was a need to seek possible indications of where in the distant past the outline of the Long Man may have been altered. For this investigation an advanced system of probing the soil with electric charges was carried out over specific areas.

At the end of the restoration and before the final white concrete block to the figure was lowered into position, a sealed container was buried. Its contents included,

> . . . items of topical interest for future generations . . .

together with full details of the work and investigations carried out. (*See* appendix 'Q').

1970

On land along the Willingdon Road at Ocklynge Hill, two houses were demolished creating a substantial area of cleared land for building new houses. With the knowledge that in 1909 Anglo-Saxon graves had been uncovered on adjacent ground, a rescue excavation was carried out seeking further evidence of past occupation.

The excavation, under the direction of Patricia M. Stevens, revealed in due course twenty-six graves aligned, except in the case of a young child, in a west-east direction. Most graves had been carefully dug, some with a scooped-out hollow for the head and with six of the bodies, iron knives had been buried.

This recent excavation is of considerable interest for when the adjoining land had been opened up in 1909, not only were large numbers of skeletons uncovered but even more remained untouched. Again, some years later on nearby land but this time on the opposite side of Willingdon Road, yet a third area of burials was discovered when skeletons were found during the digging of a trench by the G.P.O. Thus there appears little doubt that the total area of land found to contain graves indicated an ancient cemetery of considerable size, and one that must have been part of a substantial Saxon settlement.

These Saxon people died and were buried nearly thirteen hundred years ago on high ground where today, on the ancient Saxon cemetery are the new houses of Saxon Place and the busy road over Ocklynge Hill.

Once, this place two hundred feet above sea level was a dominating height, commanding to the north-east a view across the inland waters of Pevensey and to the south, there was land reaching to the coast where many hundreds of years into the future, the town of Eastbourne would develop. (*See* appendix 'U').

1971

On Sunday 4th April, Louis Francis Salzman, C.B.E., M.A., D.Litt., F.S.A. died aged ninety-three.

Educated at Haileybury and Pembroke College, Cambridge, Salzman (his name was spelt Salzmann until 1918) was a Sussex man who spent most of his early life at the house called 'Downford' built *c.* 1838 in George Street, Hailsham. In more recent years the house has been converted into council offices, a fate already suffered by 'Cortlandt', the adjoining property, but again like 'Cortlandt', this old property is now empty and awaiting its fate.

An editor of the *Victoria History of the Counties of England* from 1934 to 1939, he was also the writer of eleven books in the field of medieval history, two surveys of English trade and industries in the Middle Ages and a documentary history of building in England down to 1540. Salzman was probably the foremost scholar of Sussex history and his long life of research and lecturing, much of it with the Sussex Archaeological Society, brought him wide acclaim. It was said he,

> . . . will put all historians in his debt forever . . .

and from an H.M. Government source:

> . . . the great Sussex antiquary, the late L. F. Salzman . . .

Concerned over a lifetime with the affairs of the Sussex Archaeological Society, he was accorded the honour of the Union Jack flying from Lewes Castle on his ninety-third birthday. Sadly, this salute to the man was but days before his death and a distinguished obituary in *The Times.* His memory is respected by a special memorial panel in Barbican House, Lewes, and a handsome carved plaque in Michelham Priory.

1971

The one hundred and twenty five acre reservoir constructed for the Eastbourne Waterworks Company was completed in the area of land formerly enclosed by a wide sweep of the River Cuckmere, west of Arlington village.

While creating the reservoir shape by excavating soil from the former farmland, the remains were found at a depth of twelve inches of a fourth century Romano-British pottery kiln and workshop, together with many fragments, the remains of pottery vessels.

The evidence uncovered suggested that pottery had been made and kiln fired on a large scale and to an extent not previously found in Sussex. Expert opinion has advanced the theory that the unusual scale of manufacture could be explained by a need for such products at Pevensey, where there was a large population of Roman soldiers and their supporters.

Since the creation of the reservoir eleven years ago it has become an official nature reserve with one of the best wintering waters in the south-east. Of previous winter arrivals were some four thousand widgeon and over four hundred Canada geese while in the last ten years, one hundred and seventy-six bird species have been identified.

1971-75

Archaeological excavations during this period at Michelham Priory revealed the site of a hitherto unknown and separate large medieval hall. It was a major discovery that disclosed the hall was built before the moat existed.

Earlier excavations uncovered the sites of the priory church cloisters and a refectory destroyed at the Dissolution. During this work much medieval pottery was found together with many items once used in the daily medieval life of the priory.

1974

A Local Government Act of 1972 allowed parish councils the opportunity of elevating the status of their parish to that of a town, a change that enabled a council to replace the title of Council Chairman with that of Mayor, should a council so desire.

On 25th May 1973, following a vote taken at a meeting of the Hailsham parish council it:

> ... was unanimously agreed that the Hailsham Parish Council, when the 1972 Local Government Act becomes law in April 1974, be known as the Town Council ...

and a year later on 20th May 1974 the following changes of titles were confirmed:

'Chairman of the Parish Council' to 'Town Mayor'
'Vice-Chairman of the Parish Council' to 'Deputy Town Mayor',
'Clerk to the Parish Council' to 'Town Clerk'.

The first mayor of Hailsham T. Jeffrey Holman, in a growing community, now led a town council but the new title did not increase the power of the council.

1978

H.R.H. The Princess Anne visited Hailsham factories of the Hawkins & Tipson Group on 22nd September. The arrival of the royal party was by helicopter on the sports field adjacent to the factory of Burfield & Son in South Road, which she toured before visiting the premises of Green Bros. in Summerheath Road. Here the Princess unveiled a tablet to commemorate the occasion of her visit.

1978

Duncan Grant the artist, died aged ninety-three years, having lived at Charleston Farmhouse between West Firle and Selmeston for over sixty years.

The house, at the foot of Firle Beacon, has an interior that is unique for almost every wall of its many rooms has been painted in freehand patterns, while the countless surfaces of doors, cupboards, fireplaces, chairs and table-tops have on them designs, motifs and even simple scenes. In some areas of prominence there are impressive and colourful designs with flowers and bold figure painting.

Apart from occasional contributions by other artists the work is by both Duncan Grant and Vanessa Bell,

> . . . of a particular style, now part of art history . . .

The farmhouse has also been described as a 'habitation of genius and among its guests over many years have been: Benjamin Britten, Maynard Keynes, Lytton Strachey, T. S. Eliot, Bertrand Russell and Virginia Woolf together with several of the major artists of this century.

The work of Duncan Grant has been compared to the French Impressionist Henri Matisse.

1982

The Wealden District Council have chosen their new offices in Vicarage Lane, Hailsham, as the place in which there will be a control centre with a communication system. It is visualised that at some future date such a centre could be organised and manned as an emergency headquarters should the need arise to co-ordinate protective and survival measures in case of a nuclear attack.

BIBLIOGRAPHY

Constant reference has been made to many of the one hundred and eighteen volumes in the Collections of the Sussex Archaeological Society in addition to other titles from which the following is a selection.

Agincourt	C. Hibberd
Archaeology of Sussex	E. C. Curwen
Captain Swing Riots . . .	Hobsbawm and Rude
Chronicles of Pevensey . . .	M. A. Lower
Coast of Sussex	J. D. Parry
Concise History of England . .	F. E. Halliday
Diary of Matthias Slye . . .	Edited Monica Bowen
Diary of Thomas Turner . .	Edited Florence Turner
Dictionary of National Biography .	Edited Sidney Lee
Heathfield Memorials . . .	P. Lucas
History of the Church in England	J. R. H. Moorman
History of England (1787) . .	G. F. Raymond
History of England . . .	G. M. Trevelyan
History of Hailsham . . .	L. F. Salzman
History of Sussex	J. R. Armstrong
Honest Thieves	G. Nicholls
Island Race	W. S. Churchill
Kings and Queens of England .	Scott Moncrieff
The Last Ditch	D. Lampe
Mapping Survey of Sussex . .	H. Margary
Martyrs of Jesus	E. T. Stoneham
Michelham Priory	M. Pears
Nonconformists	N. Caplan
Parish Registers	J. C. Cox
Parochial History of Chiddingly .	M. A. Lower
Poor Relief in England and Wales .	G. W. Oxley
Posts of Hailsham	C. F. Williams
Roman Ways in the Weald . .	I. D. Margary
Secret Passages and Hiding Places .	J. Errand
Short History of Sussex . .	J. R. Lowerson
Some Early Pelhams . . .	Hon. Mrs. A. Pelham and D. Mclean
Some Smaller Manor Houses of Sussex	Viscountess Wolseley
St Wilfrids	Rev. L. E. Whatmore
Survey of the Agriculture of Sussex	R. H. B. Jesse
Sussex	Nairn and Pevsner
Sussex 1600–1660 . . .	A. Fletcher
Sussex Bells and Belfries . .	G. P. Elphick
Sussex Landscape	P. Brandon
The Thirteenth Century . .	Sir M. Powicke
Village of the Buckle . . .	W. A. Pearson
Wealden Iron	E. Straker
Wings Over Eastbourne . .	R. Armstrong
Worthies of Sussex . . .	M. A. Lower
1066: Year of the Conquest . .	D. Howarth

Appendix 'A' relating to the entries of c. 340 and 1538

The road the Romans built away from Pevensey Castle was westward, travelling to a spot close to and south of the area where at a future date, the village of Westham would be built. From here it turned sharply in a north–west direction, taking a line across the future Westham High Street until it reached Castle Farm.

The road now turned almost due west along the Old Sunken Lane, past North Breton Cottages to Ketchem Corner where it carried on into Peelings Lane and through Pickens Wood. Here, traces of the old Roman road can occasionally be discerned as far as the War Memorial at Stone Cross.

On a line due west, the route of the Roman road follows the modern road out of Stone Cross, past Hankham Place until its straight course takes it on to fields behind Brenchley Cottages. Eventually it emerges in front of Polegate station and continues in a straight line across the junction of Station Road, Hailsham Road and Polegate High Street, through the site of Polegate School until it reaches the A 22 by-pass.

At this place the Roman road was destroyed when the A 22 was built through it, but its course picks up the same straight line again after crossing the road and follows the Old Road, once called Farnestreet, where there are still surface signs of the buried Roman road. There is little doubt that this road was used by the Normans for it was mentioned in a Royal Charter of 1252 as 'the old road'.

Farnestreet, still called the Old Road, continues in a straight line uphill to Hide Farm and then on to Thornwell Cottage. At a quarter of a mile past Pickhams the Old Road turns south-west then sharply westward where the same Old Road is now called Moorshill Lane. It is along this lane we are carried to Chilver Bridge over the river Cuckmere, where much Roman pottery has been found in the past.

Once over the bridge the old Roman road follows the curve of the present road and finally crosses two fields to reach Berwick, almost at the level crossing. Continuing over the railway the route, where in places the position of the road is clearly seen, travels due west past Stonery Farm and reaches Selmeston near the church. At this place the route meets a Roman road running south to the A 27 at the *Barley Mow* inn and in the other direction, north along the present road to Poundfield Corner at Chalvington. Here again, Roman pottery has been found.

At this point it joins the site of an old Roman road that formed the eastern end of the dense grid-like layout of Roman roads covering a huge area that included Ripe and Chalvington. (*See* entry for 1538).

This Roman road from Pevensey to Chalvington, follows where possible, the higher ground and varies in width from ten to twenty-four feet with a camber, and gullies along each side for drainage.

The material used in road making was almost any hard material that may have been available close to where it was needed, and on this particular local road broken stone and flint were mostly used. Where Roman roads crossed areas of the iron industry then slag and cinder could have been used, but always, the material was rammed down hard to a thickness of between four inches up to say ten inches. On occasions when today, part of the road suffers removal, the rammed materials can sometimes be lifted in firm layers, often with traces of well worn wheel ruts.

At this time over one thousand six hundred years since many of the Roman roads were built, the distance below ground level at which they are now found varies with the road's position and its surrounding soil.

It is possible a Roman road may only be buried under say one foot of soil but it may also be found with three feet of soil above it and the reason such a road can now be so much below ground level is primarily due to countless years of vegetation growth.

The rough surface of a neglected road will soon attract its first weeds or grass which in rotting away will retain windblown dust or leaves to further encourage the next crop thus beginning the ever repeating plant life cycle of growth into decomposition which imperceptibly becomes a dusting of top soil. It is over many tens and hundreds of years that such top soil builds up into the depth of earth now covering Roman roads wherever they may be found.

Appendix 'B' relating to the entries of c. 1175 and c. 1205

When Otham Priory was founded in *c.* 1175 it stood close to the tidal waters that spread out behind Pevensey and was on a site only two miles from Hailsham's Common Pond and barely half a mile from Polegate.

The exterior walls of this very old chapel are, with buttresses, still standing firm in spite of some parts being nearly eight hundred years old. Most of the walls are now of rough local flint with stones of various sizes picked up no doubt as they were available from elsewhere and built in from time to time to maintain the structure.

A door at the rear of the south wall led, it is recorded, to the Priory and as it now opens on to a modest square lawn it may well once have been the garth that was originally surrounded by simple cloisters.

Otham Chapel lost its religious status possibly three hundred years ago and since then has been used as a farm outbuilding. Certainly in the last century it has been a barn, a stable, a cowshed and a few years ago, a chicken house. But perhaps the final indignity was the painting of an abstract mural, albeit with elegance, over the west wall as decor suitable for the use of the chapel as a disco by a former resident family. But through it all there is still clear evidence that it was once a chapel in spite of damaged stonework and many layers of whitewash.

A new owner has just transformed this old chapel and it now has the addition of an inserted damp proof course, heating system, sealed and boarded ceiling, polished wood block floor, new doors and a large new window in the formerly bricked up space of the East window above the long gone altar.

The final flourish in the history of this former Priory Chapel is that it is now blessed with a billiards table to create yet another use for this structure formerly of such historic significance.

The Tithe map of 1842 showing Hailsham parish indicates that certain fields of the original Otham Priory had in 1842 still retained their names by then over seven hundred years old.

The field closest to the priory and but a short distance from the old road used by its visitors was still recorded on the Tithe map of 1842 as Fair Place and would be on the natural site for the Otham annual fair of over seven hundred years ago.

References to Otham early in this century have quoted 'abbey', but on the few occasions it has been referred to since then it has generally been accepted as having been a priory.

Appendix 'C' relating to the entry of 1229

When long ago the Romans established themselves at Pevensey, then much later, when the Normans repaired the old Roman walls and built their castle after the defeat of King Harold, the marsh as we now know it, was a vast expanse of inland water. There was usually enough depth to enable boats to moor at Hooe, Wartling, Herstmonceux, Boreham and even within a short distance of Hailsham at any of the ridges of land that extended out from the town; they were ridges that usage eventually changed into the roads known today as Marshfoot Lane, Mill Road and Station Road.

The water was only broken by a few very small islands of which the largest were Horseye, Chilley, Manxeye and Rockhouse Bank (Normans Bay). The large houses such as Priesthawes and Glynleigh were built near the water but on land a little over fifty feet above mean sea level, and even Hailsham was only seventy-five feet above, except for its centre where the site for a church was chosen.

The land on which Otham Priory was built (*see c.* 1205) was not so well chosen, for it was a short distance from the water and on ground barely twenty-three feet high. The living conditions at such a spot proved to be disastrous and the Priory was eventually abandoned because of flooding, poor living and a total lack of even the most simple comfort.

Today, Pevensey Marsh (*see note,* p. 199) with its rivers and countless minor watercourses is all under firm control and utterly changed from the huge expanse of water the Conqueror and his army encountered. Extending westward as far as Hailsham and Willingdon, to the north Magham Down, and eastward to Hooe and Wartling, the tidal inland waterway of Pevensey allowed both the passage of boats and an important harbourage against the old town of Pevensey.

It was an area of over fourteen square miles that during many centuries was to see constant change. The dominating influence inevitably being the long coastline on which the shingle beach moved, often with devastating effect before a constantly beating sea.

From the earliest days, the perimeter landowners sought to reclaim nearby tidal areas of land to increase their wealth. They diverted watercourses and built embankments, and while some of the work survived, some proved ineffective and was swept aside. Success in reclaiming land from the inland sea water depended on many factors; there needed to be a shrewd assessment of its geographical position in relation to the tides and an honest caution against diverting water towards another landowner, a cynical practice that often provoked bitter legal disputes. But in spite of human complication and the immense forces of nature, the land field by field slowly continued to be reclaimed, changing in the course of generations the lives of the people who lived in the settlements around the water.

In early times, small boats transported materials and produce to and from the settlements around the inland waterway, and along the Wallers Haven river towards Boreham and beyond; but perhaps more surprising is the recorded evidence that as recently as 1645 certain watercourses still allowed the passage of boats carrying iron, corn, and timber, while in earlier times, the deeper channels would allow ships of even sixty tons to sail the inland waters.

On higher ground where the old town of Pevensey was built, the castle overlooked a small but thriving harbour from which ships sailed to France as well as to some English ports, while just five miles along the coast was the important quarry at (east) Bourne, where boats were loaded for sailing to Pevensey with stone for the castle and nearby large houses and parish churches.

But since those early days, changes in river courses, land reclamation, the building of sluices and finally the never-ending movement of coastal shingle that so often obstructed a sea entry, were all factors that over the centuries slowly changed the face of Pevensey.

The eventual emergence of the rich marshland pasture we know today has finally been due to the more recent expert control of the water by public authorities. But there yet remains a single factor to be added to the many other changes now part of history. It is the scarcely realised geographical fact concerning the degree to which, under certain conditions, a ground level can rise over a period of hundreds of years. This imperceptible change is due to several causes, among which are the actions of the wind moving dust and soil from high ground to low, the movement of soil by action of water and the ever-repeating cycle of vegetation growth and decay. Together with the many possible variations of circumstances, such subtleties in movement that scarcely seem to exist, can in fact and in time, serve to raise the level of low lying ground.

In 1915 the historian Louis Salzman, writing of Pevensey Marsh under the heading 'The Innings of Pevensey Levels' in volume fifty-three of the Sussex Archaeological Collections, recorded:

> ... taking into consideration the rise of the ground during the course of centuries, a rise particularly rapid in the case of land lying at the foot of hills and constantly liable to inundation, we shall probably be well within the mark if we consider that all land below 12 feet was submerged at high tide during the Roman period ...

Note: On various of the maps published by the Ordnance Survey, the particular area referred to is named more accurately as Pevensey Levels.

Appendix 'D' relating to the entry of 1546

The Pope, at war with England, excommunicated Queen Elizabeth who caused the State to ruthlessly condemn any practice of the Catholic Faith. It was a time in religion when England was a divided nation. But many were loyal to the faith of Rome, in spite of knowing that to hear Mass or receive the Sacrament according to Catholic practice was a terrible risk. There were informers ready to betray and when priests were caught, their fate could be torture, death and even the ultimate brutality of beheading and quartering. To only harbour a man was deemed a serious felony and with discovery came the risk of savage reprisal.

In 1586 a training centre was set up in Douai in Flanders and near Lille, to which selected Englishmen were sent for training in the work of reviving the catholicism of the Pope. Upon their return to England as members of the Jesuit order of Priests, these brave men were able with the utmost stealth and disguise to move from one house to another, wherein each was concealed a small room or chapel, usually with an ingenious hiding place for a priest in danger. If the house permitted and discovery was threatened, then escape was sometimes possible through a concealed tunnel or passage.

These places were called priest-holes and their disguised entrances had to be good enough to survive the most rigorous house search. Such a hiding place still exists in an old house close to Hellingly parish church.

Such silent and hidden strongholds of the Catholic Faith, more often to be found in west rather than East Sussex, were invariably in the houses of land-owners and such a house owned by the Thatcher family was 'Priesthawes', near Hailsham.

The historian M. J. Kitch has written:

> . . . other family establishments of Catholic squires were maintained in East Sussex with varying degrees of legal and financial ingenuity by the Gages at Firle . . . they were becoming what may almost be called Mass-centres for the very widely dis-persed village Catholic families . . .

Appendix 'E' relating to entry of 1610

About this time, local prisoners charged with more serious crimes were usually taken to the Assizes at East Grinstead when they could be tried within days of their arrest. A considerable number of verdicts were 'not guilty', especially with charges of witchcraft, but in many cases of guilt punishment was harsh.

When a guilty prisoner could prove he was able to read, he could be passed to the Bishop for sentencing. One such who benefited from this advantage was John Norberry of Hailsham who on 4th January 1569, broke into Wannock Mill and stole malt and wheat-meal. He was guilty but 'allowed clergy'.

> . . . of those found guilty, more than one is noted as 'clerk', that is, he read the 'neck verse' and was delivered to the Bishop; the others were hanged . . .*

Branding, though rare, was still carried out as when Anne Pyneon, spinster of Rudgwick, was in 1625 found guilty of stealing two petticoats, waistcoat, smock, two aprons and a neckerchief.

Reflecting the intense religious feeling of the time, Philip Browghowe of Lewes, an Irish labourer, was indicted for uttering seditious words. On 26th April 1600 at Cliffe, he said:

> . . . I love not the Queen, nor yet hir lawes, but I love the pope and his lawes with my hart . . .   Found guilty, Browghow was: . . . to be pilloried with a paper con-taining his words, afterwards whipped . . .

On 10th May 1571, Joan Osborne of Hailsham was charged with bewitching to death a cow belonging to John Browninge. Verdict guilty, imprisoned for one year. — On 4th August 1574, Thomas Holben a weaver of Hailsham, broke into the close of Peter Towner of Jevington and stole a black horse. He also stole horses from John Dobyne at Arlington and Richard Sommer of Folkington. Verdict guilty, to be hanged. — On 20th July 1591, John Warden a labourer of Hailsham, stole wool from the sheep of Robert Fenell of Bourne. He confessed, sentenced to be whipped. — On 20th December 1598, Agnes Luxton spinster of Hailsham, burgled the house of Abraham Esterfield and stole: piece of bread, piece of cheese, piece of butter and ½ lb. meat. Verdict guilty, to be whipped.

*Note: The neck verse, usually from the 51st psalm, was printed in black and hung round a man's neck. In reading it the prisoner confirmed an ability to read, which could transfer responsibility for his sentence to a bishop, from whom leniency might be expected.

Appendix 'F' relating to the entry of 1693

The following extracts are observations, some from men who travelled in many parts of the country and were able to make true comparisons, that convey and emphasise how isolated Sussex became in the months of wet weather with its impassable roads, and how desperately was needed the introduction of the Turnpikes of later years.

Daniel Defoe wrote in 1724

> ... I have seen one Tree on a Tug, drawn by two and twenty Oxen; and even then 'tis carry'd so little a Way, and then thrown down, and left for other Tugs to take up and carry on that sometimes 'tis two or three years before it gets to Chatham; for if once the rains come in, it stirs no more that Year and sometimes a whole Summer is not dry enough to make the road passable ... (the sending of oak to Chatham was for ship building).
>
> ... here I had a sight which indeed I never saw in any other part of England: namely going to church at a Country Village not far from Lewes, I saw an antient Lady, and a Lady of very good quality I assure you, drawn to Church in her Coach with Six Oxen, nor was it done but out of mere Necessity, the way being so stiff and deep, that no horses could go in it ...

Written in *Wealden Iron* by Ernest Straker

> ... Oxen have the special advantage in this deep and foundrous Sussex mire, as their hooves are so formed as to spread when entering the mud and to contract as they are withdrawn ...

Written in *The Sussex Landscape* by Peter Brandon

> ... so appalling were the ways across the seemingly bottomless clay and finely grained soils that visitors rarely ventured into the region after September and markets were often impossible to reach for several months of the year ...

A letter from John Fuller to Samuel Remnant, his agent,

> Sir, I have gotten 20 9 pounders of 9 feet to Lewes and they are most of them on board the 'Sussex Oak' which the promise to bring to Woolwich very speedily. These 20 have torn the roads so that nothing can follow them and the country curse us heartily.

and it was said by Horace Walpole of journeying in East Sussex:

> ... the roads grew bad beyond all badness, the night dark beyond all darkness, our guide frightened beyond all frightfulness ...

Thomas Geering of Hailsham wrote in 1844

> ... here 40 years ago the hedges met overhead all the year round ... a wagon with a load of implements stuck fast, the tools were removed and taken to the farmhouse but the wagon remained mud-bound the whole winter ... In this episode the tools were taken to Marshfoot Farm and the wagon remained mud-bound in Marshfoot Lane leading to Market Square, Hailsham.

Appendix 'G' relating to the entry of 1754

One of the Acts recorded in the Book of Statutes affecting turnpikes in the reign of George IV was passed to enable adequate repair work to be kept up '... for more effectually making, repairing and improving roads from Uckfield to Eastbourne ...'.

That part of the Act dealing with toll charges was lengthy and extremely complex since it was concerned with numerous types of carts, carriages and wagons. In the New Turnpike Act, the thinking was that the massive wagons one would find used in agriculture should have heavier steel rims, and be in the region of twelve inches wide; it was thought that the immense weight of a wide rim must surely be good for the loose stone surface of a turnpike road. But there was always the danger that the wheels of the heavy laden wagon could go off course and into the road margin where such weight, sinking disastrously into the soft earth or mud, would become immovable.

Thus the formidable work of the wheelwright was intended to render the road surface smoother and more acceptable for coaches, and in particular, the lighter carts of some refinement, whose narrow rims were made to suffer the penalty of a higher fee. In the allocation of the wide variety of toll charges an importance was placed on the type of goods or livestock being carried while, to a lesser extent, even the number of animals pulling was involved in the calculation.

A small but typical extract from the Act would be:

> ... for the first or only horse or beast of draught (except asses) drawing any wagon, cart, caravan, used for the conveyance of goods, or other such like four wheel carriage, having the fellies of the wheels thereof of the breadth of six inches or upwards at the bottom or soles thereof, in the summer part of the year the sum of sixpence and in the winter part of the year the sum of ninepence ...

Many differing charges were made for carrying different types of goods or cattle and double tolls could be charged for heavy loads such as: stone, chalk, boulders, flints, timber, bricks and iron etc.

Troublesome delays could be experienced when several transports were held up at gates while toll calculations were made and it was not unknown for gatekeepers to be less than honest when they handled the income due to the Turnpike Trust.

Appendix 'H' relating to the entry of 1775

The earliest record of the Van Cortlandt family in America was the arrival in New Amsterdam from Holland in 1638 of Oloff Van Cortlandt who was a soldier with the Dutch West India Company. Oloff decided to stay in New Amsterdam and became involved in the beaver trade which earned him enough money to allow his ventures into milling and brewing. Contrary to some recorded opinion the family was not one of the original founding families of New Amsterdam.

The commercial activities of Oloff built up into marked successes and with his by now much respected name he was in c. 1665 elected as a Burgomaster. In due course a higher honour followed of being appointed Commissioner of Indian Affairs for the Province and upon the surrender of the province to the British under the Duke of York, later to become James II of England, Oloff was chosen one of the three commissioners to negotiate the surrender terms. This no doubt accounted for the British later giving him posts of authority on behalf of the Crown.

This first American Van Cortlandt died in 1684 a remarkable, wealthy and influential man.

The family was indeed fortunate for the eldest son, Stephanus, was also to prove a man of ability. A concentration of his father's area of commerce was again to reap rich rewards for as time went on he acquired both land and property until his interests had spread in New York City (formerly New Amsterdam), Long Island and New Jersey. In contrast to this however, there was a period in his life when he was linked with the military and as a colonel he saw active service against both the French and the Indians.

In maturity Stephanus was to be acknowledged not only for his success but as a man with vast experience and considerable character and with the advantage of wealth he was readily accepted among the leading figures of the city. Working with a genuine concern in public affairs he was recognised as a candidate for high office and in the course of time was appointed Chief Justice of the Supreme Court of the Province of New York, and later in 1677 he was elected as the tenth Mayor of New York but the first native born Mayor of the City. It is also of interest that this second generation American was honoured with the specialist appointment as Chancellor of the Court of Chancery.

Over the years. Stephanus had made shrewd purchases from the Indians of extensive land along the Hudson River and in 1697 he was allowed the privilege of being granted a charter from William III that bestowed on the estate the status and title of a Manor. The Van Cortlandt Manor House was in future years to see the Methodist friend of John Wesley, the Rev. George Whitefield, preach from its porch. In the war years George Washington, the future President of America, stayed at the house and a visitor after the war was Benjamin Franklin, the scientist and politician who helped to draw up the U.S. Constitution. Stephanus died in 1700 at the age of fifty-seven leaving a wife, six sons and nine daughters.

The younger brother of Stephanus, Jacobus Van Cortlandt, enjoyed an exceptional political career for he too became a Mayor of New York. In business, Jacobus had success that brought him tremendous wealth and it was some of his land, then outside the city, that was given, to become the Van Cortlandt Park of today in the Bronx district of New York.

The eldest son of Stephanus was John who died when he was a young man. The next eldest was Philip (1683–1748) who cared for the estates passed down to him, entered commerce and maintained the family tradition of service to the government by serving a period as a member of the Governor's Council. This Philip had a daughter and five sons, the eldest of which was Stephen born in 1711.

Stephen Van Cortlandt inherited, as had others before him, properties and estates of great value but unlike others of the family male line his interests were not to be found in either business or any of the offices of public service. He was but forty-five years old when he died, leaving a daughter and two sons of whom the eldest was yet another Philip. This is the man born in 1739 who was caught up in the tragic crisis of disagreement leading to war between America and Britain, when he was destined to remain loyal to the Crown, a decision that utterly changed the life of himself and his family, bringing both injustice and sadness.

In the time of earlier generations of the Van Cortlandt family before 1739 in which the 'Hailsham Philip' was born, the new colony of America accepted the laws and demands of the British Parliament and in the beginning much was of value, but with growth in self reliance and confidence, early laws, often favourable to Britain at America's expense began to be questioned.

This new world was populated by determined, free and enterprising settlers, resolved to work and make their lives according to the materials and opportunities that presented themselves. This vast land demanded its own way of life and as the land and the lives upon it developed, so too did natural laws and attitudes.

The far away and out of touch British Parliament with serious troubles of its own was slowly but inevitably losing touch. The Americans were making their own way and moving to a natural independence, with which came a healthy confidence and well-being, provoking a drift away from the British thinking and control, taken for granted in the mother country.

With countless complications developing and in an atmosphere of growing irritation, the answer surely lay in talking and compromise, an approach that would mean the British giving ground with an understanding of the problems, but this was not to be. The mentality of the Crown and Parliament, unaccustomed to giving way, was that as in the past, strength would prevail.

One of the later and damaging impositions thrust upon the colony was the Stamp Act that required revenue stamps to be affixed to almost every piece of printed paper; licences, every type of form and pamphlet, posters, newspapers and all legal documents. Normally, it was the workers who protested and spoke out but this latest burden touched the professional classes and added to an explosive protest, the voice of the more articulate American.

The storm was indeed gathering and the anti-British feeling with the now overwhelming movement aimed at the freedom independence could give was to be seen in protest committees and organisations over the land. In 1773 the British granted to the East India Company a complete monopoly in the supply of tea to the colony, an act that overnight destroyed all other existing arrangements to import tea including even organised smuggling.

Upheaval and fury followed, resulting in the destruction of three shiploads of British tea, an occasion now known as the Boston Tea Party.

A Declaration of Rights and Grievances, together with a petition, put to the King in 1774 the American arguments for change, but in spite of the strength behind these appeals George III gave no sign of making concessions and before the end of the year the King replied with the curt message 'The die is now cast, the Colonies must either submit or triumph'.

Totally out of touch, the King's reply eliminated the last doubt that war was inevitable.

The Patriot cause was spurred on by a remarkable pamphlet called 'Common Sense' addressed to the American people and written by an Englishman, Thomas Paine. The leaflet advocated America breaking away from the Mother Country and brought a prominence that enabled him to meet and know the men destined to be America's first three Presidents: Washington, Adams and Jefferson. His writing of 'Common Sense' resulted in an award of £500 and a degree of M.A. conferred on him by the University of Pennsylvania.

Thomas Paine was an excise man from Lewes whose duty took him into the Hailsham area. The pamphlet written in his vigorous, flamboyant style had tremendous impact; it was a fierce attack on bad government and George III personally, and a scorching declaration for independence from England.

There could be few Americans who by now had not decided where their sympathies lay. An enormous voice of protest came from the patriots standing firmly for the country they had built while an unpopular minority of, in the main, more cautious people were the loyalists. They did not dispute their country's grievances but they were often thinkers who favoured stability and rather than an open break they felt a better future could be found by linking the best of America and her natural riches to the British strength in matters of commerce, defence and constitutional tradition.

The patriot feeling was overwhelming and nothing could hold the intense anger at their continued unjust rejection with what often appeared arrogance.

It was long known that arms were hidden in widespread areas and there came news to General Gage in Boston that patriots were collecting arms and military stores in Concord, Massachusetts. British soldiers were sent to confiscate the weapons and arrest the leaders and marching through the night they reached Lexington where in the early morning they were confronted by a band of armed men determined to stop them. There was firing and bloodshed in the centre of the small town where eight dead American patriots were left on the Green.

The British moved on and reached Concord where at the wooden bridge they were again attacked. The return march to Boston was through a now alerted countryside where the bright army redcoats were a target almost every mile of the way. Before Boston was finally reached, heavy casualties had been inflicted in what proved to be the start of the long War of Independence.

With the war, two Van Cortlandt cousins were to find themselves fighting on opposite sides. Indeed their futures were to be in very sad contrast, one Philip Van Cortlandt was to be a successful patriot commander in the American army with the rank of Brigadier General and to have as his friend General Washington, later to be America's first President. The other Philip was to make his personal judgement and following his principles, remain loyal to the British and in defeat, sail with his family for England.

It was in Hailsham where he spent his final years and where he was to die in 1814. It was also in the same year that his Uncle Pierre died in America and this was the man who built near the Van Cortlandt Manor House at Croton, the Methodist Chapel that is still in use today. It was Pierre who in an unusual codicil to his Will arranged for his black slaves to be given their freedom upon his death.

Thomas Paine

Thomas Paine spent several years in Lewes living for a time at Bull House in the High Street and frequenting the *White Hart* for meetings and gatherings with friends. He was an intellectual whose writing was often too violent for general acceptance. He was also an ardent whig, a visionary with ideas far ahead of his time; the abolition of slavery, the right of man to negotiate his own wages '. . . the only thing he had to sell was himself . . .', belief in the rights of women and the basic principles of the welfare state.

An idealist, Paine believed passionately that,

> . . . whatever government or form of society was right for one generation might be totally unsuitable to the differing needs of another . . .

Thomas Paine for his principles fought against the British and was rewarded after the war with three thousand dollars and an estate of three hundred acres.

During his time as a young excise man based at Lewes, he was concerned with cargoes on boats using the busy river Ouse and with riding horseback out into coastal areas to seek evidence of smuggling and contraband. Certainly he would have known Hailsham well.

General Thomas Gage

General Thomas Gage was of the distinguished Gage family of Firle Place at the foot of the Downs, east of Lewes and within a few miles of Hailsham. He was for a time Commander-in-Chief of the British Forces in America. (*See note* at foot of this page).

> The following petition was sent by Philip from his temporary home in the King's Road, Chelsea on 18th March 1784, to the Commissioners appointed by Parliament for enquiring into and awarding compensation for losses suffered by American Loyalists.

The Memorial of Philip Van Cortlandt, Major of His Majesty's 3rd Battalion New Jersey Volunteers now residing in Great Britain — Sheweth.

THAT at the commencement of the late rebellion in America your Memorialist resided at Hanover in the Province of New Jersey where refusing to bear arms against His Majesty, to resign his commissions under Government, & publickly declaring his principles averse to the measures of Congress, he was deemed inimical to their cause, subjected to fines, with every species of insult, & in consequence of an order from General Lee to take him prisoner unless he would subscribe the annexed Oath, was at last separated from his family & obliged to take refuge in the Mountains, where after being closely pursued for several days by the Rebel Light horse, joined his Majesty's Troops at New York under the orders of Sir William Howe in the year 1776 & continued in the service until the late reduction of the Army.

During your Memorialist's absence his personal property as specified in the annexed Schedule was most wantonly wasted & destroyed by the Rebel Officers & soldiers who were continually quartered in his house — his family treated in a manner that would disgrace the most savage Barbarians, reduced in the space of three months from affluence to want (of) the common necessarys of life — and then by Gen. Washington's order inhumanly turned out of doors in a snowstorm to make room for the sick of his Army.

Soon after this the property of your Memorialist was confiscated & sold in New Jersey — & exclusive (of) the actual loss expressed in the Schedule, a very considerable Estate in the possession of an aunt aged 89 years to whom your Memorialist was Heir at Law, has been, during the rebellion conveyed in a partial manner to his relations in the service of the United States by a will made under their influence, just before her death, to the great injury of your Memorialist — who now, deprived of fortune, banished (from) his native Country, with the important charge of a wife & eleven children seeks an Asylum in Great Britain, & with the fullest confidence submits his case to the patronage of your Hon. Board for such relief under your report as his losses & Services may merit.

Note: The War of Independence and the coming together of loyalist Philip Van Cortlandt and General Thomas Gage of Firle in the same cause, was ultimately responsible for the families in later years being linked by marriage.

———

Appendix 'J' relating to the entries of 1783 and 1795

The two inch scale Map of 1783 from which the enlargement of the Hailsham area was made was a considerable improvement on previous county maps, being the third of a series of four, planned to cover the southern half of the county. A set of these four old maps can be seen on display in Chichester Cathedral.

The first sheet was engraved in Paris at the expense of the Duke of Richmond, at that time Master-General of the Ordnance, but '. . . on the commencement of hostilities with France . . .' the engraving work was '. . . properly withdrawn home . . .'.

It was completed at Goodwood by Yeakel who was an engraver as well as a surveyor.

The Map of 1795 to a scale of one inch, was the last map to be completed in the 'Great Survey of Sussex' and represented a rapid advance both for the technique of surveying and the quality of cartography.

Produced under the patronage of the Duke of Richmond, Master-General of Ordnance and in charge of military defence and map-making, he instructed the surveying parties in 1792 to,

> . . . be minute in our Survey of Sussex; and to furnish Mr. Gardner with materials for correcting a map of that county . . .

The exceptionally high standard of the map of 1795 owed much to Gardner, Yeakell and Gream and their working experience with the Board of Ordnance. It was an advantage to know the Duke of Richmond was so greatly interested for with his influence, there was a close co-operation by engineer officers with their specialist knowledge of military Surveys.

Appendix 'K' relating to the entries of 1817, 1837, c. 1850 and c. 1876

Post Mills were the simplest and earliest windmills, the entire mill and sweeps (or sails) being supported by a heavy central upright post which in early days was often a tree trunk.

The mill was moved manually by a long arm projecting from the base at the opposite side to the sweeps. The arm was pushed round to revolve the mill until the sweeps faced into the wind.

Smock Mills had the sweeps fixed to a revolving cap at the top of the mill which was turned automatically by a fan-tail on the opposite side of the cap. The fan-tail with the help of gearing caused the cap to turn until the sweeps were facing the wind.

Tower Mills operated on the same principle as smock mills but instead of being built of wood they were built of brick and sometimes with stone. Being the latest type of mills their internal mechanism was more advanced in design.

Polegate Tower Windmill was restored in 1967 by the Eastbourne and District Preservation Society and after a good deal of hard work and expertise its complicated mechanism was put in working order with its sweeps and mill-stones able to turn.

This unique example of industrial history demonstrates how the immense forces of the wind acting on sweeps each sixty feet long can be controlled by working mill parts some of immense size in both wood and iron that yet are capable of the most sensitive adjustment.

However to now work the stones in their grinding position which enormously increases the pressure, would mean putting the wooden cogs (often made in Hornbeam or Apple, both of which have a natural oil that acts as a lubricant) and the original gearing, some now over one hundred and fifty years old, at a great risk.

The mill with its museum is open to the public at certain times.

Appendix 'L' relating to the entry of 1831

The population figures set out below are those recorded in 1831 of the parishes surrounding Hailsham. It is interesting to compare these parish figures with the populations in certain other places some of which have since 1831 become large towns.

Alciston	266
Alfriston	694
Arlington	727
Battle	2,852
Berwick	203
Chiddingly	902
Hailsham	1,445
Heathfield	1,801
Hellingly	1,504
Herstmonceux	1,338
Hoathly (East)	505
Hooe	525
Jevington	350
Laughton	804
Pevensey	343
Ripe	360
Selmeston	189
Waldron	997
Warbleton	1,225
Wartling	948
Westham	752
Willingdon	603
Wilmington	328
Bexhill	1,907
Brighton	40,634
Chichester	8,270
Crawley	334
Eastbourne	2,726
East Grinstead	3,153
Hastings	10,097
Horsham	4,575
Lewes	8,592
Newhaven	904
Seaford	1,098

Appendix 'M' relating to the entries of c. 1590 and 1837

The following poems are typical of John Hollamby of whom it was said,

> . . . our representative man was a minnow among tritons; but he was a true poet nevertheless. Poetry was no studied art with him; he sang his simple lays from the overflow, or impulse, of his nature . . .

To a wren who had built her nest under the eaves of Hollamby's dwelling:

> Fond, timid bird, why lookest thou so shy?
> Why keepest thou aloof when I am nigh?
> Why does my presence thus thy fears alarm?
> Thinkest thou I'll rob thy nest or do thee harm?
> No! thou the shelter of my roof shalt share,
> And undisturbed thy tender young shalt rear;
> No schoolboy's ruthless hand shall e'er molest
> Or tear thy unfledged offspring from thy nest,
> For I will be thy guardian and thy friend,
> Far as my power and humble means extend;
> Thy nest from every prying eye I'll guard,
> And in thy happiness find my reward.

This sonnet reveals a depth of feeling typical of Hollamby.

> That Love at random throws his darts,
>   And seems to make such odd mistakes;
> That he, in wounding of our hearts,
>   So many curious blunders makes;
> That some are doomed in love to mourn
>   And in their hearts endure the pain,
> Who for their love meet no return
>   But cold unkindness and disdain;
> That Fortune does not always give
>   Her favours to the most deserving;
> That some unsought her gifts receive,
>   While others seek and yet are starving;
> How can we cause for wonder find,
>   Since Love and Fortune both are blind?

In the following poem 'The Monks of Marshfoot', is a reference to the 16th century stone building that existed at the bottom of Marshfoot Lane. Strong indications are that this old structure was connected with religion but no conclusive evidence has been found.

> When the Monks came up from old Marshfoot,
>   Each man to ring his bell,
> And they rang with zeal and rang with skill,
>   And they rang the changes well.
>
> And the Monks would listen on Michelham Tower,
>   For those bells were of good renown
> And few there were who could compare
>   With St Mary's of Haylesham Town.

The following lines have been said to be his apology for putting his thoughts into words:

> I ne'er aspired to mount Pegasus,
> Nor climb the height of steep Parnassus;
> But often as my time would suit
> To saunter near some mountain's foot,
> To crop some humble sprig or flower,
> Amusement for a leisure hour;
> And if for this I have permission,
> It is the height of my ambition.

Appendix 'N' relating to the entry of 1889

The following account was published in the Eastbourne newspaper of 25th September 1889. It is a journalist's report entitled 'The Great Fire at Hailsham' and is reproduced here, less some minor passages indicated by rows of dots. It will be noted that the report continues without the use of separate paragraphs.

... On Wednesday evening the usually quiet town of Hailsham was in a state of great excitement owing to the outbreak of a fire which threatened at one time to assume alarming proportions. The scene of the conflagration was a block of buildings containing four houses and carriage works, situate in the Market square. The carriage works and three of the four houses are parish property, having been utilised formerly, in the old Poor Law days, as the parish workhouse ... The Volunteer Fire Brigade quickly responded to the call and in a very few minutes were on the spot with the manual engine, operations being at once commenced. After the fire was first observed it spread quickly, catching hold of a quantity of timber in the works and laid hold of the house inhabited by Mr. Rowland with amazing rapidity. Scores of willing hands were soon at work with buckets of water to pour on the flames. A plentiful supply was obtained from the well at the back of the house of Mr. A. Burtenshaw opposite and from the taps there. Almost immediately after the arrival of the brigade the roof of Mr. Rowland's house fell in and the flames shot up to a great height ... As it was time for the dispatch of the evening mail, great fears were entertained respecting the safety of the letters at the Post Office. Mr. Snashall, the post master, was absent from the town, and in his absence Mr. A. Burtenshaw and Dr. Gould superintended the removal of all valuables from the office and conveyed them to Mr. Burtenshaw's house, which was quickly turned into a temporary post office; the mails were made up with commendable promptitude and despatched punctually at the usual time ... As it seemed as if all the whole block must go, scores of persons assisted in getting all the goods from the four houses and stacking them in the square, which presented an extraordinary spectacle. From here they were afterwards removed to the houses of Mr. Burtenshaw, Mr. T. Vine, Mr. White, Mr. Brooks and Mr. Fuller, and some were conveyed to the Corn Exchange and to the currier's shop of the late Mr. T. Geering ... The Eastbourne steam fire engine was telegraphed for about eight o'clock, when the flames seemed beyond all control, and urgency was pleaded, as the fire was considered to be of a most serious character. The members of the Eastbourne Brigade quickly assembled in Cavendish-place, where the engine was soon ready with four horses harnessed. Amidst cheers engine was driven off at a rapid pace and arrived at Hailsham about 9.20 with hearty cheers, but the fire being completely got under they were too late to render much assistance. No use could be made of the engine because there was only one hydrant near, which was being utilised by the Hailsham Brigade. All the parish property was fully insured in the Royal Exchange Assurance Office ...

Appendix 'O' relating to the entry of 1916

The 12th Battalion Royal Sussex Regiment in which Nelson Carter fought was known as 'Lowther's Own' or 'Lowther's Lambs'. It was one of the battalions raised in 1914 of men from the South Downs by Colonel Claude Lowther, M.P. who lived at Herstmonceux Castle.

The following is an extract from a letter sent by Nelson Carter's Captain to Mrs. Carter immediately following the award of the Victoria Cross.

"I take the earliest opportunity of offering you my heartiest congratulations on the great honour that has been bestowed upon your late husband, whose memory I shall always cherish as a good and great soldier. We served together for eighteen months, and for the four months preceding his death he was my right-hand man. On 30 June, he was in command of the last platoon to go over the parapet. When I last saw him he was close to the German line, acting as leader to a small party of four or five men. I was afterwards told that he had entered the German second line, and had brought back an enemy machine gun, having put the gun team out of action. I heard that he shot one of them with his revolver. I next saw him about an hour later (I had been wounded in the meanwhile, and was lying in our trench). Your husband repeatedly went over the parapet. I saw him going over alone, and carrying in our wounded men from 'No Man's Land'. He brought them in on his back, and he could not have done this had he not possessed exceptional physical strength as well as courage. It was in going over for the sixth or seventh time that he was shot through the chest. I saw him fall just inside our trench. Somebody told me that he got back just inside our trench, but I do not know for certain. At . . . about a month previously your husband carried a man about 400 yards across the open under machine-gun fire and brought him safely into our trench. For this act I recommended him for the Military Cross. On every occasion, no matter how tight the hole we were in, he was always cheerful and hopeful, and never spared any pains to make the men comfortable and keep them cheery. In fact, it would be difficult to imagine a man better qualified to lead his comrades into action under the dangerous conditions."

The following is a further tribute to him from the Quartermaster-Sergeant of 'A' Company: 'Your husband was a man beloved by all, and a splendid soldier, and it is a little consoling to know that he did his duty even to the last moment'.

Sergeant-Major Carter was a fine athlete, and won a Medal and a Silver Cup for boxing in 1915. The Medal was for the Regimental Championship and the Cup for the Heavyweight Championship.

The following is a letter written to Nelson Carter's wife by Company Quarter-master-Sergeant T. G. D. Grigg.

'A' Company, 12th Royal Sussex Regt.,
B.E.F., France,
2 July, 1916

Dear Mrs Carter,

I am greatly grieved to inform you that your husband Company Sergeant-Major Carter, was killed in action on the 30th June, whilst gallantly performing his duty to his King and country. As Company Quartermaster-Sergt. of A Company I express the heartfelt grief of his fellow non-commissioned officers and men. Your husband was a man beloved by all, and a splendid soldier, and it is a little consoling to know that he did his duty even to the last moment. His fellow men always had the highest esteem for him, and looked upon him as their leader. There has been caused in A Company a big loss, and a big gap by the loss of your dear husband — a loss which is irreparable.

May it somewhat help you to bear the burden to know that your husband's death was instantaneous.

Please accept the sincere sympathy of A Company, one and all.

Yours very respectfully,
T. G. D. Grigg,
Company Quartermaster-Sergeant,
'A' Company, 12th Royal Sussex Regt.

The following is a letter written to Nelson Carter's wife by Lieutenant Harold C. T. Robinson.

Kye Lami, The Greys, Eastbourne.
16 July, 1916

My Dear Mrs. Carter,

I have hesitated to write to you because I could get no news of your husband, but I now hear that there is no doubt, and I have to write and tell you how deeply I sympathize with you in your loss. I should like to say how much I admired him, and how much I appreciated the work he did during the time I commanded A Company. When the time came for them to do their job, the men rose to the occasion very fairly, and I consider that it was in no small degree due to the fine example always set by Sergt.-Major Carter. Always cheerful, and working with un-ceasing energy through the long months of training and the trials in the trenches, he endeared himself to all, and the men would, I know, have gone anywhere with him. I personally feel that I have lost a very great friend, and one of the finest I ever knew. It was with pleasure that I was able to put forward his name with a recom-mendation for the Military Cross about a fortnight before he died, and I have no hesitation in saying that I should most certainly recommend him for further decora-tion for gallantry this time had he come through. At present I am unable to get about much, but I hope to get over to see you soon.

With deepest sympathy and kind regards, Believe me,

Yours very truly,

Harold C. T. Robinson,
Lieut., 12th Royal Sussex Regt.

Appendix 'P' relating to the entry of 1918

William Strickland, a Justice of the Peace who had travelled world wide, was to prove in his lifetime to be a shrewd and timely benefactor to Hailsham.

With his strong character, his association with the church and almost every aspect of Hailsham life where guidance and decisions were involved, he was inevitably for many years a dominant figure in the town. He was a fair man but he could be hard, even with his 'Cortlandt' neighbours when he would resort to law to establish his case when even threatened with minor infringements of his property.

William Strickland controlled the company of Strickland Ltd., a considerable organisation dealing in corn with shipping granaries at Newhaven. In addition, he was Chairman of the Hailsham Water Works, the Fire Brigade and the Street Watering Committee, while outside the town he was a member of the London Corn Exchange, a Commissioner of Income Tax and a Trustee of Newhaven Harbour.

The grandfather of William Strickland was Sir James Williams who was knighted at the Coronation of George IV. A man of influence, he was a Sheriff of the City of London where he had duties linked with the Session House at the Old Bailey and Newgate Prison.

As a Sheriff in 1820 he conducted Elizabeth Fry, the Quaker pioneer of prison reform, round the notorious Newgate Prison and after Mrs. Fry had spoken to the prisoners, they were addressed by Sir James, a man of the strongest Non-conformist belief. The following words are from a contemporary account of the occasion:

> ... then addressed the prisoners in a manner which reflected the greatest honour upon his humanity, and showed in a pleasing light his great desire to serve their best interest. He advised them to ... give still greater heed to all they heard; for very soon the privilege of seeing and hearing these good ladies would cease, as a warrant was expected down very soon for the departure of the prisoners for a distant part of the world ...

The condemned men and women were to be taken to the London docks from where their convict ship would sail.

Appendix 'Q' relating to the entries of 1873, 1925 and 1969

The age of the Long Man of Wilmington is unknown, but through the years many theories have been advanced, suggesting origins that have varied from prehistoric to post-medieval periods. It was the restoration of this famous figure on the Downs overlooking Wilmington in 1969 that enabled serious work to be carried out on the site, with the aim of seeking evidence of age or of any physical change in the figure.

With opinion still conflicting on the precise shape of the outline, it is of interest to recall a drawing made in *c.* 1780 for Sir William Burrell's Sussex history (*see* entry of 1733). The Long Man is drawn with the stave of a rake in his right hand and the stave of a scythe in his left hand. Another intriguing difference the drawing indicates is the left foot pointing to the west and not to the east as does the figure of today.

It is, of course, possible that at the time of the drawing, the chalk outline of the Long Man would have in places been somewhat obscured, for it is unlikely to have been given any great care.

During the restoration, however, the opportunity was taken to dig four exploratory trenches at places on a shoulder, leg, stave and on the head. In two of the trenches a limited quantity of very small pieces of fired clay was recovered. Examined in turn by Dr. I. W. Cornwall of the Institute of Archaeology in London and Professor B. W. Cunliffe of the University of Southampton, it was agreed the finds were, in fact, linked with pottery and Professor Cunliffe has commented,

> ... my own feeling is that the fragments are of Roman tile ...

but the finds were too limited to allow a firm explanation of such remains.

Still with the hope of tracing a previous and now obliterated outline of the Long Man, an advanced technique was used over areas of turf at the top of each stave and over the figure's head. Controlled electrical charges effective to a depth of three feet were fed into the soil at measured intervals spread evenly over an area, and readings of soil restivity were taken. By assessing the varying soil reactions it became possible by plotting the results to detect lines or patches of past soil disturbance.

Such disturbances that were indicated became apparent at the top of both staves and to a lesser degree above the Long Man's head, these places were not without significance when compared with the old drawing, but no precise outline emerged.

While opinion still differs on the age of the Long Man of Wilmington there is reason to doubt that the outline so firmly established in the turf today is exactly as it was two to three hundred years ago.

Appendix 'R' relating to the entry of 1940

From a small office in Whitehall Place near the War Office, Colonel Colin McVean Gubbins, a man widely experienced in military intelligence work, was given the awesome and vital task of organising with the greatest speed a network of underground Resistance units behind those English coastlines thought likely to be assaulted, should the German army. attempt to invade.

The plan was to bring into being throughout the south-eastern countryside a series of Auxiliary Units; an intentionally vague title chosen in the interest of total security. The units were, however, in due course to be recognised as British Resistance, an underground organisation dedicated to the disruption and destruction of the enemy by any means. And so little time was available for the creation of a Resistance that Winston Churchill personally asked for weekly progress reports.

To aid him with all speed in this critical organisation, Colonel Gubbins was granted a remarkable authority to select those officers he could find, who, by their initiative and proven service experience, could each take command of sectors extending up to say thirty miles inland from the coast.

In turn, these officers were faced with the task of seeking out, vetting and carefully choosing certain local civilians whose background and character would prove suitable for undercover work. When the right men were found and sworn to secrecy, they often proved to be members of the farming community, all of whom with the experience of years, could offer a combined and deep knowledge of the hedges, fields and woods of the countryside that spread between the villages concerned in this book. It was in this countryside that hideouts were positioned and manned.

The civilians chosen to be members of the British Resistance were each given secret training in many areas of subversive activity including sabotage and the use of various explosives. As a cover for their training and on the occasions when these men would be out and about, usually at night and often with the Canadian soldiers stationed in East Sussex, the uniform of the Home Guard was worn, but with a shoulder flash indicating they were not connected with a local unit. Indeed so successful did this cover prove, that friends, and sometimes wives, were completely unaware of the underground organisation or the identity of its members.

Usually, six or seven men were trained to work together as a cell, and a network of such cells was strategically positioned, each operating from a securely hidden hide-away which in the early days had been dug, often at night, by men of the cell or by specially briefed men of the Royal Engineers. Later versions were of concrete but always the structure was deep, roomy and so designed that its entrances were ingeniously sited and camouflaged as to be invisible to the closest observer.

One such hide-away was in a Heathfield wood and its entrance had to be opened by a switch in a tree behind a small moveable panel of bark. The switch operated an earth-concealed entrance some thirty feet away below which was a ladder down to a small room with ammunition and explosives. Here a concealed switch allowed entry into two further underground rooms fitted with weapons, bunks, a cooker with food for a month, spare clothing, a generator for lighting and ventilation and a compartment with a chemical lavatory. Leading away from these underground chambers was a cramped tunnel as an emergency escape route.

A wartime Senior Commander, Miss Beatrice Temple was in charge of those members of the A.T.S. who had been chosen to act as secret radio operators in certain underground hide-aways. In the course of her duty Miss Temple regularly visited her operators wherever they were in the South of England and one such transmitter was in the Heathfield hide-away.

Many years after the war, Miss Temple, a mayor of Lewes in 1972, journeyed to the Heathfield wood and looked for the secret hide-away of the Resistance she had known so well in 1940, but her search failed to discover either the loose panel of bark or the nearby entrance to the underground chambers.

Several such hide-aways still remain in secluded parts of the countryside and have after many years become hidden by nature, and sadly now remembered but by very few.

The Colonel Colin Gubbins of 1940 was eventually in 1946, after being much decorated by several allied nations, Major-General Sir Colin Gubbins.

Appendix 'S' relating to the entry of 1939-45

Record of bombs dropped on Hailsham and the surrounding parishes during the war years 1939–45.

Parish	High explosive	Incendiary
Alfriston	38	575
Arlington	46	100
Berwick	2	75
Chalvington	33	250
Chiddingly	60	1,350
East Hoathly	33	605
Folkington	22	170
Hailsham	110	1,225
Hellingly	54	215
Herstmonceux	97	2,385
Jevington	17	45
Pevensey	93	630
Polegate	20	5
Ripe	14	4
Selmeston	6	0
Warbleton	96	120
Westham	57	75
Willingdon	12	7
Wilmington	6	0

Appendix 'T' relating to the entry of 1960

Ashburnham Place has been the home of the Ashburnham family for at least 800 years. Following the death of Lady Catherine Ashburnham in 1953, the estate was inherited by the Reverend John D. Bickersteth, a great-grandson of the Fourth Earl, who saw crippling death duties necessitate the sale of about 4,000 acres of land and nearly all the valuable pictures and furniture in the house, which then remained empty for about five years.

In 1958 over three-quarters of the building was demolished to ensure what was left could be economically maintained. The remainder has been progressively adapted for its present use and supplemented at various times since then, and it was in 1960 that Mr. Bickersteth gave away the mansion and 220 acres of surrounding gardens, woods and lakes to the Trustees of the newly formed Ashburnham Christian Trust.

The huge volume of people who travel to Ashburnham each year come from every quarter and represent a wide variety of groups who use the house for Christian Conferences drawn from churches of all the major denominations, from school and hospital Christian unions, and from ecumenical groups formed for specific purposes, such as for prayer or spiritual renewal. Such groups draw up their own training programmes and invite speakers of their choice.

The fine and extensive stable buildings built *c.* 1730 are being converted for use by Christians of all denominations in East Sussex as a centre for united worship, prayer and ministry. The hope is that the offering of praise and intercession, which such Christians go there to make, will soon be continuously maintained by day and night. Christian teaching, counselling and fellowship are also available from time to time.

On an historic site in an area that once was famous for its intensely prosperous iron making activities, and to a lesser extent its brick industry, this inspired Christian enterprise has in a very few years achieved a truly remarkable success.

Appendix 'U' relating to the entries of 1909 and 1970

In determining the importance of the ancient cemetery below the ground on what is now the summit of Ocklynge Hill, it can be said that the discoveries revealed in the entries of 1909 and 1970 do not represent the complete story.

In the previous century a gang of labourers engaged on removing soil from the top of Ocklynge Hill, uncovered a number of graves with skeletons that indicated burials dating back many hundreds of years. In 1822, the object of the work on this old road passing through what was then the village of Willingdon, on its way to East Bourne (now Old Town in Eastbourne), was to re-make the road into a turnpike.

Recorded in 1876 were the words of an old labouring man who remembered when he was very young, and one of a gang of some ten men employed in laborious road work. It was said by him that when the digging had reached down to a few feet below the stones of the road surface, a large number of skeletons began to be found lying close together. The digging continued for several weeks and the old man described how every day more graves would be found with sometimes six skeletons uncovered in a single day while on one occasion as many as fourteen were found.

At this early date, with no great concern or appreciation at unearthing history, the occasion passed without the attention of an expert or a written account of the discovery. Thus the simple record of the 1822 episode that survives today is due to the eye witness who actually laboured on improving the road at that time. It was also he who recollected the hugh quantity of bones being loaded into a cart and taken down the hill to the parish church at East Bourne, where they were buried in a pit.

INDEX

LIST OF SUBSCRIBERS

Mrs. J. D. Adam
Mr. A. Adam
Kenneth H. Aherne
Mrs. O. E. Airey
Sister Alban (Lourdes)
Douglas E. Allen
His Hon. Judge M. J. Anwyl-
    Davies, Q.C.
Dennis G. F. Ardouin
Mrs. J. Ayres
Aubrey A. Baker
B. E. Baker
Eileen Baker
Geoffrey Baker
Mary Ball
Peter F. Barnes
Kevin Edward P. Barnett
Maurice Hamish Barnett
Mr. D. Barton
Mary Bear
Derek R. Beck
Dr. S. A. Belshaw
Winifred Bennett
John and Jennifer Berkett
Sidney and Louise Berkett
Ivy G. Bettney
E. A. P. Bircher
C. E. J. Bishop
Ernest Booth
James Albert Bourne
F. J. Bower
Maxwell and Berenger Bowie
Paul E. Bowler
Mrs. J. Brabyn
D. F. Bracey
Mr. R. Brandley
Eric L. Bridges
G. Bridges
Miss Karen Bridgman
Kenneth and Lily Briggs
R. J. Brockway
Mr. T. J. Brook
K. Brooks
George Brown
Phyllis Joan Brown
Phyllis Bruton
Jean Burfield
A. J. Burgess
Margaret M. J. Burr
O. L. Burrell, O.B.E.
M. L. Buss
C. G. Calder
Arthur H. Cameron
Elizabeth A. Capon
Ruby Elizabeth Carley
W. S. Carter Esq. C.M.G., C.V.O.
Graham M. E. Castell
W. F. Caton
Mr. F. S. Catt
Anna Champney-Warrener
Brian Cheele
Mrs. E. Chewter
Mrs. Eileen D. Chowen
Herbert Clarke
Peter B. Clarke
Mr. and Mrs. C. E. Clay
A. L. Clissold
Christine Edin Coates

Christopher Cole
A. J. Coleman
J. R. Coleman
Mr. Peter Collins
Lieut. Col. and Mrs. R. K.
    Constantine
Mr. and Mrs. Geoffrey Cook
P. I. E. Corbett
Barbara and Tim Cordner
Ronald Leslie Cornwall
J. Victor Craig
I. M. Crosweller
H. G. Crouch
J. G. Crouch
Asenath A. Crowe
Malcolm William Rowland Crowe
Mrs. G. E. Crowhurst (Clarice)
Mrs. Eileen Mary Dalgety
H. L. Dann
Pauline Davies
Mr. Geoffrey Davis
K. T. Daw
Eileen F. Dawes
Ivy F. Dean
Mrs. I. B. Dearle
J. G. de Geus
B. S. Delves
A. B. and H. M. Denney
Bridget C. Dimond
Tim and Liz Dowsett
E. A. Drury
Mrs. Ivy Dunk
Judy Dupree
Mr. R. J. Earl
Basil Ede
Andrew T. Edgoose
A. F. Edmonds
A. J. Edwards Esq., B.A. (Cantab)
Hugh M. Edwards
David Elfick
K. G. Elphick
Marjorie Freda Elphick
Neil Elphick
Rev. Robin Elphick
Martin John Falkner
Mary Jo Fanaroff
George Farebrother
John S. Farrier
Rosina Filsell
Mr. E. A. Ford
Helene Ford
Col. F. H. Foster
Alec L. Fox
Hugh Francis
Kerry French
Hilary Frizell
Mrs. E. M. Funnell
Gerald L. Gadd, F.R.I.C.S.
Mr. and Mrs. Quentin Gage
Barbara Gardner
John Leslie Gardner
Lord Garner of Chiddingly
M. C. Gibbs
Mrs. D. L. Girling
R. J. Girling
Americ and Sarah Godley
Hilary Goodwin
D. Goring

M. N. Gosden
Peter N. Gosden
Mr. and Mrs. V. C. Gothard
Mr. Wyndham Gould
Richard J. Goulden
Mrs. G. E. Green
Peter K. Green
Eva Griffin
J. M. Griffin
Joyce Lucy Grove
Doris Irene Guy
Mr. and Mrs. Nigel Hadow
Hailsham Historical and Natural History
    Society
Nigel E. Hammond-Williams, M.A. (Cantab).
    B.D.S. Lond. L.D.S.R.C.S. Eng.
Mr. and Mrs. C. Harding
Mr. Vivien Harper
Mr. B. J. Harris
Mr. G. E. Harris
P. W. Harris
Dr. K. F. Hartley
Mavis Harvey
Richard Harvey
Alan J. Hassell
Pamela Joan Hassell
Rev. W. A. Hawkins
Christopher M. Hayes
M. D. Hayes
C. S. Hayler
Gordon Head
Ian R. Henderson
Edwin Herbert
Annie Heseltine Harding
Mrs. E. V. Hill
Gordon C. Hillman
F. D. H. Hoad
Graham David Hobden
Jeffrey Holman
John Holt
Michael Hone, M.B.E.
Carole Hordley
Maj. Gen. R. D. Houghton
Mrs. Olive House
Mick Howells
Ian Howie
K. Hubbard
Major Laurie B. Hubbard
Edgar A. Humphrey
Mrs. N. Humphrey
Stephen Humphreys
Adrian Clark Hunkin
Leslie M. Hunnisett
R. E. G. Hunt
Harry Hurdle
Richard A. Inskip, Esq.
Alison Mary Ivemy
Michael James
Mr. and Mrs. P. K. Jelly
Mrs. A. Jenkins
A. J. Johnson
Dr. R. Johnson
Grahame A. Jones
Lionel D. Jones
K. M. Kennard
J. M. Kitchener
R. Kitcher
R. Knight

Miss E. M. Lamb
N. W. Lancaster
Nicholas Leonard
Mrs. J. M. Linford-Jones
Christina Llewellyn
Christopher Lloyd
Barbara Lock
L. F. Lockwood, Esq.
Mrs. P. Gwynne Longland
L. E. Loose
T. M. McAll
Dr. and Mrs. R. Maggs
Stephen Mann
Kathleen I. Marshall
Mr. J. S. Martin
Henry W. Maryan
Mr. and Mrs. A. J. B. Middleton
A. H. Miles
Eric Miller
Joan Miller
John Mobbs
Roger Mobsby
Mr. and Mrs. M. Moloney
Moonraker Restaurant, Alfriston
Wade Douglas Moore
Prof. C. F. D. Moule
Thomas H. Mount
George R. F. Muggeridge
Donald J. Munro
Margaret E. Nicholson
Elspet Nicol
Michael and Christine Notley
Denis Sayer O'Callaghan
Denis H. O'Dell
David George Oakenfold
Mrs. J. E. G. Oaks
Jack Ogier
R. W. Olesen and family
Barbara Ovenden
Mrs. Sheila M. Owen
Mrs. Eileen Page
Barry Pannett
Joan M. Parry
F. G. Parsons
J. E. Parsons
Mrs. Sylvia E. Partridge
Charles L. Payne
Christopher L. Payne
J. H. M. P. Payne
P. E. Peake
B. H. Pengilley and family
E. V. and F. Penrose
Sir Roland Penrose
Colin Keith Perry
J. B. Petrides
Pevensey Town Trust
John Phillips
P. J. Pigott
C. G. Piper
Mr. and Mrs. C. S. Piper
Bernard Porter

Hilary Edmondes Preedy
John and Eileen Proctor
Major and Mrs. G. W. Pullen
Arthur Puttock
Margaret Pye
Reginald H. Pye
Timothy Reade
Rupert Reed
Edwin J. Reeve
L. Reinholds
Mrs. C. V. Relf
W. A. Relph
Residents of Havelock House
  Rest Home
Charles A. Reynolds
E. J. Reynolds
Elizabeth Ann Rhodes
Dr. David Rice
David Alan Richards
N. Richardson
Peter H. Richardson, Esq.
Enza Riddiford
J. A. Riddle
Brian K. Rivett
Brian R. Roberts
Clifford A. Robertson
Paul Robertson
Susan Robertson
Daphne Robinson
Eve and Dudley Robinson
Rev. Hugh Robinson
Mrs. M. E. Rolfe
J. G. Romer
Dudley E. Rose
Rotary Club of Hailsham
R. P. Rousset
Royal Greenwich Observatory
S. Salvage
R. H. J. Sandy
Albert George Saunders
B. R. Saunders
Peter W. Scarnell
A. G. and I. Scarlett
Reg Searle
F. C. R. Sharp
Phil Shaw
Anthony Sherwin,
  D. Arch. R.I.B.A.
Gladys L. Simmons
A. H. Simms
Christopher E. Slade
Dora H. Slowgrove
Rev. H. R. Smart
A. F. Smith, Ltd.
M. J. Smith
D. Smithers
Hugh G. Soper
Evelyn M. Spencer
Margaret E. Spencer
Ivy-Irene Spikins
Mr. D. G. Squier

Mrs. H. Y. Squier
Mrs. K. J. M. Stacy
R. Stacy-Marks
Harry Staplehurst
Joan Stapley
Alan Peter Statham
H. J. F. Stenhouse
J. W. Stretton
Mrs. W. M. A. Surman
Sussex Archaeological Society
Geoffrey Sutton
Mrs. H. A. Taylor
Mrs. Dorothy Terry
B. C. Thomas
Mrs. Dorothy Thompson
Mr. and Mrs. R. Thorne
Maurice Thornton
Susan E. Thrower
Ronald B. Tibble
Alan M. Ticehurst
Charles H. Tidmas
Eric A. Tippett
Elizabeth Turner
John and Betty Turrell
William Henry Twine
Ernest Tysall
George L. Umbers
Mr. and Mrs. J. J. Van Rietschoten
Jill D. van Slogteren
V. A. and J. A. Veck
Frank Herbert Verrall
Vicar of Hailsham
Trevor Vincent
W. E. Vine
Raili Waite
G. S. Wake
Roy W. Walter
Denise R. Ward
Stanley Washbourn
Winifred E. Waters
Anthony Watson
Mrs. J. V. Watson
W. H. Watts
Kathryn M. Weller
Miss B. M. Wells
R. J. Westgate
Mrs. L. Wheatley
John and Alice White
John and Priscilla White
P. W. C. White
Mrs. J. D. Whiter
Coral Whyman
Ann St. John Wilkes
S. J. Wilson
Alan G. Winchester
Hetty L. Wood
Graham R. Woods
John Albert Wybrow
David William Wye
Mrs. Patricia B. Yeulett
Rosemary A. Yallop.